# The Progress Trap

# THE PROGRESS TRAP

## The Modern Left and the False Authority of History

Ben Cobley

polity

Copyright © Ben Cobley 2025

The right of Ben Cobley to be identified as Author of this Work has been asserted in accordance with the UK Copyright, Designs and Patents Act 1988.

First published in 2025 by Polity Press

Polity Press
65 Bridge Street
Cambridge CB2 1UR, UK

Polity Press
111 River Street
Hoboken, NJ 07030, USA

All rights reserved. Except for the quotation of short passages for the purpose of criticism and review, no part of this publication may be reproduced, stored in a retrieval system or transmitted, in any form or by any means, electronic, mechanical, photocopying, recording or otherwise, without the prior permission of the publisher.

ISBN-13: 978-1-5095-6762-1
A catalogue record for this book is available from the British Library.

Library of Congress Control Number: 2024948790

Typeset in 11.5 on 14 pt Adobe Garamond
by Cheshire Typesetting Ltd, Cuddington, Cheshire
Printed and bound in Great Britain by CPI Group (UK) Ltd, Croydon

The publisher has used its best endeavours to ensure that the URLs for external websites referred to in this book are correct and active at the time of going to press. However, the publisher has no responsibility for the websites and can make no guarantee that a site will remain live or that the content is or will remain appropriate.

Every effort has been made to trace all copyright holders, but if any have been overlooked the publisher will be pleased to include any necessary credits in any subsequent reprint or edition.

For further information on Polity, visit our website:
politybooks.com

# Contents

Preface ... vi

1. Introduction: From colonialism to decolonization ... 1

**Part One: How progressives win**
2. Taking the place of God ... 31
3. The uses of social science ... 47
4. Progressivism as promotion ... 62
5. Eliminating opponents ... 77
6. The politics of expertise ... 91

**Part Two: The progressive society**
7. From art to activism ... 111
8. Progressive capitalism ... 125
9. The technocratic state ... 144
10. Nationalisms, good and bad ... 156
11. Playing Jesus: The activist as narcissist ... 171

12. Conclusions: How should we respond? ... 182

Notes ... 207
Index ... 219

# *Preface*

Our world today sometimes feels like it is spinning out of control. The spread of radical political and religious ideologies – and the elevation of their ideologues by our institutions – feels inexorable. Panic seems to be everywhere. There is panic about the far right, racism, xenophobia, misogyny and Islamophobia; about Islamism, anti-Semitism, multiculturalism, diversity and unprecedented immigration feeding into each of them; about our housing crisis, Brexit, Trump, Elon Musk's Twitter/X; Putin, Israel, Hamas, Iran, China and Russia; Western decline, climate catastrophe and the destruction of nature. Our political leaders and institutions either appear powerless and irrelevant, or are an active source of the problems we identify. Visions of a new dark age present themselves.

Yet at the same time corporations continue to sell us very different visions of a world redeemed by their products and technology. Economic growth remains the core measurement for how we are doing: and it continues, leading some to suggest that things are better than they ever were. We are told that 'diversity is our strength'; mass immigration and multiculturalism are only beneficial. Communist China, Putin's Russia and the Iran of the mullahs have serious issues of their own and will inevitably collapse. Islamism in the West and the anti-Semitism that accompanies it will die out as immigrants become more liberal and Western. The climate is not changing or it does not matter if it is, so we should continue on our path of maximal consumption.

These contrary accounts are inextricably linked. They emerge from the same world. They are concerned with the same things. And we sometimes hear them in turn from the same people. You may switch between them yourself: between pessimism and optimism, fear and faith, despair and hope. It is worth lingering for a moment on Donald Trump's victory in the 2024 American Presidential Election. This event has clearly delivered a massive jolt to the Western progressive consensus, making it doubt itself more than ever before. This book gives further grounding to that doubt, focusing in particular on the British context, where progressive hegemony in the institutions remains almost total but is now under sustained attack.

This book seeks to unravel how the narratives of Establishment progressives and their opponents are linked. Its subject matter is the notionally optimistic, progressive narratives that tell us how things are getting better, particularly those promoted from the liberal-left. As I see it, most people who we call 'progressive' do not embrace so much an idea of progress as the comforting illusion that things will inevitably get better so long as they and their allies are in control of things. This has various negative consequences when they do have control of things, not least the denial that, when things go awry, it has anything to do with them and their actions. We can see a similar thing with neoliberal, right-wing, progressives: they refuse outright to admit that their focus on economic growth alone has deleterious consequences on society and maybe on the economy itself in the longer term.

As George Orwell said, 'To see what is in front of one's nose needs a constant struggle.' As I see it, the incapability, decline and discord we see all around us nowadays arises largely from a failure to do this: a failure to recognize what is going on in front of our noses. And I think this failure arises partly from the assumption that we are right and good and can only cause good to occur in the world, while our opponents can only cause bad.

This is the progressive mindset in action. Variations of this mindset have pervaded Western culture in various guises for centuries – and they have now gone global. They confer confidence and hope. They encourage us to do things, to see ourselves in a good light, as capable of improving the world around us. As some say, the progressive mindset shows 'a faith in humanity'.

In this way it can appear to be a blessing – and certainly many of us cling to it as a source of faith in ourselves and the world around us. Our current political, administrative and business elites seemingly cannot do without it, their airy, empty optimism grounded in a combination of faith and the exalted positions in which they find themselves. After all, since history has placed them at the top, it must be a good thing, surely?

But not all the evidence points this way. Following the equivocations of Western elites about Hamas's murderous rampage in Israel in 2023, the Jewish-Canadian academic Gad Saad said:

I am unsure that the West can recover from its multifront civilizational suicide.... It will be a long and ultimately bloody demise and the West will be the first society in recorded history to fully self-implode due to its parasitic ideological rapture.... Your grandchildren will pay a very high price for your 'progressive' arrogance rooted in the pursuit of Unicornia that only exists in the recesses of deeply flawed parasitized minds.[1]

Well, quite. The arrogance Saad identifies is very real. However it is really nothing new. The imperialism of European nations used to display similar traits: assumptions of superiority not just in the technological domain, but in moral and political matters too, practically overriding objections from those outside the charmed circle of knowers. Nowadays the same spirit comes at us in the guise of 'decolonization', a new drive to re-educate the masses to submit to those with a superior morality grounded in historical knowledge. The arrogance of this – and the lies and distortions that come with it – have blossomed in societies that are meant to be guided by knowledge.

But how does this process work? And why is it so successful? Hopefully in this book we will find out; and maybe start to find a way out.

The book is divided into two parts, with an additional Introduction and a chapter of conclusions. The Introduction lays out the primary theme, 'From colonialism to decolonization', of how progressivism has given impetus to European colonialism and now gives 'decolonization' necessary authority. The final chapter of conclusions looks at how we should respond to progressivism – practically, politically and philosophically. In between, Part One looks at why progressivism is so successful and Part Two considers particular aspects of the progressive society today, from the arts, the economy and technocratic government to nationalisms and the behaviour of prominent activists.

The book might be best seen as a sequel to my first, *The Tribe*, broadening out the scope from the politics of identity to the nature and practice of particularly progressive ideology. My ambition in taking this on has posed difficulties, but it has also proved rewarding and I hope readers will find it so.

To get to this stage, I owe particular thanks to George Owers, who initially commissioned the book and paid rigorous attention to it, something rare from editors nowadays. As a typically insecure but self-regarding writer, I found George's comments on my efforts at time brutal and intimidating. However they were valuable and necessary and have led to a much better final version. Thanks also to Polity for taking the book on and to Jane Fricker for spotting glitches and errors. Then there is my agent, Matthew Hamilton, who has offered calm, sound advice when called upon. Lastly, and most of all, I should thank my long-suffering family for just about sticking with me despite everything. This is what proper families do. Anyone who proposes to 'abolish the family', as some progressives want to, should not be trusted.

# 1
# *Introduction: From colonialism to decolonization*

## *Progressive history*

To open to civilization the only part of our globe which it has not yet penetrated, to pierce the darkness which hangs over entire peoples, is, I dare say, a crusade worthy of this century of progress.[1]

With these words on 12 September 1876, King Leopold II of Belgium reached out to fellow Europeans with his project to capture the giant Congo region of West Africa. At a lavish Geographical Conference in his palace in Brussels, the king spoke of how 'pacification bases' would be set up in the Congo river region 'as a means of abolishing the slave trade, establishing peace among the chiefs, and procuring them just and impartial arbitration'.[2]

To many of those who heard it, this clarion call sounded wonderful. Ferdinand de Lesseps, the French developer of the Suez Canal, suggested that Leopold's venture was 'the greatest humanitarian work of this time'.[3] British attendees at the conference were greatly impressed and the positive feeling towards Leopold lingered for years. In 1884, the *Daily Telegraph* glowingly reported, with a nod to the British-American adventurer Henry Morton Stanley, how 'Leopold II . . . has knit adventurers, traders and missionaries of many races into one band of men, under the most illustrious of modern travellers to carry into the interior of Africa new ideas of law, order, humanity, and protection of the natives'.[4]

By around 1890, much of the Congo Basin was under Leopold's control. Local people were being killed, mutilated and taken hostage, their villages burned down and their crops destroyed in order to ensure deliveries of rubber and ivory to pay off the king's investment and fund his extravagant lifestyle. The population of the Congo Free State area dropped by an estimated 10 million people between 1880 and the 1920s, due to a combination of mass murder, starvation, exhaustion and exposure to disease and the much reduced birth rate which resulted from these things.[5] Leopold's public assertions had sounded great to his audience, but the reality on the ground, once his representatives had got to work, was a nightmare of brutality and despair.

Leopold's Congo is an extreme example of how Europeans and their descendants in America and elsewhere used ideas of progress and civilization to justify colonial expansion and control. Progress, as a belief in change, directed by its believers, remains the animating idea of Western civilization today, including among those movements that are trying to abolish it.

Leopold himself was particularly influenced by the British example, having a personal copy of *The Times* brought across the Channel daily to keep him abreast of developments. He spoke of how he wanted Belgium to follow in the footsteps of Britain, taking her part in the great work of civilization. There was cynicism behind Leopold's words. But they were well chosen. For these sentiments were held genuinely – if rather naively – by many in Britain and elsewhere. The hero-explorer Dr David Livingstone had moved many with his talk of a worldwide crusade to open up Africa, defeat the powerful Arab-Swahili slave trade and bring in the '3 cs': Commerce, Christianity and Civilization. By that time, the humanitarian movement had become a major force in British public life. Already, in 1807, Britain had passed a law to ban *trade* in slaves followed by another in 1833 to ban slavery itself within its Empire, accompanied by pressure on others to do the same. It deployed squadrons of warships off the West and East coasts of Africa to intercept slavers, confiscate their ships and return captured slaves.

The push against slavery arose largely out of evangelical religion which merged into a much wider missionary zeal, 'to save . . . Africa from itself' as the historian Thomas Pakenham has put it.[6] The religious impulse to save and convert Africans found itself aligned to a wider, secular notion of bringing civilization and progress to the continent, thereby saving its people from barbarous ways and oppressive rulers. This merging of Christian and progressive standpoints has endured, as has the Western idea of *saving* Africa and telling Africans how to behave. President Macron of France for example caused a storm in 2017 by referring to the problems the continent faces as 'civilizational' in character, evoking France's colonial 'civilizing mission' on the continent. Previously, Tony

Blair had offended many by linking his 'passion for Africa' to its status as an apparent 'scar on the conscience of the world'. The writer Richard Dowden has said of Blair, 'His messianic mission to save Africa was reminiscent of the nineteenth-century missionary zeal that set teeth on edge. It sounded like saving Africa from the Africans.'[7] There is another similarity in the way many non-governmental organizations (NGOs), in Dowden's words, 'find themselves operating like mini-governments, responsible for everything from providing food aid to employing their own private armies'.[8] Back where the NGOs are based and raise their money all the talk is of doing good and saving lives, but on the ground much more earthy political realities often prevail – a very similar dynamic to that of colonial times.

Dr Livingstone was followed by a host of other missionaries and explorers, many inspired more by dreams of wealth and glory than the ideals he passionately held. Pakenham says that the Brits who followed Livingstone 'all conceived of the crusade in terms of romantic nationalism'.[9] Their French counterparts shared a similar feeling about extending French civilization to the world. The explicit idea of progress had largely been a French invention: and colonialism was a way to spread it around the world.*

To gain necessary support in circles of power and in public opinion for colonial ventures, the idea that these European countries had an historical mission and destiny to export their superior ways was essential. Of the British experience, the historian Robert Tombs writes of how:

> Ideas of Progress had burrowed to the centre of the Victorian world view. The Scottish Enlightenment had already elaborated the idea of successive stages of civilization: from the decline of savage and violent feudalism to the growth of peaceful and civilized 'commercial society', which England seemed to epitomize. Historians wrote a saga of Progress: the Great Men of history, seen by Carlyle as crucial, were to be judged by progressive criteria: 'Were their faces set in the right or wrong direction? . . . Did they exert themselves to

---

* As with elsewhere, such ideas offered cover for other, more visceral motivations: in the French case enduring envy and bitterness towards the British stretching back to the Napoleonic Wars and beyond, plus more recent humiliation in the Franco-Prussian War in 1870.

help onward the great movement of the human race, or to stop it?' Central to the 'great movement' was the growth of freedom, associated in England with Protestantism and Parliament, and enshrined in the Whig interpretation of history by writers such as Macaulay.[10]

He adds:

> It was strongly felt to be an obligation to provide leadership and assist the forces of progress, preferably by peaceful means, but by force if necessary against 'barbarity'. The moralizing, missionary aspect of nineteenth-century politics should not be underestimated, despite Cecil Rhodes' cynical quip that empire was philanthropy plus 5 per cent profit.[11]

Tombs talks of a 'progressive colonialism' which was meant not so much to conquer as to *civilize* foreign domains, with Christianity, free trade and ending slavery all part of the mix. One of the most prominent imperialists, Lord Curzon, wrote of how, 'In the Empire, we have found not merely the key to glory and wealth, but the call to duty, and the means of service to mankind.'[12] There was significant support for this vision of imperialism even on the left of politics, notably from the Fabian Society.

However, the actions and interests of settlers, traders and officials often stood in stark contrast to the noble ideals of pontificators thousands of miles away in Europe. Being on the spot, they were also able to mould the realities and exploit possibilities to impose their will. Rhodes made a fortune in the Kimberley diamond mines and came to dominate Cape Colony politics largely by balancing the interests of British settlers and the white majority Boers of mainly Dutch descent. Exploiting his wealth and power on the ground, Rhodes also succeeded in bending the untrusting British authorities to give him a Royal Charter to move into what is now Zimbabwe and Zambia, exploiting fear of German and Portuguese strategic threats in the area. For Rhodes and his colleagues, land and lucrative mineral concessions were there for the taking. The promise of free trade, which British Liberal Prime Minister William Gladstone and others regarded as a sort of moral law, proved to be a mere abstraction and irrelevance when set against the interests of those on the spot. In practice, in Africa as elsewhere, progress and civilization often appeared as the assertion of power, backed up by modern weaponry.

## INTRODUCTION: FROM COLONIALISM TO DECOLONIZATION

In 1883, the pioneer historian of the British Empire John Seeley concluded that imperial expansion was now the 'goal of English history' since constitutional liberty within Britain itself was 'a completed development'. As Tombs points out, a variant of this view became part of the national myth of America,[13] reflecting the many parallels between American expansion into the West and British imperial expansion. For a start, it was driven largely by desire for trade, land and valuable natural resources. However, it was also backed up by more abstract ideas about spreading 'civilization', commerce and religion to the 'savage' populations: so changing them into better people.

One Commissioner for Indian Affairs said the existing populations of North America were prevented from learning the benefits of civilization,

> by their *possession of too great an extent of country held in common*, and the right to large money annuities; the one giving them ample scope for their indulgence in their unsettled and vagrant habits, and preventing their *acquiring a knowledge of individuality in property* and the advantage of settled homes; the other fostering idleness and want of thrift, and giving them means of gratifying their depraved tastes and appetites.[14]

As the Marxist historian Eric Hobsbawm put it with more than a little justification, 'To deprive them of their lands by fraud, robbery and any other suitable kind of pressure was therefore as moral as it was profitable.'[15] Even those who sympathized tended to share the same wider perspective. Artist George Catlin travelled among the Great Plains tribes in the 1830s. Despite noting how the native populations were in many ways more honourable and trustworthy than the whites who were pushing into their territories, he still saw it as a duty of whites to teach them civilization and justice. Of his favourite Mandan tribe, Catlin said, 'he is capable of improvement' and 'his mind is a beautiful blank on which anything can be written if the proper means be taken'.[16]

The American Indian experience shows how progress in practice has always depended on the *submission* of the relatively powerless to the powerful, and the enforcement of power by the latter on the former. This has much wider ramifications. As the American educational writer Audrey Watters says, 'The frontier . . . remains an important metaphor in the American conceptualization of the future. New places, new fields for exploration and conquest.'[17] Tombs writes of how, 'we have generally accepted the idealized vision of the American Revolution as a noble struggle for freedom and democracy. Here indeed is a case of history being written by the victors.' Furthermore: 'America's flattering foundation myth is itself of immense historical importance.'[18]

In retrospect, we can see this in the words of John Adams, one of the founding fathers. 'I always consider the settlement of America as the opening of a grand scheme and design in Providence', Adams said, 'for the illumination of the ignorant and the emancipation of the slavish part of mankind all over the earth.'[19]

That last phrase, 'all over the earth' is telling in view of what happened in time. Once there was no more land left to acquire on the continent itself, the striving, improving, pioneering spirit blessed by Providence had to find new outlets. Techniques for internal self-improvement and for external world improvement have both proliferated in this context. Here we can see a new version of European efforts to civilize the world, offering similar openings to the greedy, venal and ambitious, the warlike, the wannabe heroes, and the weapons makers and traders.

The Second World War offered a perfect stage for this spirit, with the Greatest Generation saving the world from tyranny and looking mighty good in doing it, embodying the spirit of the New World to tired Europeans. However, when vanity and overreach culminated in the disaster of Vietnam, the self-confident American zeitgeist struggled to deal with it. Philip Caputo, a Marine in Vietnam, notes how, 'Our self-image as a progressive, virtuous, and triumphant people exempt from the burdens and tragedies of history came apart in Vietnam, and we had no way to integrate the war or its consequences into our collective and individual consciousness.'[20] Journalist Neil Sheehan adds: 'We thought we were the exceptions to history, we Americans. History didn't apply to us. We could never fight a bad war. We could never represent the wrong cause. We were Americans.'[21] The conservative former governor of Georgia George Wallace responded to the My Lai massacre of 1968 by refusing to believe how any American soldier could possibly shoot a civilian. 'Any atrocities in this war were caused by the Communists', he said.[22]

In the latter suggestion, we find a theory of causation which is inherently progressive, showing an almost touching faith in one's own side, detached from the brutal realities of war, assuming moral superiority and superior knowledge. *What we do causes good things to happen; bad things cannot result from our actions.* It is a story we find in many settings.

The French Revolution took a lot of inspiration from the preceding American one. Ideas about the progress of knowledge had been gestating in the salons and writings of French intellectuals and early scientists for years. During the Revolutionary period they reached a full flowering in the social theory of Nicolas de Condorcet, who believed he and other men of the revolution were inaugurating a new and better reality for mankind. Another major influence was Jean-Jacques Rousseau, who saw civilization as a corrupting force, justifying the overthrow of institutions. He invested goodness in the people, in their 'general will'. As Hannah Arendt has written, 'The outstanding quality of this popular will . . . was its unanimity, and when [Revolutionary leader] Robespierre constantly referred to "public opinion," he meant by it the unanimity of the general will; he did not think of an opinion upon which many publicly were in agreement.'[23] Rousseau legitimized the idea that there is a single righteousness within the people that is available in abstract form to the intellectual. This has been seized upon by progressives claiming possession of the general good ever since. The general will potentially legitimizes anyone who claims to represent the people, but with reference to his own superior knowledge rather than to the people themselves. And when such persons gain in power, this translates easily into a *greater realization* of the general will, meaning that things as a whole are getting better. And this is an *historical* process of change, progress, improvement.

A century later, Vladimir Lenin built on these ideas by giving the intelligentsia a crucial role in the preparation and instigation of revolution – and in any government that followed. The intellectuals were the knowers. They understood the progress of society and would make public affairs work in harmony with how things were moving. Soviet leaders constantly reached to intellectual authority to justify their power. Among the many titles Joseph Stalin took were, 'Leader of Progressive Humanity', 'Great Genius of Marxism-Leninism', 'Builder of Socialism', 'Architect of Communism', 'Gardener of Human Happiness' and 'coryphaeus of learning' (a 'coryphaeus' being a chorus-leader or spokesperson).

On the first ever visit of a Soviet premier to the United States in 1959, Nikita Khrushchev startled his hosts by lecturing them about how their superior productivity in agriculture would not last. As he told them, 'you will have to jump onto the running board of the train of socialism, which is about to leave for the future. Otherwise you'll be left far behind, and we will wave goodbye to you from the rear platform of the last carriage.' Another time he told a group of Western ambassadors in Moscow that the triumph of Communism was inevitable. 'Like it or not', he said, 'history is on our side. We will bury you.'[24]

For the Soviet state and its leaders, history appeared as a process in which Communism would inevitably triumph over capitalism; good triumphing over evil. The Soviets would also, eventually, get ahead technologically, thereby winning a sort of world-historical Great Game and burying their ideological opponents in the grave of history.

The Cold War was in this sense a clash of two forms of progressivism. As Martin Sixsmith writes, 'It was a conflict in which the battleground was, to an unprecedented extent, the human mind: the aim was control not just of territory, resources and power, but of loyalties, belief and the nature of reality.'[25] It pitted the supposedly open, liberal, democratic capitalist societies of the West, epitomized by the United States, against a closed, top-down, highly-controlled socialist kind of polity, exemplified by the Soviets and Maoist China. And these two forms of polity map on to two distinct versions of progressive theory.

J.B. Bury, in his defining tome *The Idea of Progress*, published in 1920, said:

> Theories of Progress are ... differentiating into two distinct types, corresponding to two radically opposed political theories and appealing to two antagonistic temperaments. The one type is that of constructive idealists and socialists, who can name all the streets and towers of 'the city of gold,' which they imagine as situated just round a promontory. The development of man is a closed system; its term is known and within reach. The other type is that of those who, surveying the gradual ascent of man, believe that by the same interplay of forces which have conducted him so far and by a further development of the liberty which he has fought to win, he will move slowly towards conditions of increasing harmony and happiness. Here the development is infinite; its term is unknown, and lies in the remote future. Individual liberty is the motive force, and the corresponding political theory is liberalism; whereas the first doctrine naturally leads to a symmetrical system in which

the authority of the state is preponderant, and the intellectual has little more value than a cog in a well-oiled wheel: his place is assigned; it is not his right to go his own way.[26]

Sometimes, these two types get summed up as, respectively, 'Progress as Power' versus 'Progress as Freedom'.[27] Embodying the former is the Communist Party of the Soviet Union. Historian Catherine Merridale points out that it portrayed human progress as a struggle between good and evil, proclaiming 'strict morality, the virtue of the citizen who aligns himself with history, devoting his life to the creation of a better world'.[28] By contrast, Western liberal societies have over time come to embrace lax morality, the elevation of the consumer over the citizen, while portraying progress in terms of individuals becoming more liberal, taking more and more control of their own lives without constraint from others or from the state. Here we can see the 'closed system' in which things are 'known and within reach' waged against a mindset which is open to the elements and happy to go wherever history takes it, having faith that it will be the right way.* It seems no coincidence that the latter version has found its fullest expression in places with a strong Protestant and Puritan background like the United States, where the dominant Christian churches upheld individual faith above centralized organization and ritual.

However, this open, liberal version of progressivism is not completely open and liberal. Its faith in history and openness to whatever the future will bring is itself a form of dogma. It is a form of core knowledge that cannot be stepped on. Robert Nisbet, author of another classic book on the idea of progress, is a staunch advocate of Progress as Freedom. He says that the concept of progress 'is distinct and pivotal' as a developmental context for other ideas like freedom, equality, popular sovereignty. Set in the context of the idea of progress, he says 'each could seem not merely desirable but historically necessary, inevitable of eventual achievement'. And, 'Clearly, any value that can be made to seem an integral part of historical necessity has a strategic superiority in the area of political and social action.'[29]

---

* In reading this book, readers should assume that 'progressive' and 'progressivism' refer to the closed, systemic, generally left-wing kind, unless specified.

Now the notion of *strategic superiority* is a very different idea to truth. It is the perspective of the committed participant rather than the objective observer. This is the sense in which Nisbet sees the idea of progress itself as *necessary* – similar to how Marxists and other advocates of closed progressivism have. His fear is that, without the belief in progress, progress will come to an end. In this sense faith is instrumental and superstitious. He blames writers from Alexis de Tocqueville to Max Weber for causing us to have doubts about progress in the West, at a time when the East is embracing the concept and the sense of destiny it confers. Again, we might recognize a religious echo here: the need for belief in progress in order to receive the blessings of progress matches the Protestant need for faith in God in order to be saved by God.

In practice, the controlled openness of the liberal perspective defers to power, by giving way to whatever forces happen to be powerful at the moment: normally economic power. But at the same time liberal openness relies on power to survive. The historian John Lewis Gaddis wrote in 2005, 'No one today worries about a new global war, or a total triumph of dictators, or the prospect that civilization itself might end.' For him, the Cold War 'was a necessary contest that settled fundamental issues once and for all'.[30] Now, such a perspective seems naive and premature, mistaking a fleeting victory for eternity, drawing an historical arc into the future based on a limited number of events in the recent past. According to this liberal triumphalism, the game had been won and liberal progress could now proceed uninterrupted.

The complacency of this perspective combined with its dogmatic openness allowed the opponents of liberalism to thrive. Progress as Freedom contained inside it the seeds of Progress as Power, both in its theory and in its politics. It acknowledged the need to control opinion, to intervene and maintain faith in progress, thereby stepping on freedom. Its openness was really an openness to power within a liberal society that it thought guaranteed freedom. So when its antagonists started to rise up from within that society, it happily gave way to them. In practice, to be fully open to the future meant being open to becoming closed; and to being consigned to the dustbin of history yourself. Clever, politically-motivated antagonists exploited progressive liberal openness in order to establish themselves in places like universities and the media before using their inside power to remove and exclude those who had let them in.

This has been happening for a while now in the upper reaches of Western society.

The second coming of Donald Trump looks like the first major challenge to this state of affairs. Mainstream progressives have popularized a view that the brash and uncouth President and his new confrères like Elon Musk and Vice President JD Vance are far-right reactionaries and fascists. Labour's London Mayor Sadiq Khan released a statement about the election to console Londoners, saying: 'The lesson of today is that progress is not inevitable. But asserting our progressive values is more important than ever – re-committing to building a world where racism and hatred is rejected, the fundamental rights of women and girls are upheld, and where we continue to tackle the crisis of climate change head on.'[31]

Trump has also made economic liberals despair with his pledges to bring in a raft of tariff protections for the American economy. With Trump's victory, it seems, the world is at risk of returning to the dark ages.

But this is not someone in whom the spirit of progress is absent. Claire Lehmann, the Australian founder of *Quillette*, wrote of meeting Trump supporters on election night in New York:

> This tension between achievement and resentment explains much about our current moment. The young men I met that night in Manhattan weren't just voting for policies. They were voting for a different view of history and human nature. In their world, individual greatness matters. Male ambition serves a purpose. Risk-taking and defiance create progress.[32]

She added: 'They saw in Trump not just a candidate, but a challenge to a psychosocial orthodoxy that has dominated American institutions for a generation. Their votes marked not just a political preference, but a cultural correction.'[33] The historian Niall Ferguson highlighted the presence of Elon Musk, the world's richest man, in Trump's inner circle. As he said, Trump's win 'was a victory for SpaceX, for Starlink, for Polymarket, for Bitcoin, for Anduril, for Palantir' and others; 'in short, for the new generation of builders whose autistic-virile qualities Musk exemplifies'. [34]

These are not people who reject progress. Rather, they want to return to an older, more productive form of it that the hegemonic version has threatened to destroy. Trump's big slogan is Make America Great *Again* (shortened to the acronym MAGA), which points to how he is targeting a restoration of sorts. Trump is seeking to reimpose American hegemony through a twenty-first-century version of the frontier spirit, deploying a powerful, apparently 'authoritarian' state to support individual freedom and uphold merit. New technology will be allowed to rip through the economy, just as long as it is not controlled by hostile outsiders. His politics is a progressivism of a different kind, with limits and limitlessness in different places to those versions that we have got used to in the last few decades.

The closed, idealistic and hegemonic version of progressivism that Trump is trying to destroy takes its knowledge of society and historical change from the twin disciplines of sociology and history. Indeed, it accords an exalted status to the sociologist and historian, seeing them as important participants in the historical process that help to push progress onwards.* They are objective, not because they collate facts from society and the past, but because they understand the bigger picture: the historical movement from past to present and future and how the latter is an improvement on the former. They are committed to rejecting the past in favour of the future, to embracing social trends and the power that is driving them. Indeed, they are part of that power, part of its driving force.†

E.H. Carr, one of the most influential theorists of the historian's role, explained how this process works in practice.

> Educators at all levels are nowadays more and more consciously concerned to make their contribution to the shaping of society in a particular mould, and to inculcate in the rising generation the attitudes, loyalties, and opinions appropriate to that type of society.[35]

Carr had a Hegelian-Marxist perspective, seeing modern history as the development of humans' consciousness of themselves, progressively

---

\* Sociology was born to track and theorize about historical progress, as we'll see in chapter 3.
† This means that social trends that are not aligned to the sociologist or historian's own aims can and indeed should be rejected for not properly representing the bigger picture of historical movement. In this way, we see political commitment laundered into objective knowledge.

## INTRODUCTION: FROM COLONIALISM TO DECOLONIZATION

uniting subjective perspective with objective reality. We can see this perspective in the idea that educators *at all levels* are getting more and more motivated towards *shaping society* based on knowledge of that society that is by definition correct: it sees a continual, inexorable improvement in consciousness uniting theory and practice. And the historian has a special place in this schema. As Carr writes, 'It is only today that it has become possible for the first time even to imagine a whole world consisting of peoples who have in the fullest sense entered into history and become the concern, no longer of the colonial administrator or of the anthropologist, but of the historian.'[36]

In this conception, the historian presides and oversees, replacing the colonial administrator and anthropologist. They are someone who knows and dictates what should be done. They are superior to their forebears for having an overarching historical knowledge, giving them a full view of society and history. They are effectively an expert in the whole of human existence. In a following passage Carr presents this 'widening horizon' of historical practice as a contrast to the 'history of elites', but in reality it is just a new version of it, with historians like himself appearing in the elite role, their knowledge existing on a higher level than that of previous elites.

While Carr's perspective operates at the exalted level of world-history, the jobbing sociologist's role in our present society is very much that of the cog in the wheel: to keep tabs on the population, using monitoring and surveillance to identify threats to progress in order for them to be stamped out; rather similar to how colonial administrators and anthropologists sought to understand the 'native' populations they presided over.

While Nisbet frets about non-Western parts of the world embracing progress and their historical destiny just as the West has been abandoning it, Carr says that progress needs to embrace those parts of the world and those people, to acknowledge that their rise is right and just. The historian and sociologist should therefore side with Russians, Asians and Africans as representatives of historical improvement: a broad-sweep politics based on a broad-sweep idea of historical progress. And we find this perspective now applied widely not just in looking abroad *from Western societies*, but *within those societies*, as a way of relating different racial, ethnic and other identity groups to each other: favouring some over others as of the future and not the past.

Understandably, non-Western leaders are keen to seize on the authority this perspective can confer on them. Chinese and Russian leaders in particular are naturally well versed in this sort of theory, having grown up under Communism. Both Vladimir Putin in Russia and current Chinese premier Xi Jinping regularly invoke a sense of historical destiny as they seek to grow their own and their countries' power. Xi himself is a stern advocate of Marxist progressivism, telling the Moscow State Institute of International Relations in 2013:

> History always moves forward according to its own laws despite twists and turns, and no force can hold back its rolling wheels. The tide of the world is surging forward. Those who submit to it will prosper, and those who resist will perish.[37]

Here we find again how in this *closed system* of progressivism, the individual's role is to submit, firstly in order to prosper, but actually also to just survive. By submitting to the theory, you submit to the leader's own authority and power. By presenting his theory as incontrovertible, Xi's power likewise appears as necessarily absolute.

## *The role of identity*

The strength and power of this theory is its relation to ordinary people. For those with ethnic origins in places that were formerly colonized or intervened upon by Western powers, it provides a simple and potentially attractive framework in which to understand their lives, one in which they are moving from victim-status to that of power. Progress is a form of power. But identity politics makes it into a superpower: fissile and dangerous.

This treatment of people peppers the history of progressive politics, giving it meaning and purpose way beyond the ranks of ideologues with their theories and claims to authority. Identity groups take on roles as heroes and villains of history who either need to be rewarded with the fruits of progress or punished as enemies of it. In the French Revolution, the *sans-culottes* took on the former role. The Marxists similarly embraced

## INTRODUCTION: FROM COLONIALISM TO DECOLONIZATION

the proletariat or working class. Race, ethnicity, religion, sex/gender and sexuality have all cropped up at different points, in different places.

In fact identity is intrinsic to the progressive story. Valuing the new over the old, 'change' and 'the future' naturally leads to valuing younger people as better than older, which is a form of identity politics. And when brought into contact with reality, this natural logic to value younger people more than older triggers other forms of valuation. In Britain and the wider West at the moment, the greater ethnic diversity and more international origins of younger generations naturally suggest that progressives should confer a higher value based on skin colour, ethnicity and national background. For Britain it means valuing people with non-white skin colour and non-English, non-British identities, associating them with a better, progressive future. Meanwhile people with white skin and what might be called English or British identity appear associated with the tainted past and are to be accorded lower status and lower value.

These negative associations are especially powerful when put into the context of a past consisting of British Empire and power around the world. However this is something that earlier versions of the progressive story treated as positive. For progressives of the past, white skin, Britishness and British power carried progress into backward parts of the world where they were new, *making change happen* in today's jargon. Nowadays these things appear very much as of the negative past, except for the continuing Whig tendency which expresses itself primarily through free market ideology.

There is a sort of remorseless existential logic to how the identity politics works. The association of Britain, British power and British assertion with imperialism in turn associates any positive expression of Britishness with the past as something negative, regressive and oppressive. The fact that British imperial rule was conducted with white-skinned people at the top of the hierarchy and that Britain was an overwhelmingly white population during this time makes another easy association of this negative past with 'whiteness'.

This progressive narrative played a major part in the political convulsions around Brexit, clashing heavily with the assertion of continuing British identity ('Take Back Control'). Relatively new European and cosmopolitan globalist identities gathered around the European Union as a sort of totem of progress, but the EU has also drawn in Scottish and Irish nationalist identities given their opposition to British national identity. In fact, Brexit developed into something of a perfect storm of identity politics, made worse by anti-British, anti-English and anti-Brexit expressions appearing in the idiom of knowledge, as apparently incontestable assertions grounded in history and the authority of professional expertise. As Jonathan Rutherford says: 'A war of position over defining Brexit was prosecuted and a story was established on the progressive left that Brexit was a consequence of the authoritarian personalities of Leave voters who were unable to cope with change.'[38]

Some of the assertions coming out of this *war of position* were quite remarkable in their vehemence and spread like wildfire. The imperial association was a constant theme. Another was the concentration of negativity onto specifically *English* people and English identity, so dividing them from other parts of Britain. The Cambridge University Professor of German and British Academy Fellow Nicholas Boyle for example said that,

> Brexit is the result of an English delusion, a crisis of identity resulting from a failure to come to terms with the loss of empire and the end of its own exceptionalism.[39]

Boyle called the vote 'an outgrowth of English narcissism', adding, 'Like resentful ruffians uprooting the new trees in the park and trashing the new play area, 17 million English, the lager louts of Europe, voted for Brexit in an act of geopolitical vandalism.'[40] Elsewhere he has referred to Brexit as, 'a collective English mental breakdown . . . English people living on dreams of empire never learned to see others as equals'.[41]

In Professor Boyle's account, English people and Englishness are malign forces, obstructing historical progress through their very existence. In its simplicity, internal unity and racial overtones, his interpretation follows a pattern of ideology, finding in human identity its distinction between good and evil.

The Irish journalist Fintan O'Toole has written extensively along similar lines, calling Brexit 'imperial England's last stand' in the tradition of British 'heroic failure', from the Charge of the Light Brigade and Isandlwana to the Somme and Dunkirk. 'The English are no longer dominant and powerful', he has said. 'They are a mid-sized, fairly average western European nation.'[42] Ideas of 'post-imperial delusion' and 'the pathology of Brexit' continue to get thrown around with abandon.[43]

These assertions present aspects of the current moment (the Brexit vote, England and the English people, the existence of the United Kingdom) as leftovers of a negative past (imperial times, failures in battles and world wars) that are threatening what is new and better (*new* trees in the park, the *new* play area). In O'Toole's framing, they appear as a *last* stand before history inevitably rubs them out.

This theme of *ending* and weakness also appeared in association with skin colour. In a campaign email before the Brexit vote, Ricken Patel, the founder of online activist network Avaaz, referred to Leave voters as 'xenophobes', 'small minded' and 'backward', adding that, if choosing Leave, Britain 'can turn away from Great Britain to become little England: small, weak, and white'.[44]* Here Englishness appears associated with white skin colour, despite England being much more ethnically diverse than the other UK nations. However, like in O'Toole's version it also appears alongside notions of weakness, as *diminutive* and *lacking power*. The bigotry, stupidity and also crucially *backwardness* of this diseased identity of Englishness mean that a negative past continues to hold on in the present.

These narratives typically invoke ideas of *causation*. 'Brexit is exacerbating underlying problems in our society', the Labour MP and leadership challenger Owen Smith said; 'it is a racist, xenophobic, right-wing reactionary project.'[45] After returning home from a stint at *The Guardian* in London, the Dutch progressive Joris Luyendijk wrote, in an article entitled 'How I learnt to loathe England', that 'the Brexit vote should . . . be seen as the logical and overdue outcome of a set of English pathologies'.[46]

There is a relatively simple and reasonably consistent narrative going on here, whereby an unfavoured identity and the people who hold it are serving as a source of negativity. They are effectively holding back historical destiny and those who stand on the right side of history, preventing everyone from moving into the sunny uplands of progress. It is simple cause and effect, spoken in the argot of calm, mature spectators

---

* Ironically, the post-Brexit immigration policies of Boris Johnson and Rishi Sunak loosened controls for non-European countries, so while predominantly *white* immigration fell back, non-white immigration soared.

rather than political participants who are invested in the matter. Political opponents, rather than merely having a different perspective, are in fact deficient in their knowledge and understanding, are morally and rationally defective, even mentally ill. The historian Robert Saunders, himself a committed Remain voter, had some choice words about this perspective, saying that, 'when it comes to Brexit, too many of us treat it as a mental disorder that is beyond the category of rational analysis. We march around like quack doctors in a psychiatric ward, diagnosing "imperial nostalgia", "xenophobia", "postcolonial melancholia" & other pathologies.'[47]

This may be so. However the doctor's role is a powerful and appealing one, not least when broadened out to cover the whole of social reality and history. The writer Yascha Mounk, formerly executive director of Tony Blair's Institute for Global Change, invoked it when talking of populism as a virus: 'By fighting off the current infection', he said, 'we might just build up the necessary antibodies to remain immune against new bouts of the populist disease for decades to come.'[48] This kind of doctor-expert diagnoses social sickness, identifies its origin and prescribes solutions to get rid of it. The doctor's role confers natural authority, having generally high trust, grounded largely in traditions of discipline, rigour and evidence. It points towards how progressivism tends to act as a parasite on other things like language, institutions, identities and social roles. Because it knows best, it can deploy these things as it pleases for its own ends, for the greater good.

As a result, during the Brexit spats and Trump's campaigns, various identity groups found themselves being politicized as props to support the right side and oppose the bad people. A couple of years after the Brexit vote, the feminist campaigner Caroline Criado-Perez told us how, 'Women no longer want to leave the European Union. The failure to listen to their voices is a national scandal and it stops now.'[49] The Labour MP Rosie Duffield, who has since given up the party whip over gender issues, said: 'make no mistake: Brexit is a feminist issue. It has been negotiated by and for white men, yet it will be economically worse off women, ethnic minorities, and LGBT+ communities who will be hit the hardest.'[50] Alastair Campbell's daughter Grace added: 'If Brexit had a face, it would be that of a man. It would look a lot like Voldemort.'[51]

## INTRODUCTION: FROM COLONIALISM TO DECOLONIZATION

At one point *Sky News* even led its bulletins with football anti-racist organization Kick It Out claiming that Brexit was causing Islamophobic attacks in football, albeit it provided no evidence for this link and did not even attempt to explain it.[52] One of the complainants featured in the piece attacked the Football Association (FA) as a bunch of white men who were therefore ignorant and did not care. The identity of the accusers and their assertion of knowledge, of causation, was enough for them to be accepted as authority figures. In this framing, the white-skinned man is an unsympathetic leftover of a discredited past, linked to Brexit as an assertion of British national identity. In turn the framing legitimizes marginalizing this identity group and removing it from power: similar to how totalitarian regimes of the twentieth century justified the exclusion of their unfavoured groups.

We might see this sort of activity as bigotry, but it appears as the exact opposite: as *combatting* bigotry; fighting for right and good. Progressive identity politics discriminates with justification, in the name of justice and even rationality. By preventing bad identity groups from asserting themselves, the logic goes, you prevent bad consequences for society as a whole. There is a sense of mission and a sense of historical good about it to the extent that it appears as higher than politics. The progressive story gives discrimination a sheen of authority and legitimacy that makes broad denunciations of identity groups and voters appear either uncontroversial or as something that is needed more.

In the Soviet Union, the aristocracy, bourgeoisie, kulaks (wealthier peasants), Ukrainians and Jews all became targets of general, legitimized denunciation of this kind, justified by Party leaders' apparent knowledge of historical destiny. In Maoist China, those listed as capitalists, landlords and rich peasants were denounced and their property expropriated, while for Hitler's Nazis, Jews, gypsies and Slavs were all targets, apparently in order to fulfil the historical destiny of the German Aryan people.

In those regimes, as today, the workplace was a crucial forum for embedding processes of inclusion and exclusion, of favoured and unfavoured groups according to the accepted ideology. The attachment to ideas of historical progress and destiny lends credence to this discrimination, as does their promotion by authority figures. In applying identity politics in modern Britain, civil service managers routinely call themselves things like 'the agents of change' and 'managers of tomorrow'.[53]

In Britain the adoption of progressive identity politics to govern the workplace properly started back in the 1980s through initiatives of radical left-wing local authorities like Lambeth and Haringey, both in London. By employing Race Officers to range across the whole organization, the idea was to combat racism by teaching correct behaviour and identifying, disciplining and removing wrong-doers. James Heartfield writes, 'The disciplinary process was in the hands of the management, which would lodge the original complaint, prepare the charges, and organise the initial hearings, under the terms of the policy. ... The disciplinary process enhanced the authority of the employers over the employees.'[54] Now this approach has become standard in medium-to-large organizations through the employment of Diversity, Equity and Inclusion ('DEI' or 'EDI') officers and directors. Their roles are more or less the same except they cover a much broader range of identity categories, giving them more of a presiding role over the organizations they serve. These roles have increasingly come to police general relations between different identity groups in the workplace, including the bosses: giving them potentially great power on the lines of political officers or commissars in the Soviet Union.

This inflation of DEI or EDI officers' authority over employees' and members' everyday behaviour and communication has been helped along by a conceptual expansion which associates wrong-doing with the past, particularly the time of imperialism and colonialism. Often appearing as a uniting of moral and historical necessity, it therefore unites what should be with what will be, while denigrating the past and the people in it: classic progressive optimism.

One of the most striking examples of conceptual expansion in practice is the movement to 'decolonize' parts of social and institutional existence: notably curricula and reading lists in schools and universities.

## *Decolonization: a new colonialism*

A guide to decolonizing the curriculum produced by the University of Sheffield explains:

## INTRODUCTION: FROM COLONIALISM TO DECOLONIZATION

Decolonisation is broadly about confronting how European imperialism, colonialism, and racism have shaped our modern world. It is a framework that helps to tackle racial injustice – but more than that, it seeks to interrogate and tear down the structures that embed racism in our society. For us, as academics and students working in a UK university, this starts with acknowledging and reflecting on the whiteness and Eurocentrism of our science.[55]

The heady combination of absolutist assertion and technical instruction in the document reflects an approach which assumes the need for decolonization has already been established; all that remains is to convince those remaining people who do not properly understand it and put their plans into practice. The authors and their ideological commitments appear as established and unassailable.

The movement of decolonization grounds itself in the familiar narrative in which white-skinned British colonizers used the Empire to oppress non-white populations around the world, including via slavery. However they retain Empire as a story of the present as well as the past. According to decolonizers, colonial oppression is continuing today, notwithstanding previous 'decolonization' of the territories of Empire. It takes place via legacy practices and values which have lodged in the minds of colonizers and colonized people alike, discriminating against the cultures and persons of the previously colonized. This perspective leads to a simple political project: that, in order to end colonization and attain justice, the colonizers' society must be overturned: destroyed or effectively colonized itself.

Priya Satia, a professor at Stanford University in California, is one of a battery of anti-colonial historians who offer a theoretical underpinning to this perspective. For them, the British Empire is a continuing phenomenon which still needs to be eliminated, primarily from the minds of the British people. In Satia's book, *Time's Monster: History, Conscience and Britain's Empire*, Brexit appears as a prime example of this tendency. She says:

> The Brexit movement . . . is a sort of memorial in the antithetical direction, the very opposite of coming to terms with the imperial past in favour of glorifying its memory – without bad conscience, making penance both impossible and even more urgently necessary.[56]

She does not explain this in any detail; nor her suggestion that anti-immigration sentiment in Britain is a continuation of Nazism.[57] However she recognizes that the idea of progress had a crucial role in supporting British colonization, effectively excusing its depredations via the assumption that history would *later* vindicate the enterprise as a whole. Indeed, this perspective gives her book its primary theme.

Nevertheless, despite its criticisms of progress, we find signs of another version of it in Satia's argument, from her belief that Brexit supporters are *behind the times* (pushing in an 'antithetical' direction) to her celebration of how history-writing has moved from being the preserve of white males to 'the inclusion of women and people of color' like her. In fact her book is marinated in the progressive ideology of its time, just like those of historian-participants like Winston Churchill and John Stuart Mill, who she argues had an 'outsized policymaking influence' during the Empire.[58] Perhaps the main difference from conventional progressivism is how she rejects the idea that historians *will* judge *later*, asserting that she and her colleagues can do so perfectly well now. This works in their favour though, allowing them – and the decolonizers who follow them – to discard any lingering rhetorical restraints on their authority.

The Sheffield guide to decolonization seeks to preside over the whole of academia and intellectual life. It tells us that, 'UK science is inherently white, since the discipline developed from the European scientific enlightenment'. Also: 'Colonisation is perpetuated in academia by the imbalance of power and wealth between universities in the Global North and those in the Global South. Historically, Western universities have been financed through colonial plunder and enslavement, and the modern practice, language, and publication of science continues to be under Western control.'[59]

Clearly, there is some truth in these assertions. However, saying the higher *reputation* of universities in Europe and America is *an example* of *colonization* stretches the definition beyond literal description of colonial practice into something much bigger and more sinister, associated above all with skin colour. The same goes for the reduction of universities to being products of 'colonial plunder and enslavement' and the idea science is under 'Western' control. Both pick up examples from history and use them to define universities now, in totality: a huge leap. It is all a bit strange and dubious given that universities and other institutions are so vigorously promoting these theories and the people who promote them.

There is a confidence and flair on display in the Sheffield guide that matches the slickest of presentations by a corporate leader promoting a new product. This professional presentation aligns to the habits of power, both in universities and wider civil society, habits which the document assumes are imbued with racism and colonialism. The sheer scale of the authority claimed, over society, history and individual psychology, is striking and impressive. At one point, in discussing any doubts we might have about the ideology, the document casts its gaze over the inner world, stating how, 'Our brain wishes to protect us, to assert our innocence and deflect our privileged identity by disowning or downplaying our identity, distancing ourselves from colonial events, being unwilling to see how the past leads to the present, or tokenising minorities etc.'[60]

In its suggestions, we find a mixture of the reasonable and the anti-intellectual: from advising academics to avoid stereotyping to instructions that they include 'discussions about papers concerned with anti-racism and decolonisation within your subject area'.[61] If the rest of the document is to be taken seriously, this will mean stereotyping aggressively on racial grounds. Academics are also told they must 'Engage positively' with a group of undergraduates established 'to identify problematic areas in the curriculum'.[62] This reproduces the practices of Mao's Cultural Revolution, with students supervising teachers to ensure ideological rectitude. In the workplace, this practice has appeared in recent times as 'reverse mentoring', with young activists employed to tell multinational bosses how to put racialized thinking at the forefront of what they do.

Towards the end, the Sheffield writers suggestively list 'Problematic key figures in science', including no less than Charles Darwin and James Watson (of the Watson and Crick team) for apparent racist things they said, followed by a list of scientists who have apparently been overlooked or excluded based on their race. The logic here is clear: that a scientist's authority – the amount to which they should be pushed forward and listened to – does not follow from their scientific achievements, but relates to how they fit into an ideological schema. Those to be favoured appear as representatives of approved victim groups who need to be compensated for past discrimination and neglect. Here, science appears not so much as a discipline in its own right but as something that is subject to racial politics, to be administered according to the rules of racial ideology rather than scientific traditions.

Matching its wider racial politics, the document sees whiteness as an oppressive category, reiterating that core idea of critical race theory (CRT) popularized by writers such as Robyn DiAngelo and Ibram X. Kendi. Kendi has said: 'There is no neutrality in the racial struggle. The question for each of us is: What side of history will we stand on?'[63] The notion of 'racial struggle' and a world that is defined by race should ring alarm bells. It was shared by Adolf Hitler among others, who said, 'The racial question gives the key not only to world history but to all human culture.'[64] Hitler's thinking has strong parallels with progressive politics, both historically and nowadays. Ian Kershaw tells us how, by the time he wrote *Mein Kampf* in the mid-1920s, Hitler 'had developed a philosophy that afforded him a complete interpretation of history, of the ills of the world, and how to overcome them. Tersely summarized, it boiled down to a simplistic, Manichean view of history as a racial struggle, in which the highest racial entity, the Aryan, was being undermined and destroyed by the lowest, the parasitic Jew.'[65] He talked about how the power of Jewish people 'murders the future'.[66] This matches current progressive thinking in several ways, for seeing the future as desirable but also as something threatened by unfavoured identity groups occupying positions of influence.

Messaging like this emerged once more in 2023 after Hamas's murderous attacks on Israel on 7 October and Israel's vengeful response. One of the favoured slogans chanted at protests in Britain and America was 'From the river to the sea, Palestine will be free'. This comes straight from the progressive playbook, in framing the desired event as inevitable. Time appears in the slogan as a redeemer, a deliverer, bringing freedom and justice to an occupied land. The role for Israel and Jewish people is implicit in it, but nonetheless clear. They are the entities which will be respectively destroyed and defeated: and Hamas's brutal attacks on Israelis in their homes, on the streets and at the Nova Festival showed how. The anti-Semitism that floated around the marches and protests of following months and years is simply a logical extension of this positioning, infusing it and then springing out of it renewed and strengthened.

While the Israelis were retaliating against Hamas, Scotland's First Minister Humza Yousaf tweeted, 'If you are not calling for an immediate ceasefire, you are frankly enabling the suffering of so many innocent people.' Here we find another version of the far-left assertion that 'silence is complicity', inviting hostility and guilt not just towards anyone who supports Israel's resistance, but to anyone not actively calling for a ceasefire (one that would have practically benefitted Hamas). British Jews, overwhelmingly sympathetic to the situation of Israelis, therefore appeared automatically in the role of enablers for the suffering of others, so as unfavoured and targets for blame and hostility. Yousaf added a progressive, historical flourish to his positioning, saying that, through his leadership, 'Scotland will be on the right side of history and of humanity'.[67]

The academics who said that the 7 October attacks on Israel and its people were what 'decolonization' meant in practice demonstrated how progressive support for Hamas and its interests arises in particular from the keenest advocates of identity politics on the left, especially supporters of racial, ethnic and ethno-religious politics. From this 'decolonizing' perspective, Jews appear as privileged, white-skinned and as colonizers in the Middle East through the existence of the Jewish State of Israel. Decolonizing the Middle East means getting rid of that state and anyone who believes in it (the 'Zionists').

For this movement of 'decolonization', existing structures of power in Western academia, schools and other institutions express the dominance of an oppressive whiteness which needs to be abolished. This means removing or marginalizing people who represent that oppression, but also dismantling customs which articulate what it means to be 'at home' in an organization. It replaces these things with the rule of the racial ideologues themselves. Others must ultimately give way or face punishment. Legitimacy has already been established. The time for debate is over. As Professor Sunny Singh of London Metropolitan University explains it, 'debate is an imperialist capitalist white supremacist cis heteropatriarchal technique that transforms a potential exchange of knowledge into a tool of exclusion & oppression'.[68]

All that is left is control and technique: to impose your power through promotional techniques and removing obstacles, not least people who get in the way. Professor Singh's own university, London Metropolitan, has pledged to embed critical race theory and 'decolonial discourse' in all subject areas. It also created a fund worth £15 million to hire minority-only staff.* As James Muldoon of Exeter University noted, 'decolonising universities is not about completely eliminating white men from the curriculum. It's about challenging longstanding biases and omissions that limit how we understand politics and society.'[69] Here again we find the characteristic combination of the reasonable – challenging longstanding biases and omissions – with the ideological and threatening: an apparent reassurance that this agenda is 'not about *completely* eliminating' an identity group rather suggests that it is at least *partly* trying to do that.

In practice, decolonization emerges as a form of existential colonization: a set of techniques used to remove existing sources of authority in a certain location, whether in libraries, classrooms or lecture halls, the media, local government or even a whole society. In that sense it matches other instances of progressive optimism in uniting an abstract general interest (the progress of history through the abolition of the past), a sense of tangible group interest (rescuing oppressed identity groups from their oppressors) and self-interest (removing potential competitors in the workplace and preventing views and interests other than your own from being expressed). Its targeting of white people specifically emulates the worst of European colonization too, in treating the bulk of the population as *natives* with dangerous 'nativist' instincts, whose culture is inherently damaging and needs to be suppressed. Taking a wider definition of genocide like that applied to Ukraine in recent times, we might even attribute a genocidal impulse to decolonization in this form. It is not just another relatively harmless theory.

Like all ideological progressives, the decolonizers place themselves existentially *ahead* of the rest of us, as if they have already got to a better place in the future. From this standpoint, all that is left for them to do is to shepherd us away from the tainted, oppressive past and towards the better state of being that they have already attained. This can justify all sorts of unpleasantness if we do not comply: students denouncing teachers; teachers denouncing their colleagues; false accusations against those who fail to submit; attempts to shame staff into conformity or get them sacked – the same things that happened during Mao's Cultural

---

* This will likely not fall foul of equalities legislation on account of a loophole in the 2010 Equality Act, the Labour Party's last act in government, which permits discrimination in order to correct 'under-representation'.

Revolution. Sometimes this agenda appears as a wholesale attack on inheritance and established authority, the destruction of the existing meaning of institutions and the targeting of identity groups which the theory treats as beneficiaries of oppression in both present and past.

The self-certainty of the decolonizers, like that of colonizers in past times, can help trick us into submission to them and their very political agenda. However it also traps us into patterns of dishonesty. The habit of claiming authority on the back of knowledge you do not have has been honed into sophisticated technique that arises almost naturally out of the nature of progressivism.

If you are the guardian of progress and all that is true and right, then all that remains is the need to attain and maintain power.

All is technique. All is power. This is the Progress Trap.

PART ONE

# HOW PROGRESSIVES WIN

# 2

# *Taking the place of God*

In January 2017, the polling company Gallup asked a sample of Americans how they thought Barack Obama would go down in history – 'as an outstanding president, above average, average, below average or poor?' As it turned out, 18 per cent thought he would be judged 'outstanding' and 29 per cent said 'above average' while 35 per cent thought he would be seen as 'below average' or 'poor'.[1]

At least for our purposes here, it is more interesting that this question was asked at all. How would a cross-section of ordinary Americans know how anyone would 'go down in history'? What does the phrase even mean?

In fact Gallup has been asking Americans this question since the end of the Gerald Ford administration in 1977. But the framing goes back much further. Google's NGram Viewer traces use of the term 'history will judge' back to the start of the nineteenth century – as far as it can see. American presidents have used it widely over the years. Obama himself told Americans that history would judge them harshly if they were not generous to refugees. John F. Kennedy, who retains the highest ratings of any president according to the method, expounded at length along these lines as he prepared to take office:

> For of those to whom much is given, much is required. And when at some future date the high court of history sits in judgement on each one of us – recording whether in our brief span of service we fulfilled our responsibilities to the state – our success or failure, in whatever office we may hold, will be measured by the answers to four questions.

According to JFK, these questions related to a person's 'courage', 'judgement', 'integrity' and 'dedication'. In this famous 'City Upon A Hill' address, he spoke of himself and other leaders in the past tense, looking back from the future to ask if 'we' showed 'perceptive judgement of the future as well as the past – of our own mistakes as well as the mistakes of others', whether they showed 'enough wisdom to know that we did not know, and enough candour to admit it?'[2]

Several years later, after JFK had been assassinated, his brother Senator Robert F. Kennedy told students that 'history will judge you on the extent to which you have used your gifts to lighten and enrich the lives of your fellow man'.

> The future does not belong to those who are content with today, apathetic toward common problems and their fellow man alike, timid and fearful in the face of new ideas and bold projects. Rather it will belong to those who blend passion, reason, and courage in a personal commitment to the ideals and great enterprises of American society.[3]

All this is heady, stirring stuff: showing knowledge of the future, of how *it will judge* and *who it will belong to*. Both JFK and his brother are apparently already there, looking back. They are using it to address core existential issues: the meaning of life, whether someone's life is worthwhile, whether a nation and its people have been good or bad. Bobby's invocation of 'light' signals where all this is coming from. Swap out 'history' for 'God' in 'history will judge' and we are left with a pretty straightforward account of the Christian Day of Judgement where, 'at the last', God will judge whether we deserve to go to heaven or hell. In this language, the abstract idea of 'history' is taking the place of God and making those judgements. *History*, as a singular entity, *will judge* the present and everyone in it in the way that we say it will. By saying 'history will judge', we take on for ourselves the responsibility of doing this. We give ourselves privileged insight into the future. We make ourselves the representatives of the future on Earth, like unofficial priests. And, it must be said, the likes of Obama and the Kennedys have looked pretty impressive in doing so.

However, you will rarely hear anyone dragging out the logic this far. The framing almost always passes by without being questioned. It seems to be sacred in a sense. Certainly, to be a successful politician in twentieth- and now twenty-first-century America, it helps to be accomplished in this language. It is a way of demonstrating authority, effectively of *manufacturing* it like a good marketing or public relations executive would.

In a democratic, equalitarian society, this source of authority is potentially available to all of us. It therefore makes a kind of sense that pollsters will consult the people on how *history* might *judge* their presidents in the future, as if the mass in aggregate has inherent wisdom in judgements of this type. Added together, 'the people' could give us a provisional verdict on JFK and Obama and Trump: an indication of grace (albeit there will be no vindication until the mysterious force of History makes a final decision at some point to be determined in the future). All the leader can do is strive to secure their reputation – and making out that they speak on behalf of the future or of history is clearly an effective way of doing this.

Of course, we also hear this style regularly in British political discourse. Bonnie Greer, the British-American commentator and writer, tapped into it in tweeting, 'History will record that #Brexit is the greatest national self-own in history.'[4] On another occasion, she said, '#Brexiteers & #Trump voters are the same phenomenon Both are out of history and out of time.'[5]

In these statements Greer goes a step further than the Kennedys did, mobilizing history and time not just to attract authority to the self by saying she *knows* how history will judge, but by making the judgements that history will make *herself*, now: judging millions of real people, separating them into good and bad, those who are chosen from those who are not, according to how they voted. For her, Remain and Hillary Clinton voters appear on the good, chosen side, while Brexit and Trump voters are on the bad side, obviously bound for a progressive equivalent of Hell.

London Mayor Sadiq Khan used the same framing on a 'no-deal Brexit', intoning solemnly, 'History will judge our Parliamentarians on this issue like few before. So MPs must think carefully about how they will be remembered if they fail to use their position at this pivotal moment to help stop a damaging no-deal Brexit.'[6] He thereby placed himself existentially in the future, speaking on behalf of a single, mythical historian who will one day (not specified) look back and cast a final judgement on all Members of Parliament. The phraseology magicks up the mysterious, impenetrable but all-seeing, all-knowing qualities that a God would have, transferring those qualities to the self via the idea of history. It is a position of complete, unquestionable authority; also a pure invention.

Through this language the progressive self presents itself to us as an entity that fully understands the future/history and how it will judge people in the present. This self has free rein to judge while not being judged; to hold accountable while not being held accountable. It ultimately cannot be touched, vanishing in a puff of smoke as soon as you try to grab hold of it.

Anyone who thinks that this framing is exclusive to left-wingers, to so-called 'Remainers' in Britain, or Democrats in the United States, should think again. Public figures across our political spectrum employ it, invariably when they feel they need to make themselves look bigger. Lee Anderson, the abrasive right-wing MP who defected from the Conservatives to the Reform Party in 2024, justified his claim that 'Islamists' had 'got control' of Sadiq Khan by telling *ITV News* that the public supported his comments and 'history will judge me on this', albeit qualified with the caveat 'I think'.[7] Political classes around the world use it, almost without exception: from Western liberals, socialists and right-wingers to Chinese Communist leaders and Vladimir Putin, that nostalgist for the Soviet Empire; from decolonizers, Islamists and black race activists to European nationalists, anti-immigrationists and supporters of Israel.

Talk of how 'the history books will say' or how someone 'will be judged' in a certain way, are all variations of the same implicit idea: that at some point in the future this abstract idea of 'history', perhaps represented by a mythical 'future historian' or 'historians', will come together into a single whole, drawing the substance of all life together to make a series of final judgements. These judgements will be both singular and incontestable, divining good and bad, dividing right from wrong just as God will do in the Last Judgement.

## *An inherited temporality*

As E.H. Carr says in *What is History?* 'It was the Jews, and after them the Christians, who introduced an entirely new element by postulating a goal towards which the historical process is moving – the teleological view of history.'[8]* Christianity is particularly future-oriented. For most

---

* A teleology explains things happening in the world in terms of the purpose they serve, so giving history 'a meaning and a purpose'.

versions of it, and more than for the Jewish faith, fallen humankind will only find the good life *later*, normally in the next life but sometimes also in this one through God's supportive influence. The various forms of progressivism inherit this temporality, this 'meaning' and 'purpose' as Carr puts it, seeing resolution and righteousness in the future, either through incremental improvements to society or through the necessary ruptures of revolution. And from the future, history *will* look back and judge us without reservation and without fault.

The German G.W.F. Hegel has been one of the most important synthesizers of this way of seeing history, a major influence on both left and right. Carr writes as one of the former:

> Hegel is rooted in the idea of laws of providence converted into laws of reason. Hegel's world spirit grasps providence firmly with one hand and reason with the other. He echoes Adam Smith. Individuals 'gratify their own interests; but something more is thereby accomplished, which is latent in their action though not present in their consciousness'.[9]

This way, our everyday lives of surviving, grasping and striving attain a magical aspect. Bigger phenomena of *change* like exploration, colonialism and mass migration meanwhile become world-historical, as if ordained by history: and therefore, by definition, a good thing – at least for the time being.

In his *History of the Idea of Progress*, Robert Nisbet points out that the dialectic Hegel and Karl Marx employed to propel history forward has a 'supra-rational, neo-religious character'. He says, 'Even Saint-Simon, often credited with the founding of modern socialism and also the then new science of sociology, recanted his earlier atheism and came increasingly to see his imagined utopia under the label of "the New Christianity".' Auguste Comte, the founder of systematic sociology and 'arch-exponent of science', became an ardent believer in 'the Religion of Humanity'.[10] Voltaire, torch-bearer for the Enlightenment, argued that faith in one god was more *rational* and natural to humanity than belief in numerous deities as was customary in the ancient world – so implying a progress of rationality through monotheism.[11] Maximilien Robespierre, radical leader of the French Revolution, took up Voltaire's faith in a Supreme Being with his Cult of the Supreme Being, apparently justified by science and rational philosophy. Herbert Spencer, 'without doubt the most influential social philosopher and social scientist of his day', Nisbet writes, employed the concept of the First Cause which he saw 'as Infinite and Absolute': 'attributes, obviously, of the Augustinian God'.[12]

## George Floyd: twenty-first-century martyr

An Ashes Test Match between England and Australia at Lords Cricket Ground is one of the flagship games of cricket: an occasion for keen anticipation and indulgence in the glories of summer sport. However, the first day of the fixture in June 2023 was completely overshadowed by a cricket event with little relation to the game taking place. The Independent Commission for Equity in Cricket (ICEC), appointed by the England and Wales Cricket Board (ECB), had chosen this moment to release its report on discrimination and prejudice in the domestic game.[13] The findings were incendiary; and the publicity could hardly have been worse. '"Absolutely horrific" stories show "culture is rotten"', blazed the top headline on the *BBC News* website, based on an interview with Commission Chair Cindy Butts.[14]

In her Foreword to the report, Butts wrote:

> The Commission's work was instigated as a consequence of the broad reactive introspection generated by the public outcry following the tragic murder of George Floyd. Readers will no doubt recall their own personal response to witnessing such inhumane actions undertaken by the very members of society entrusted with the role of protection. There was a spontaneous extension of this visceral response into collective protests for a renewed scrutiny of society's institutions to ensure that they represented the highest principles of our beliefs in fairness, equity, meritocratic process and fair competition.[15]

All across Britain as well as America, institutions were engaging in similar exercises of interrogation and reckoning based around race, confessing their guilt and committing to change. The ICEC report is pregnant with the assumption that the whole game and its administration must change. In the Commissioners' words, 'the game will need to apply a steadfast commitment and relentless vigilance to ensure that the policies, practices and systems are reformed and embedded into all aspects of cricket in

England and Wales'.[16] By this they meant institutionalizing 'EDI' (otherwise known as DEI – Diversity, Equity and Inclusion): 'We recommend that the ECB substantially increases the money allocated towards advancing EDI in all areas of the game, particularly at recreational and talent pathway level.'[17] Basically, it was demanding that the ECB becomes a political organization, run on the lines of progressive political organizations and publicly supporting progressive political causes, as many state institutions do.

Across the Pond, the same transformational spirit had already swept its way through state and civil society. City police forces were gutted as campaigners led by the Black Lives Matter movement (BLM) demanded they be 'defunded'. In America, as in Britain, the justification always seemed to be the same: the killing of George Floyd, a black man, by the white-skinned policeman Derek Chauvin in Minneapolis.

As Butts had said in her cricket report, this process was 'a spontaneous extension', leading into 'collective protests' and a focus on the 'renewed scrutiny of society's institutions'. The killing of Floyd and its interpretation as an example of systemic racism *whooshed up* into world consciousness, driven on by mass support, effective promotion and instant global communications. The story of Floyd, as a black man dying under the knee of a white authority figure, obviously resonated with many black people. Race activists and academics were not backward in pushing the idea that it reflected a wider history and present reality, not just in the United States but in Britain and elsewhere. From Sir Keir Starmer to the England football team, public figures 'took the knee' in recognition, showing that they were actively anti-racist rather than just not-racist.

This would all have been incomprehensible if the Floyd story had not fitted an archetype that is ingrained in the culture and history of the West.

Floyd himself was a troubled man, a drug abuser and serial criminal who had been brought up in poverty and experienced a string of tragedies in his life. At one point he rapped on a music track,

> I've been broke for so long/
> I've been stuck in last place for so long/
> Loaded with potential, but I'm still going wrong. . .

Apparently he had told high-school classmates: 'I'm going to be big. I'm going to touch the world.'[18] To many, the footage of him struggling to breathe under the knee of Chauvin was a defining moment, pregnant with meaning and implied purpose. It linked past, present and future in a story of necessary movement from past and present oppression to future redemption. After he died, Floyd started to shine as he never had in life.

The activists and others who spoke on his behalf fitted his death into a familiar story harking back more than 2000 years. Jesus Christ had died like a slave on the cross at the hands of an oppressive empire in order to redeem the sins of humankind. This descendant of a slave seemed to have emulated him, specifically on behalf of black people. He seemed to have been martyred, as if spontaneously, like Cindy Butts suggests in her cricket report. His story tapped into that Christian narrative that has returned again and again over the generations: that, as Tom Holland put it in his book *Dominion: The Making of the Western Mind*, 'God was closer to the weak than to the mighty, to the poor than to the rich. Any beggar, any criminal, might be Christ. "So the last will be first, and the first last".'[19]

Especially when taken out of the context in which they appear, these last words from the Gospel of Matthew are revolutionary, promising an overturning of our existing society.[20] Those who jumped onto the Black Lives Matter bandwagon after the killing of George Floyd inserted themselves into a modern version of this story. By placing their faith, money and promotional clout behind BLM, it seemed that they might change society from a state of systemic oppression to one of justice, where the beaten-down victims would *rise up* and break the chains that hold them.

In the years since his death, George Floyd has continued to shine almost as a pure symbol of black victimhood, his story representing wholesale racial oppression in places where white- and black- and indeed brown-skinned people coexist. In the House of Commons, the Labour MP Dawn Butler talked of the need 'to get the Government's knee off the neck of the Black, African Caribbean, Asian and minority ethnic community', so drawing a parallel between Conservative government attitudes and the killing of Floyd.[21] And then we find Butts, in an official report, drawing parallels between Floyd's death and the game of cricket in England and Wales, presenting offensive banter towards Muslim players and unwanted advances to women as part of the same phenomenon as a white policeman suffocating a black man in Minneapolis. Through his death, Floyd had achieved something remarkable, evoking what Holland says: 'Not as a leader of armies, not as the conqueror of Caesars, but as a victim the Messiah had come.'[22]

Just as much of the light that shined on Jesus also shined onto his disciples, so has that which continues to shine on Floyd refracted onto those who have done the shining.* 'Christians brought a conviction as potent as it was subversive', Holland says: that they were 'actors in a cosmic drama'.[23] The same goes for the activists, celebrities and institutional leaders who committed themselves to BLM and demanded change. However, they generally saw themselves not as agents of the Word, but of progress in society. They had a responsibility and destiny to change the world. Those who resisted the actions they took, like the fans who opposed the England football team 'taking the knee', appeared as *guilty* for resisting necessary change and for supporting historical, systemic racism. They were *on the wrong side of history*. They were not just heretics but bad people who deserved to be condemned and marginalized in this world.

## *A un-Christian Christianity?*

Holland says, 'So profound has been the impact of Christianity on the development of Western civilisation that it has come to be hidden from view.' He describes the religion as 'subversive and disruptive' and that, 'in a West that is often doubtful of religion's claims, so many of its instincts remain – for good and ill – thoroughly Christian'.[24]

In practice nowadays, progressive politics often operates in concert with advocacy from Christian leaders, notably on issues such as immigration and asylum, finding enough common ground to advocate for the same goals with the same justifications. The two traditions are instantly recognizable to each other, sharing a universality, a future-based temporality, a sense of righteousness and an elevation of the victim. Some

---

* Nurjahan Khatun, a 'Social Impacter' and senior official at the UK Health Security Agency, told colleagues of the post-Floyd moment: 'it is a great time as an ethnic minority to leverage that in a positive way and where possible use that as an opportunity to develop and grow yourself'. A month later she was promoted to a position in the Home Office.

dioceses in the Church of England have even jettisoned the word 'church' in describing the new faith communities they have been establishing, instead using the description 'new things'. A report on this development explained how, 'loosed from theological roots, the conceptual framework inevitably looks for other sources for its guidance, namely business and management theory'.[25]

As we have seen, many thinkers and political actors have found ideas of progress and *providence* (describing God's beneficent influence on earthly affairs) amenable to each other. The Founding Fathers of the United States believed in both, seeing in their own burgeoning country a demonstration of inevitable growth and improvement, tied to God's will. Nisbet writes that the likes of Thomas Jefferson, John Adams, Benjamin Franklin and Thomas Paine 'were emphatic in their conviction of past progress over vast lengths of time for humanity, and of progress, with America in the vanguard, through a long future'. The Puritans from whom they descended saw progress as essentially divine.[26]

In political terms, progress and Christianity have aided each other in certain ways at certain times. The progress trumpeted by European imperialists occurred hand-in-hand with Christian missionary activity. Imperialists justified territorial expansion by their obligation to protect missionaries, while missionaries used the protection to spread the word of God. Meanwhile secular revolutionaries have emulated religious 'reformation' in approach and style.

The commonalities between modern progressivism and Christianity have no doubt assisted the rise of the former by adding a sense of familiarity to this new form of belief system. It has also perhaps helped the latter at least to try and find some traction in an apparently secular modern world.

It all poses the question of whether progressivism in its many guises represents the rise of an alternative, modern type of religion: even a new version of Christianity, with many of the supposedly irrational and unnecessary elements, like God, stripped out.

Against this idea, it is worth emphasizing that while progressivism may have arisen out of Christian societies, shared some of Christianity's attributes, and existed alongside it quite comfortably in certain situations like the rise of the USA, it was a departure from actual religion. Many of its advocates strongly rejected religion and the idea of God – even when this was socially and legally problematic. Nowadays, talk of how progressivism or 'wokism' represents 'a new religion' can seem somewhat trite, particularly to Christians, with the continuities seeming superficial and far outweighed by differences.

One example of this is the doctrine of 'original sin', developed by St Augustine in the fourth century and becoming a core of Western Christian doctrine. As Augustine explained it, by eating the forbidden fruit in the Garden of Eden, Adam had condemned us all to eternal damnation on Earth. It is a notion of deep sadness, while progressivism is inherently optimistic, essentially believing the words of the song, that 'heaven is a place on earth' (or at least that its secular equivalent will be realized at some point in the future). Progressivism rejects the idea of the human being *per se* as *fallen* and *guilty*. Progressive humanism believes that people are essentially good: and all we need to do is remove the social constraints that prevent them from being good. The Augustinian view aligns much more to a conservative viewpoint, in which we are better off seeking to mitigate the harm done by humans when on Earth rather than having faith in them to do good. Among modern British public figures, Peter Hitchens is an outlier in fitting this mould.

Here is a gaping chasm of philosophical (or theological) difference. However I think we can see that a version of original sin has crept back into progressive ideology. This is through its tendency to identify certain groups of people as favoured groups: as *agents of progress*. At the very least this *implies* that other groups are *not* agents of progress: that they are backward and holding back improvement in the world by retaining any power they have and oppressing the favoured groups. Karl Marx's system gave favoured status to the working classes and unfavoured status to the bourgeoisie, but saw that this distinction would be dissolved once the communist society came into being. Our present world of 'diversity, equity and inclusion' (DEI) shows even less interest in the utopian society that it assumes will follow from its prescriptions. It delineates a whole matrix of favoured and unfavoured categories, with the white-skinned 'cisgender' man attaining maximal unfavoured status for having apparently dominated and oppressed all other groups all over the world in the past, continuing into the present.

The stain that attaches to this maximally unfavoured 'male, pale and stale' figure, and indeed to all of those unfavoured categories, looks uncannily like a form of original sin.* It is a mark for life from which the individual cannot escape while on Earth. The only way out of eternal disfavour is accept it and transcend it: to embrace the judgement of History. Unfavoured group members may still be marked by the stain of sin passed down by their forebears, but they can at least attain the progressive version of salvation by acting on behalf of History, by acting in favour of the favoured groups, protecting the chosen people, just as God protected the Israelites on their journey out of Egypt. And this can, paradoxically yet conveniently, see them be blessed on Earth, at least by their fellow travellers.

I think this is the contortion made by present Western progressive elites. They manage to retain their overseeing role by pledging their allegiance to progress, change and the relentless march of history, by helping the favoured groups on their way to redeem humankind. Their scripture or 'tablets of stone' can be found in 'the rule of law': not the law passed by transitory governments, but permanent international (and therefore universal) rules, codes and judgements, particularly on human rights. This form of law is absolute and all governments are subject to it. Its authority refracts onto the group which wrote and believes in it: giving its members a quasi-religious role as interpreters. By aligning to this form of law, the politicians, bureaucrats, NGO officers, lawyers and corporate bosses can feel like they are representatives and voices of History and sleep comfortably in their beds at night.

## *More appropriation than continuation*

From these examples, I think it is clear that the Judaeo-Christian tradition retains a major influence in the progressive world of today. However it is a bit like a pick'n'mix' in the supermarket. Some doctrines remain, but in a different form with different significance. What we see is more

---

\* According to a bastardized Augustinian interpretation, this would mean that the fallen, guilty side of humankind is available to us only through our unfavoured group attributes. Only the straight white man is fully human in this sense, for being fully guilty. Everyone else is infantilized to some degree, like children who are not legally responsible for their actions. The white-skinned woman can only be guilty on account of her skin colour (the 'Karen'), while the black- or brown-skinned man is absolved from guilt unless it is assigned to a general male misogyny, or if they renounce their identity and destiny.

*appropriation* than *continuation*. And that appropriation is more of *styles* and *habits* than set doctrines. Original sin remains with us, but in a bastardized form with a different meaning. It is not called 'original sin' nor even related to a thing called 'sin'. Jesus dying on the cross retains its power, but with Jesus and the cross stripped out of the story, leaving only the victim and the oppression. The ideal 'love your enemies and pray for those who persecute you' endures, but relates to certain identity categories and not others.*

Certainly, as a category of its own, that of the 'progressive' can seem awfully *thin* compared to the depths of the Christian religion from which it sprang. Beyond the basic story of history as improvement and the potentially boundless assertion of authority that springs from it, plus appropriations like the blanket embrace of victimhood, it is distinctly lacking in positive content. This allows for huge variations in practical doctrine and belief, from free-wheeling liberal capitalism to the totalitarian control of Soviet and Chinese Communism and present 'woke' activism.

Against this, however, it must be said that lack of content or 'thinness' was never a problem for pagan religion – at least until Judaism and Christianity came along. Neither was it for early versions of these monotheistic religions, whose more sophisticated theology developed over time and also varies significantly to this day. The flexibility of belief available to the progressive style has allowed its different forms to morph and recreate themselves over time, not least when their failures have become overpowering, as with twentieth-century totalitarianism. In today's hyper-networked world, specific doctrine can shift rapidly, but the basic styles endure.

Loosely, we might divide those styles into left-wing and liberal, a division that first articulated itself fully during the extended Protestant Reformation, with its double movement of action and reaction. First came the revolutionary, evangelical movement that has come to be known as Puritanism in the Anglo-American tradition, smashing the idols and sacking the monasteries of sixteenth-century England, emphasizing the individual's personal relationship to God and lack of agency in the face of God. Then there was the reaction, consecrated in England through the 'Glorious Revolution' of 1688, which brought in a new settlement

---

* See the contrast in elite attitudes towards radical Islam and those denounced as 'far right'.

of relative tolerance and freedom, recasting the Protestant revolt against Rome in a new, more *moderate* form.

The revolutionary, overturning spirit never went away though. Indeed, it had been present in Christianity since the beginning. In mainland Europe this spirit burst out once more through the (openly anti-clerical) French Revolution of 1789, when the term 'the left' was inaugurated. This in turn inspired the very left-wing Russian Revolution of 1917 and further Communist takeovers in China and elsewhere.

As James Simpson writes in his book *Permanent Revolution*, 'Party rigour, enforced by internationalist intellectuals wholly dedicated to a totalizing cause, mark[s] out Puritanism as a proto-revolutionary movement.'[27] Simpson appraises the theology of Calvinism and its offshoots as 'fundamentally expressive of European revolutionary modernity' and quotes the pre-Civil War English Presbyterian Edmund Calamy: 'God hath an absolute power over all Kingdoms and Nations, to pluck them up, pull them down, and destroy them as he pleaseth.'[28]

Whether 'God' or 'history' is doing the work here might seem like a mere detail. Both appear as deterministic. Both, almost as a reflex, encourage a sense of righteousness and entitlement in their followers: *to act*, to smash and overturn that which displeases them. Both reject the past and the people and institutions that populate it. As Simpson says: 'The core of the puritan position is the supremacy of scripture against human traditions – the fact that the "Word is above the Church".'[29] But this goes back further. As Tom Holland points out of the Puritans: 'their rejection of tradition was itself a Christian tradition'.[30] And this feeds into the drive to change and transform the world: rulers, traditions, institutions, the lot.

### *Deploying mystery*

In her book *A History of God*, Karen Armstrong tells us how pagan gods existed in the ancient world *to serve a purpose*. Above all, people demanded *effectiveness* from their gods. They were meant to help human beings to survive and prosper. 'This pragmatism', she says, 'would always be a factor in the history of God. People would continue to adopt a particular conception of the divine because it worked for them, not because it was scientifically or philosophically sound.'[31]

Progressives do not see themselves having a connection to the divine. Rather they see themselves as *rational* and right because they are rational. They are not making a leap of faith as followers of religion are with God. Rather, they are expressing *knowledge*. However, this knowledge is necessarily denied to non-believers or mere followers, because the future is not accessible to them. In effect it does require divine qualities in the wannabe theorist of history. Indeed, we might say that all the talk of 'history' or 'the future' plays a divine *role*. It is mysterious and unknown – and to accept someone's description of it means passing authority over as you would to a God or a representative of God. And this establishment of rational authority, grounded in mystery, combining the religious and rational styles, makes progressivism *effective* above all, which Armstrong maintains is a hallmark of any successful religion.

This religious-yet-rational style has reproduced itself again and again over the years of modernity, helping to prop up elites in power and then overthrow them when their self-justifications are no longer sustainable. For those of us in the Anglophone West right now, leftist moralism plus economic and social liberalism combine to do this job. The former contributes a base of moral authority and mystical dreaminess underlying the necessary quasi-religious commitment. The latter offers up stern laws of necessary economic rationality and the leeway for a multicultural society to endure, at least in the short term. Underlying each is an assumption that they are propelling us forward. Sometimes they do this in unison, as on the civilization-defining matter of mass immigration. Each narrative helps to keep proponents in the ring, generating mountains of rhetoric and deterring challengers. Eventually, actual history tells us, they will become exhausted, tainted by consistent failure. The sea will rush in – and a new version with a new hegemonic doctrine will take over.

To address the essence of religion, Armstrong echoes the early twentieth-century German writer Rudolf Otto, emphasizing the 'numinous', which is to say the mysterious, unknown forces present in the world around us, as intrinsic to the religious spirit.

> When people began to devise their myths and worship their gods, they were not seeking to find a literal explanation for natural phenomena. The symbolic stories, cave paintings and carvings were an attempt to express their wonder

and to link this pervasive mystery with their own lives; indeed, poets, artists and musicians are often impelled by a similar desire today.[32]

By invoking the authority of the future and of 'history', the progressive retains that sense of wonder and mystery. But they discard it for themselves. The mysteries of the unknown are *for the others*, for those they are talking to and managing as the overseers of society. Assuming a quasi-scientific authority, they assume literal – and total – understanding of 'natural' phenomena, including human society. The most strident of ideologues in our circles of power present their perspectives as totally rational, moral and internally consistent, not relying on any sort of faith or unproven elements. Employing sophisticated language and defended by more talk than you can shake a stick at, this perspective is of course a fabrication. In 1931, Kurt Gödel proved mathematically that internally consistent, self-contained systems of knowledge like this are impossible. There is always an unknown, faith-based element to all justification. We are never – and cannot ever be – *completely* right. To assume that we are relies on an appeal to something outside. For progressives this is an invented future which looks back on us all now, judging us, as a God would.

# 3

# *The uses of social science*

Shaykh Dr Umar Al-Qadri, chair of the Irish Muslim Council, put the discipline of sociology to good use in November 2023 following Hamas's attacks on Israel and the Israeli response.

Al-Qadri tweeted:

> the side responsible for all violence is undoubtedly the one that has occupied, oppressed, and systematically cleansed the native population. If Israel had not oppressed and treated Palestinians poorly, Hamas would not have come into existence. Hamas is a result of the Israeli occupation. To address the underlying cause of all violence, it is crucial to focus on the root issue.[1]

Similar sentiments continue to be echoed widely during these febrile times. Islamist leaders, 'decolonizing' academics and their various followers from Asia to North America spoke almost robotically of how the brutal attacks of 7 October were merely 'consequences' of what the Jews of Israel had done to Palestinians.

Of course we may think they have a point. Actions tend to provoke reactions. However, this characteristic framing has consequences of its own. By placing the actions of Hamas fighters into the language of science – of cause and effect – you withdraw any ethical agency from them and place it all on their victims. This clears the way for the effective blessing of the mass murder, kidnapping and rape of Israeli civilians by this 'resistance'.

By situating human actions in the language of science, you end up laundering them into something else: stripping them of a crucial human element, thereby helping to make the unpalatable palatable and the horrific acceptable. The disciplines of social science and history turn out to be great tools for justifying hatred, violence and killing. All we need to do is utter often enough the playground slur that 'he started it', make it into a social truth shared among the group, and then anything goes. Ethics do not apply.

From Adam Smith's *The Wealth of Nations* in 1776 to Auguste Comte's *Course in Positive Philosophy* starting in 1830, social science was drenched in assumptions of progress. Robert Nisbet argues that 'political economy, sociology, anthropology, social psychology, cultural geography, and others – were almost literally founded upon the rock of faith in human progress'.[2]

J.B. Bury says that the Frenchman Comte laid the foundations of sociology, 'convincing many minds that the history of civilisation is subject to general laws, or, in other words, that a science of society is possible'.[3] Bury adds that Comte's synthesis of human Progress is, like Hegel's, a closed system. 'Just as his own absolute philosophy marked for Hegel the highest and ultimate term of human development, so for Comte the coming society whose organisation he adumbrated was the final state of humanity beyond which there would be no further movement.'[4]

Comte was not a fan of equality, popular sovereignty nor what he called the right of free examination. He believed that freedom of thought and liberty more generally were absurd and counterproductive. If the laws of society have the absolute character of scientific laws, then there is no place for diversity of opinion. Like Karl Marx, his sociological predictions did not come true for the most part. 'However', as one observer has pointed out, 'the underlying tendency towards technocratic managerialism, detected by Comte, continues to make itself felt with almost deterministic force in most advanced industrial societies.'[5] In fact, through his scientific sociology, Comte believed that politics itself could be eliminated. He believed that the scientist of society like himself would speak solely as the facts dictated. It is a style that should be familiar from today in an era when even politicians talk of 'taking the politics out' of public affairs.

## *The sociology of hate*

It was a March morning in 2017 and the ticker headline on *Sky News* boomed 'BREXIT RACISM'. It was accompanying a discussion around a report from the Trades Union Congress (TUC) entitled *Challenging racism after the EU referendum*, which highlighted apparently increased racism in UK since the EU referendum, claiming that a third of ethnic minority people had seen or experienced racism between June 2016 and March 2017.

As an expert to discuss the report, *Sky* had invited Rose Simkins, the chief executive of a charity named Stop Hate UK which provides phone lines for people to report hate incidents without going to the police. Simkins said that the report's findings were not surprising and you just had to look around you to see the truth of it.

Asked whether the reported increase was down to Brexit, she said,

> What's happened immediately after the referendum was a rapid increase in hate crime reporting that stayed high for some months and that's what's unusual about it. When we have an event it normally spikes and comes back down again. It was a combination of many things, many things such as people saying to us, 'I've never experienced this before, why am I experiencing it now?' Or 'I'm experiencing a lot more than I used to so now I want to report.' Or, just 'I'm more frightened. I'm actually very fearful what might happen next.'[6]

Simkins went further in an interview with the London *Evening Standard* a couple of years later, discussing data her charity had collected from British Transport Police (BTP) showing a big rise in racially and religiously aggravated offences on London's tube and other rail networks. This time the headline was of 'Brexit tensions'. Simkins said, 'The figures don't surprise me. Everybody working to combat hate crime is aware there are tensions causing these increases. After the referendum, the number of hate crimes increased and there is also evidence of a slow increase at the moment.'[7]

For this, she blamed pro-Brexit campaigners making an issue of immigration. 'There are definitely feelings of increased hostility towards people who are different', she said. 'The current situation of political uncertainty, and some people using Leave as an anti-immigration platform, means there is greater hostility towards people who are perceived to be from another country.'[8]

Giving the example of a Spanish woman being punched in the face in London, with the assailant apparently saying it was for her speaking Spanish, she said, 'Language [of elected officials] is really important in not fuelling this. We often see politicians using antagonistic and divisive language.'

Here we find the crucial explanation of how and why this increased reporting arose: of what *caused* it. Simkins pins increased hate crime reporting specifically (albeit implicitly) on those with a British or English identity, gives victim status to 'people who are different' while blaming pro-Brexit politicians and campaigners for inflaming hostility among the former towards the latter.

This is applied sociology: identifying something bad going on in society and explaining the causes for it, thereby helping authorities to address and hopefully stop it. The charity's name is, after all, Stop Hate. Its aim is to stop hate from arising.

Or is it?

The facts around hate crime are more than a little murky. A lot of the statistics informing it rely on automatically trusting that people's *perceptions*, their motives and their perceptions of other people's motives are correct and consistent – something I think we can say from experience is not always the case, not least when there are barriers of language and culture. The numbers reported are also low – just three per day on average across what is a huge transport network in London. This means that raising awareness among people can deliver large percentage increases in reporting. Simkins herself said in her *Standard* interview, 'Institutions like ourselves, British Transport Police and the government have campaigned to raise more awareness on how to report hate crimes.' A spokesperson for London Mayor Sadiq Khan added: 'The increase in offences reflects national and London-wide trends, and is partly as a result of high-profile public campaigns that have encouraged more people to come forward and report hate crime.' There was a particularly concerted campaigning push around the EU referendum of course as authorities *anticipated* an increase in incidents.

A rise in reports is therefore in one sense a sign that the Mayoralty and partner organizations like Stop Hate have *succeeded*. They have successfully raised awareness. Yet they present the increases which they have helped to secure through their work as reflecting a real increase. Moreover, they use these delivered increases as ammunition to attack certain political figures and demand the suppression of certain types of political speech – notably that which advocates immigration control. The reports of increased hate crimes around the Brexit referendum attracted huge publicity not just in Britain but within the EU and in North America, where it was a crucial prop to turn opinion against 'Brexit Britain'. This helped to generate repeated waves of hostility towards Britain and pro-Brexit campaigners, with even many erstwhile respectable commentators denouncing the likes of Boris Johnson and Nigel Farage as fascist and racist and blaming them for apparently greater racial violence and xenophobia.

As with the actual reality behind all this, the lines between expertise and campaigning, facts and desire, are difficult to discern here. However, I think it is clear that what is presented to us uncritically as evidence-based sociology ends up having significant political effects: indeed almost dictating to us what our political perspectives should be.

I think we can also see that there is a paradox here, whereby charities, state bodies and other groups which are on the surface of things trying to *prevent* hatred are providing an evidence base that *justifies* it against certain political figures and groups. This phenomenon is particularly stark among the wider ecosystem of professed anti-hate organizations which have no statutory responsibilities to stay out of politics (like Stop Hate does as a charity). One organization called Stop Funding Hate became notorious for mobilizing people to bully businesses into severing relations with those they denounce as purveyors of 'hate': specifically organizations which resist the progressive left's politics of identity like *The Spectator* and *GB News*. Hope Not Hate has not always been so aggressive, but was radicalized by Brexit to the extent of calling an end to free movement with the EU 'morally wrong' and joining in with demands from Labour politicians and others that Nigel Farage should be arrested.

In a book they edited called *Hate, Politics and Law*, Danish scholars Thomas Brudholm and Birgitte Schepelern Johansen write: 'In public discourse, hate is typically ascribed to the other (criminals, enemies, strangers, or terrorists) and to label something as a matter of hate is typically a call for action: new or more elaborate statistics, criminalization or penalty enhancement clauses, police training, human rights advocacy, and sometimes even war.' They add: 'The scholarly concern with hatred mirrors the activist in so far as this concern is also often pushing for extension of the scope or rules of engagement.'[9]

Claiming that you are trying to *stop* hate while also successfully providing a justification for it might seem like a contradiction; blatant hypocrisy even. However, under this sort of approach that we have been seeing, where politics and sociology appear to merge, this is not necessarily the case. The idea is that if you remove the *root cause* of hatred, then you will also remove the reason for any hatred in return. The original source of hatred disappears and so peace is created. *Give back* Palestine to the Palestinians and there will be no reason for anti-Semitism anymore; it will disappear. Jews will be able to live happily in the new state created. Progress will have been achieved.

In this way the left-wing progressive language of 'hate' does not refer to a *behaviour* of hating, something that it embraces, but rather looks towards the root cause of *all* hatred: as if to a single source, like the Devil, who resides in some people and not others. Recognizing it depends on expert sociological knowledge, which invariably aligns to a certain type of politics. 'Zionists' and other 'far right' types like Johnson, Farage and Trump appear as *the source* of all hatred in the world, including the (justified) hatred thrown back at them. Hatred refers to what *they* do, but not to what *we* do. Progressives can therefore justifiably hate others without their hate counting as original hate. Indeed, you might say that hatred is a *requirement* of a just politics which understands the world correctly. This is the same logic that leads Islamist propagandists to remove any blame from Hamas for their brutal attacks on Israeli civilians during their incursion of 7 October 2023.

Brudholm and Schepelern Johansen point out that 'it would seem safe to assume that we, in our study of the combating of hate today, should include scrutiny of questions about the nature of hatred as such. This is, however, exactly what many scholars of hate crime and hate speech deny.'[10]

It might seem staggering that so-called scholars do not define the terms of what they are investigating. However this helps their enterprise politically, allowing for a successful 'pushing for extension of the scope or rules of engagement' as Brudholm and Schepelern Johansen put it. Of course, this includes expansion of university departments apparently devoted to the phenomena of hate.

The actual study of 'hate' originates in the American civil rights movement, which was confronting open, explicit racism and segregationist attitudes, not least among state governors and other senior politicians in Southern states like Alabama and Mississippi. These attitudes were associated clearly and obviously with racial violence. To apply it in the same way to the Britain of 2016, for example by calling Britain a 'racist society', widens the scope of what words like 'hate' and 'racism' mean, but in an undefined manner, allowing the terms of reference to be expanded and contracted pretty much as researchers and commentators require. The authority to choose who is guilty of 'hate' appears to reside widely in the personal choices and group norms of the people involved, rather than in any method which is open to scrutiny. In this way it can be attributed only to political opponents, being used to call for more concerted action against them, while skating over similar or even worse behaviour among your allies.

In the United Kingdom, this merging of research with activism always seems to lead to the same place: to demands for the suppression of the same people, perhaps by police arrest (marking the likes of Johnson and Farage as political criminals) or simply by media organizations removing the ability of these 'fascists' or 'populists' to contribute to public life on their own terms, refusing to cover them in anything other than a bad light – rather like the way Emmanuel Goldstein is treated in George Orwell's *1984*.

## *A style made for media*

James O'Brien, perhaps Britain's most successful current radio talk-show host, is a keen proponent of this language and this approach. He has produced three books in recent years, entitled *How To Be Right* (2018), *How Not To Be Wrong* (2020) and *How They Broke Britain* (2023) – notably didactic titles that reflect the content within rather well.

In the second of these works we find alongside the usual self-righteousness and denunciations of opponents a sort of confession-and-redemption story. As he writes at the end of it:

> I now know that almost all of our most toxic attitudes towards blameless, innocent people are born of buried pain, shame and guilt about ourselves and our own experiences, but it took me a long time. I have finally learned that admitting to being wrong is infinitely more important than using skills and tricks and weapons and tools to look 'right', and that there is no point having a mind if you never change it.[11]

This appears to be more about positioning than reality. For the learning experience he talks of does not take him to a place where he is humbler about what he does not know, but to one in which he understands *better*, that 'toxic attitudes' towards 'blameless, innocent people' have their roots in the past, in our psychology. It is a theory of genesis, causation, with the authority of 'lived experience', of personal change, to back it up.

At one point he says:

> In the history books of the future, it will be impossible to explain the election of Donald Trump without reference to the undiagnosed psychic damage visited upon millions of white Americans by the election of Barack Obama eight years previously.[12]

And,

> long before various fraudsters and charlatans started bleating about 'cancel culture' in an attempt to avoid justifying their own bigoted rhetoric, I was compelled to step down from [the BBC] because of my now proven convictions about the depravity of Donald Trump and the impossibility of Brexit delivering any of the benefits promised by its cheerleaders.[13]

The first passage, if taken seriously, mobilizes a remarkable personal authority, again grounded in the expertise of sociology and psychology. As he puts it, the 'psychic damage' on 'millions of white Americans' is *undiagnosed* so far but will be fully accounted for *in the history books of the future*; in other words, once the world catches up with people like him and his advanced opinions. These future history books will it seems *all* say what he is saying now. People with opposing views will, we must assume, either cease to exist or will at least no longer write history books: all for the better either way.

The second passage suggests that *he has already* been proved right both on Trump and on Brexit, that his authority has been fully vindicated. Leaving aside the sometimes horrifying spectacle that is Donald Trump, on Brexit he does not give any evidence for how he has been proved right or any explanation of his methodology. Certainly, some right-leaning Brexit campaigners treated Britain leaving the EU as a sort of launchpad to embrace global and open rather than mere regional and regulated free trade – and there is a strong case for saying they were mistaken in this. However, such a verdict can only be honestly given many years down the line in a rigorous study that attempts to take everything into account, rather than in an obviously biased rant about how the writer was obviously right all along.

There is a bigger point here however, which is that treating Brexit as a rationalist, technocratic policy decision as he does is a category error. As a vote it was an act of *preference*: an act of identity with a certain political entity over another and a choice of one *source* of government over another rather than a question of knowledge which is either right or wrong. To claim you have already been proven right on it is premature in technocratic terms, but it is mistaken to reduce it to those terms in the first place.

O'Brien says at one point, 'If I have become an expert at anything, it is unpicking the false (or at least utterly unprovable) "certainties" with which we all sometimes insulate ourselves from the myriad confusions of life.'[14] This is a nice line, but inaccurate. For, when not engaging in such false modesty, his default position in print, on his radio show and on his notoriously strident social media is that of an expert in the totality of society, history and even individual psychology. Indeed, he presents himself effectively as a *doctor of society*: able to diagnose its ills and prescribe cures to eliminate the root causes of social and psychological sickness. Invariably the root cause which the body politic needs to excise from its being is his political opponents: specifically that motley crew of right-wingers, conservatives and Brexiteers who he knows have done so much damage.

In one passage in *How Not To Be Wrong*, he speaks of our society's continuing enslavement to 'false equivalence', whereby institutions, especially the media, persist in giving airtime to people he does not like to argue against those who have facts and evidence on their side. As he puts it, 'I think we have become so completely inured to the tyranny of right and, these days, far-right talking points that we have come to see the neutral middle as the "left".'[15] This appears like a version of Comte's anti-political vision, updated for the present day: a call for the world to only listen to experts like him.

Emily Maitlis, one of the most senior broadcast journalists in Britain and former presenter of the BBC's flagship *Newsnight* news programme, agrees with O'Brien's diagnosis. Having been invited to deliver the flagship MacTaggart Lecture to the 2022 Edinburgh International Television Festival, she railed against 'the impact that populist rhetoric is having on the way we do our job'. Her theme and title was, 'We have to stop normalising the absurd', which suggests a sort of neutral stance between the group of *us* (who are normal – and therefore in a sense neutral) and *them* (who are absurd and biased). Focusing almost exclusively on Conservatives, Brexiteers and Trumpists, she lumped them all together as variations of the same dangerous phenomenon that the media needs to *defend itself against*. 'The frog should be leaping out of the boiling water and phoning all its friends to warn them', she said.[16]

However Maitlis also claimed she was not offering 'a critique of left or right, Conservative versus Labour, Democrat v Republican'. Populism is entirely cynical, she suggested: 'It's not an ideology. It is a means to achieve and retain power.' Ranged against it are 'the checks and balances on the executive', the judiciary, civil service and 'a media free from interference or vilification'. She dismissed any possibility that these nasty populists might have a point on some things, for example on bias in the media, judicial activism and on the existence of the 'deep state' which thwarts democratically-elected government.* She spoke of 'our objectivity' at *Newsnight*, despite herself repeatedly revealing political commitments on air and on social media – perhaps the most egregious example being her 'liking' a tweet in which David Lammy, later made Foreign Secretary in the 2024 Labour government, said the Conservative European Research Group was like the Nazis.

Like O'Brien and many others in the media and elite circles, Maitlis is still obsessed with a vote that happened in 2016, claiming that, 'Here in the UK we spent early summer watching the havoc at Dover customs meet with a wall of silence around Brexit.' A wall of silence there most certainly was not. She justifies continuing to point fingers at the same people by seeing the job of the journalist not being just to report events but to *explain* them in terms of historical *causation* rather than individual agency. 'Our job is to make sense of what we are seeing and anticipate

---

* Anyone looking for the existence of a 'deep state' need only watch the TV satirical sitcom *Yes, Minister*, never mind study the era of Brexit and how the British state has clutched progressive identity politics to its bosom.

the next move', she said. This gives leeway to blame whoever you like, just as long as you can find an *expert* to provide an *independent* view – the more partial and interested the better. In the case of queues at Dover she mentions, Brexit can be made to appear as an original root cause in history, while the role of the French in withholding border services, helping to fulfil the Macron government's predictions that Brexit would cause problems, can pass by without comment. Maitlis passes over any agency they have, just as she passes over her own during her time at the BBC. In her account, she and they all appear as neutral actors who are responding almost out of necessity to threats posed by negative forces outside themselves. As much as anything, this is a style of *politics*: one that approaches political life as causation rather than agency. You present your own stance and that of allies as non-political, not interfering, just being interfered against. And this invariably precedes a call for action, so justifying the exertion of power, before returning to claim neutrality in the next breath.

Claiming to be above politics is above all a political technique: and an effective and popular one, not least for elites who have a privileged ability to get themselves heard in public. It is not a technique 'to achieve and retain power' as Maitlis talks of populist efforts, but to apply and defend existing power: for example by taking the unchallenged 'expert' position in debates. The stance presents already-existing authority as neutral or as a mere variation of privileged knowledge, expertise, so insulated from legitimate contradiction.

Paradoxically, presenting yourself as impartial frees you up to be as partial as you like: it is a way of manufacturing authority for political action. For societal leaders, this stance offers security. However, it begs the question: what comes first? The politics or the knowledge? Does the politics depend on knowledge or does this knowledge arise out of the political concern to defend existing power and authority? Are the wrong people really wrong while we are right? Or do we just *disagree* on matters of politics?

These questions cannot be answered conclusively. Most of the time in political debate, true knowledge, false knowledge and guesswork mix chaotically with self-interest, group interest and other political considerations – always feeding off each other and breaking apart to find new combinations. Even looking at quite narrow individual instances like the politics of James O'Brien and Emily Maitlis, untangling these things is often difficult if not impossible.

Nevertheless, I think we *can* say conclusively that *no one* approaches the world solely on the basis of objective and impartial knowledge. Even the best social science is not and cannot be totally neutral. We all exist in a political world and have done since we came out of the womb. Our desires and defensive instincts are always pressing upon us. The idea of the 'independent' and impartial contributor to politics is largely a fantasy and a contradiction in terms (albeit those with a genuine respect for the limits of knowledge and of their roles – as we used to see in the BBC of old for example – can come close).

Nevertheless, the technocratic approach to claiming political authority has a strong appeal. To many, it appears to solve the problem of who should rule and how they should be appointed – not just at the level of high politics but in every institution, including the media. Having a body of knowledge and story of causation at your fingertips means you can go out into the world and do the right thing, this narrative tells us. However, as important politically is the way it gives you a basis on which *to say* you are doing the right thing. It helps to manufacture that necessary authority, building up the idea that you are right, generally, on all things; that you have it all in your grasp, under control. A logical consequence of this is that, by definition, those who oppose and criticize you are wrong. And a logical consequence of this is that they need to be crushed or at least silenced for good.

### *Sociology as technique*

In his great essay 'Rationalism in politics', the conservative philosopher Michael Oakeshott deals with this sort of style, which he calls 'modern Rationalism'. He says:

> The heart of the matter is the pre-occupation of the Rationalist with certainty. Technique and certainty are, for him, inseparably joined because certain knowledge is, for him, knowledge which does not require to look beyond itself for its certainty; knowledge, that is, which not only ends with certainty but begins with certainty and is certain throughout. . . . It has the aspect of knowledge that can be contained wholly between the two covers of a book,

whose application is, as nearly as possible, purely mechanical, and which does not assume a knowledge not provided in the technique.[17]

James O'Brien for one seems unable to see human activity except in terms of judgement: right and wrong. As Oakeshott describes the 'Rationalist', 'much of his political activity consists in bringing the social, political, legal and institutional inheritance of his society before the tribunal of his intellect; and the rest is rational administration, "reason" exercising an uncontrolled jurisdiction over the circumstances of the case'.[18] In *How Not To Be Wrong*, O'Brien does not quote opponents directly. Rather, he inserts himself in their place, speaking on their behalf as judge, jury, prosecution and defence all in one. At one point he says, apparently of his unreformed self before he wrote that book, 'I can think very quickly, identify intellectual and emotional weaknesses in others and exploit them. I have always been able to bend people to my will and spin complex webs of words.'[19] All of this speaks of someone who has come to understand technique as a source of authority, his power as a form of right – and challenges to that power as illegitimate. For both him and Maitlis and their many allies, knowledge appears as something to be used and directed as an instrument to achieve certain ends, like a piece of military technology that can batter one's opponents. Far from being independent and autonomous, it is a tool, a weapon, an indispensable aspect of which is its apparent autonomy and independence.

There are many other advantages to the rationalist-progressive style. Treating ideas of social causation as fact allows you to freely project into the future and treat your projections as factual. The boundaries between theory and fact, fact and invention, become cloudy. By merging politics with this applied social science, you end up eliminating the need for thinking unless it is purely practical and instrumental. After all, if you can anticipate what will happen as a result of any action that concerns you – and also know its significance, any further explorations of society become superfluous. You already have the formulae at your fingertips. New facts must match these formulae. You simply need to fit them in – and if they do not fit, then they do not count and may as well not exist.

Social science in a bastardized form like this appears to rule over our politics. However perhaps it is the other way around. For, by dispensing with the need for significant new knowledge of the world, sociology and related disciplines, *as disciplines*, find themselves subsumed and appropriated: placed into the straitjacket of formulae and subject to the same imperatives. By treating disciplines of knowledge in this way, we ossify the world. We also end up creating a sort of a pure politics where *doing* and winning is all that matters. This pure politics takes over even the institutions of knowledge: the *intelligence functions* our society relies upon to protect and renew itself. As with political campaigns, our activity becomes reduced to technique: everything else must follow. The academic disciplines become servants to politics and power, which is to say the ability to form and shape. The aim is to ensure that the right people with the right ideas prevail according to pre-existing formulae. This in turn justifies the suppression of opponents.* It also incentivizes the employment of promotional techniques to bring a reluctant and ignorant population into line. And it justifies controlling speech: pushing some forms of language forward, while marginalizing others and their users.

Of course this style is not really new. As George Orwell wrote in his essay 'The prevention of literature', 'In Communist literature the attack on intellectual liberty is usually masked by oratory about "petty-bourgeois individualism", "the illusions of nineteenth-century liberalism", etc., and backed up by words of abuse such as "romantic" and "sentimental", which, since they do not have any agreed meaning, are difficult to answer. In this way the controversy is maneuvered away from its real issue.'[20]

These are political tactics, but every step of the way they are grounded in the idiom of applied social science: knowledge of negative consequences if certain people speak certain truths. 'The argument that to tell the truth would be "inopportune" or would "play into the hands of" somebody or other is felt to be unanswerable', Orwell writes, 'and few people are bothered by the prospect of the lies which they condone getting out of the newspapers and into the history books.'[21]

And so we might see how the appeal to truth and facts, to social causation, can be deployed as a technique to *suppress* truth and facts. It is carried out in the name of truth, as a *rational* process based on an understanding of how certain things and people cause bad things to happen.

Oakeshott says: 'By one road or another, by conviction, by its supposed inevitability, by its alleged success, or even quite unreflectively,

---

* Perhaps in the service of 'democracy', 'truth' or 'justice'.

almost all politics today have become Rationalist or near-Rationalist.'[22] This is as true today as it was in 1947 when he wrote 'Rationalism in politics'. 'But', he adds, 'so far as authority is concerned, nothing in this field can compare with the work of Marx and Engels. . . . No other technique has so imposed itself upon the world as if it were concrete knowledge; none has created so vast an intellectual proletariat, with nothing but its technique to lose.'[23]

Edgar Snow, the American journalist who did propaganda for Mao Zedong and the Chinese Communists, once wrote of their success in resisting China's Japanese occupiers: 'The job was done by men who worked with history as if it were a tool, and with peasants as if they were raw material.'[24]

History as a tool and peasants as raw material: it sounds pretty cold-hearted, even brutal – as indeed it was in Mao's China. However, this style has many different appearances – and it remains all around us in the West today. Under it, reality and history are things to be deployed in the service of power. People meanwhile appear as human resources, whose role is to support power, rather than to question and participate in it. Applied sociology ends up merging into a sort of pure politics which does not just seek to control government and institutions, but reality itself.

# 4

## *Progressivism as promotion*

> My voice gives the illusion of unity to what I say.
> Mikhail Bakhtin, *The Dialogic Imagination*

In his famous inaugural speech as American President in January 1961, John F. Kennedy came up with one of the greatest, most famous lines in history: 'Ask not what your country can do for you – ask what you can do for your country.' Kennedy's voice matched the words perfectly, expressing gravitas and determination, but also passion and confidence. His words and voice combined to have a powerful, magical effect on millions who heard the speech, both in the United States and abroad.

One such listener was Philip Caputo, a nineteen-year-old from Westchester, Illinois, who later described himself and his fellow Vietnam War veterans as having been 'seduced into uniform by Kennedy's challenge'.[1] Caputo was bored at the dullness of life in suburban America and yearned to find some of the heroism that had existed in that country 'before America became a land of salesmen and shopping centres' as he puts it.[2] Of Vietnam, he writes in his memoir, *A Rumor of War*,

> I guess we believed in our own publicity – Asian guerrillas did not stand a chance against U.S. Marines – as we believed in all the myths created by that most articulate and elegant mythmaker, John Kennedy. If he was the King of Camelot, then we were his knights and Vietnam our crusade. There was nothing we could not do because we were Americans, and for the same reason, whatever we did was right.[3]

Robert Dallek, one of Kennedy's biographers, has written of his subject: 'He and those closest to him were extraordinarily skilful at creating positive images that continue to shape public impressions.'[4] You can get a further flavour of this from Kennedy's acceptance speech for the Democratic Party presidential nomination on 15 July 1960. As Dallek relates it, 'Too many Americans have lost their way, their will and their sense of historic purpose', Kennedy asserted. 'It is a time, in short, for a new generation of leadership – new men to cope with new problems and new opportunities.'

> 'I stand tonight facing west on what was once the last frontier,' Kennedy said with evident passion and conviction. 'From the lands that stretch three thousand miles behind me, the pioneers of old gave up their safety, their comfort and sometimes their lives to build a new world here in the West. They were not the captives of their own doubts, the prisoners of their own price tags. Their motto was not "every man for himself" . . . but "all for the common cause." . . . We stand today on the edge of a New Frontier – the frontier of the 1960s – a frontier of unknown opportunities and perils – a frontier of unfulfilled hopes and threats.'[5]

It is heady stuff: more than enough to inspire any nineteen-year-old to try and change the world, to fight against whatever evils come into view, whether it be Southern segregationists, Vietnamese Communists or mere boredom and lack of purpose. Kennedy's message is that the old frontier may be gone, but there is a new one that needs to be pushed out by a new generation with the same vigour and sense of purpose as the old pioneers showed.

The Kennedy era was when the American civil rights movement properly got going – and its successors continue in the present day, campaigning vociferously to defeat racism and other forms of oppression, not just in America but around the world. As a matter of course, major and minor institutions and corporations in English-speaking countries have been keen to get on board, publicly committing to 'change' and 'transformation' while denouncing their past and present for any association with slavery and colonialism or anything else that the activists may not like. The wider movement consists of an awful lot of *talking and campaigning*, along the same vague, general lines, with the same aims, applied to every corner of American and wider Anglophone society.

Before the British General Election of 2010, major intellectuals including George Monbiot, Richard Dawkins, Noreena Hertz, Brian Eno and John le Carré wrote an open letter to *The Guardian* newspaper entitled, 'Lib Dems are the party of progress'. It said, 'The Liberal

Democrats are today's change-makers. They have already changed the election; next they could drive fundamental change in our political and economic landscape.'[6] Alas, things remained pretty much the same once the Lib Dems entered government in coalition with the Conservatives. Perhaps we should not be surprised by that however, given how such rhetoric matches that of the man who had been in government for most of the previous thirteen years. Tony Blair has been remarkably consistent in his language over the years, for example in talking recently about how progressives winning back power 'will require innovation, not the status quo; and the mentality of change-makers, not "small c" conservatives'.[7]

*The Guardian* newspaper has similar promotional messaging: 'We're used to being the outliers', it says. 'The change makers. A cat among the pigeons. Because, like our readers, we've never been ones to follow the herd.'[8] From the Royal Society of Arts (RSA) we find the same energy: 'Change was and will be hard fought', it tells us. 'The RSA is ready to fight for change; for a better, more equal, sustainable future.'[9]

Sometimes it seems as if there is barely an institution or corporation left that has not embraced this sort of messaging, of change, transformation, 'making a difference' and changing the world. Indeed *change*, the desire to become something different, appears as a sort of social mission and moral necessity, not dissimilar to how JFK presented it. When given substance it normally links into sociological ideas of systemic oppression based on race, gender and other identity attributes. As part of a decolonization initiative, the University of Leicester adopted the slogan 'Citizens of Change' to reflect this, describing its students as 'forward looking ... globally connected ... agitators and instigators' and 'diverse in our make-up'.[10]

The cacophony of more or less identical messaging is a powerful political force in Britain as in North America, building bonds of mutual commitment and creating a critical mass that has overwhelmed countervailing forces in the country, including those arising out of democratic politics. However, in recent years, one rather loose grouping hit on a sweet spot of language that brought the promotional power and impact of progressive politics to a new level, enlisting public and private institutions which normally avoid politics to promote it for free in public, helping to raise billions of dollars in funding.

## *BLM Inc.*

You could perhaps gauge the power of this movement best in trying to get *away* from politics and the incessant noise of political messaging during the Covid pandemic. Tuning in to watch the football following the Premier League's 'Project Restart' in June 2020 meant being plied with same slogan repeatedly: BLACK LIVES MATTER. It was on the players' shirts. Broadcasters displayed it across the screen during matches. Arsenal Football Club placed a huge BLACK LIVES MATTER banner in its stands: meaning that fan noise had been replaced with this strange statement that hardly anyone could disagree with. Premier League broadcasters *BT Sport* and *Sky Sports* produced videos promoting the movement, with their presenters and commentators delivering reverent monologues about its importance. Black-skinned players and ex-players were engaged as racial activists to speak on its behalf, with white-skinned colleagues offering uncritical support.

Alongside this, before every game for two years in England, football players 'took the knee': a gesture pioneered by the American Football player Colin Kaepernick as a protest against racial oppression while the American national anthem was being played before NFL games. Initially, all of this activity was in reaction to the shocking killing of George Floyd in Minneapolis by white policeman Derek Chauvin on 25 May 2020.

The reaction of the football world was just one part of how this movement *whooshed up* to capture British institutions and wider public life, despite the killing of Floyd taking place thousands of miles away in a different country. Many used it to justify further promotion of activist messaging and to remould their own organizations to privilege activist voices more. Senior civil servants, who are meant to be apolitical, sent messages to their staff backing the movement.

As one interested observer wrote,

> On 3 June, Jonathan Slater, Permanent Secretary of the Department for Education, responded to the DEFRA Permanent Secretary Tamara Finkelstein's call to 'fight racism' by tweeting the Black Lives Matter hashtag and declaring his quest to 'tackle the whiteness of Senior Whitehall' (both these Whitehall heads are white, incidentally). On 5 June, Stephen Lovegrove, Permanent Secretary of the Ministry of Defence, sent an email . . . declaring

that 'Systemic racial inequality . . . has deep roots within UK society, including Defence' and, like the DfE head, signed off with #BlackLivesMatter.[11]

In its pre-Musk days, Twitter/X used its 'Help Center' to push an article by a couple of staff members, entitled 'Allyship right now: #BlackLivesMatter'. The piece consisted of a lecture on systemic racism in the US and instructions on how to behave towards 'Black' and 'Brown' people, the capital letters pushing forward skin colour as a fundamental existential category. It said, 'Continuously leverage your voice and privilege to amplify Black and Brown communities. Violence, police brutality, racism, and discrimination aren't isolated incidents. They're happening everywhere everyday.'[12] On the BBC the Christmas edition of *The Vicar of Dibley* sitcom was used to deliver a BLM-themed political lecture. *BBC News* also made a five-minute segment entitled 'Britain's colonial legacy in Ireland under spotlight after Black Lives Matter protests', thereby using the promotion of this rather tenuous link by activists to promote it further themselves.[13]

One of the key things here was momentum: the way the thing happened so quickly, drawing so many political commitments with so little questioning (and later often denied as political at all). It was a defining example of what, in my previous book, I called 'the system of diversity' in action.[14] Activists claiming victimhood based on skin colour demanded special favour from authorities, institutions and corporations, which was granted almost automatically and *en masse*, creating a tidal wave of special dispensation across the Western world, especially the English-speaking part of it. This was something already up-and-running which was *activated* and exploited by the Black Lives Matter movement.

The *decentralized* model that the BLM movement employs, detaching central and local elements from each other organizationally along the lines of a wartime resistance organization or spying network, helped. This enabled 'plausible deniability' about each other's activities, diluting responsibility and accountability from one to the other and helping to protect all from attack. It also allowed the name *Black Lives Matter* to float freely away from the organization and its objectives, leaving us to project onto it our own vision of its meaning – most likely a literal one. The title existed on two levels, as a name and as a concept which surely no decent person could deny. This piece of marketing genius enabled the mass media, politically neutral civil service and other institutions to promote for free the brand name of an organization which hardly any of them knew anything about, parading their own virtue and directing money to the purveyors of what was pretty heavy-duty racial ideology.

In 2020, the year of the George Floyd killing, the Black Lives Matter Global Network Foundation (BLMGNF) umbrella organization alone raised US$90 million. In the same year, roughly US$12 billion of funding was pledged to what are called 'racial equity organizations' according to data compiled by the philanthropy research body Candid.[15] Between the start of 2020 and mid-October 2022, 76,970 grants had been made in the United States, valued at US$16.6 billion, in addition to 205 pledges valued at US$11.6 billion. The biggest donors to such causes since 2011 have been the Ford Foundation and Amazon founder Jeff Bezos's ex-wife, Mackenzie Scott, with more than US$3 billion apiece, Ford's President explaining, 'We support issues that are about progress and inclusion and justice.'[16]

Other billion dollar-plus donors have included the Silicon Valley Community Foundation, the Howard Hughes Medical Institute, the W.K. Kellogg Foundation, the Bill & Melinda Gates Foundation and the Robert Wood Johnson Foundation – showing how this is very much a US Establishment endeavour, with a distinct Big Tech new economy flavour.[17]

However, as the money flowed, the startling success of BLM and its fellow travellers brought with it increased scrutiny. This revealed a few uncomfortable facts about its financial management as well as its political aims. Concrete information about the organization's finances and make-up is sparse, since the parent was registered in the low-regulation, 'tax shelter' state of Delaware. However, in 2021 it emerged that BLMGNF's sole executive director, Patrisse Cullors, had bought four properties for herself worth several millions of dollars using donated funds. Then in May 2022, the *Associated Press* produced tax documents showing that during Cullors's tenure BLMGNF had paid out millions to entities controlled by her relatives and close associates. The man who succeeded her in the role, Shalomyah Bowers, had received a US$2,167,890 payment to his consulting firm.[18] He was later accused by others within the BLM network of taking out a further US$10 million himself.

On the politics, in Britain BLM UK issued a list of six 'key demands' in September 2020, echoing those made previously by the US organization, with the hashtag #theukisnotinnocent. The first of these was, 'We call for the police to be defunded and our communities to be invested in', so advocating the abolition of the police plus the channelling of power and money to activists like themselves. Others included an end to border controls and immigration enforcement plus a 'transformation of our education', with a 'decriminalisation of black students in the classroom', which we might presume to mean exempting black students from school discipline.[19]

For the movement's *moderate*, Establishment supporters, this reality was distinctly inconvenient. Though irritating however, in a sense it was irrelevant. For what Labour leader Keir Starmer called the 'BLM moment' had already achieved what a campaign is supposed to achieve. It had generated a frankly staggering level of publicity and support in which it was widely presented as beyond criticism in mainstream public life on both sides of the Atlantic. A lot of people in positions of power made commitments to it – and once commitments are made, they are difficult to withdraw from. This provided political heft to push back against the reaction that did arise. James O'Brien said that Black Lives Matter was simply about 'support for basic equality' and denounced those who questioned and criticized it as 'consciously and subconsciously racist'.[20] This messaging was echoed widely – and extended to the gesture of 'taking the knee' by many, including the England football team and management. O'Brien added, 'Working once again on the probably false premise that this stuff actually *needs* explaining, the BLM movement's mission is, very simply, to create societies in which a citizen's treatment at the hands of the police, employers, the education system or simply the wider public will not be in any way determined by the colour of their skin.'[21]

Of course, this is the opposite of what the BLM movement's mission is, if we understand that mission to be what the various parts of BLM organizations have publicly stated as their mission. The award of resources to people based on their skin colour, whether through 'reparations' or other means, is its core purpose and policy platform. This is grounded in the ideology of 'systemic racism', which O'Brien supports. He is on board with the ideology at the same time as claiming it to be something else: something nice and cosy, something that anti-racist opponents of the ideology would support. The football authorities, players and media made similar moves, but came to distance themselves from BLM, saying that 'taking the knee' had nothing to do with it. Commentators started earnestly telling us how this gesture was devoted to more nebulous things such as 'ending injustice', having previously linked it explicitly to this political organization.

Black Lives Matter was a phenomenon: a slogan with a campaign attached and a trenchant political ideology lurking in the background. No doubt, it was a sophisticated campaign. But all good mass marketing campaigns also rely on simplicity. In this case, the name was the most crucial thing. A masterpiece of political marketing, on first hearing it may sound nice and harmless, indeed the perfect dividing line between decent people and genuine racists. And this gives a great deal of protection to the organization behind it. In effect it cannot be criticized without the person doing so appearing to oppose the idea that black lives do indeed matter.

The result of all this was a sort of rhetorical blackmail, where everyone is at least vaguely aware that here is something that cannot be questioned and criticized without *making a scene* and putting your reputation – and perhaps your livelihood – at risk. It sends powerful signals to potential critics: either get on board or you will be slammed as a racist.* It also sends powerful signals to advocates, that this is their core weapon, their core advantage, the core thing to be exploited in order to get their way.

This was a big part in the remarkable success of BLM, helping to make it perhaps one of the most successful marketing campaigns in history. It succeeded brilliantly in exploiting elite social norms to make the corporate and wider institutional sector do its promotion for free, providing millions of dollars' worth of advertising for nothing and helping to raise billions for activists and their campaigns.

Of course, it is an old trick of politics to take the name of something nice or popular or respectable in order to build general appeal. Progressive politics is littered with the ghosts of organizations and campaigns past

---

* If you are black and dare to question the movement, you appear as a race traitor and servant of white oppression. Sasha Johnson, the activist who was badly injured in an apparent gangland shooting at a party in South London, is on film ordering a black man who was questioning her statistical claims to 'shut up' and calling him 'a coon', while also denying that it was possible for her to be racist in using this insult.

whose names have proclaimed their inherent righteousness. In the current moment this tendency is linking itself assertively with race, racial victimhood and the need for preference to be made based on race.

## *The progressive alignment*

The idea of progress has always been an effective promotional tool, appearing as a source of authority and destiny that has in some ways replaced the Christian God in Western societies. If you get the masses to accept that you have special knowledge of a better future, and can shepherd it in for everyone, then you are onto a winner. American democracy in particular has been built largely around this style of presentation alongside its market-based economy.

This quasi-religious style – with support of existing power and money – helps you to put yourself *out there*, in front of others, ahead of them, ready to mould discourse and guide it onto ground that is convenient for you. This goes for both commercial and political interests. As we have already seen, progressive social science offers a ready-made tool to do this: effectively *to occupy* existential space in the public sphere. It gives us something to say and a claim to higher status. Indeed, we might say that progressivism fulfils a public relations need, offering a necessary form of authority to justify certain buying habits or political choices. The progressive form of authority is attractive not just to the promotional industries but to media and journalists who rely on authority figures to support the angles they are taking on things. By presenting themselves as experts not in a single discrete discipline but in the world, history and politics, progressive ideologues fulfil a need. They appear as authority figures who know how historical causation works. This means among other things that they are experts in what their opponents are up to: they know that their opponents will always cause bad things to happen. They can create a bogeyman as well as anyone, not just based on tribalism but on knowledge.

In this way, progressive politics and the promotional industries are pretty much made for each other. The latter feeds off the authority that the former offers, while the latter has the ability to put the former out there in front of people. Progressivism is particularly aligned to corporate *disrupters* or innovators who are seeking to create new markets and refashion existing ones. Just like political progressives want to change society, not least to make people more willing to accept *them*, so these disrupters want to change habits and customs in order to make way for their products. In their most advanced iterations, like Big Tech companies and smartphone makers, they need to create *new worlds* of activity in order to prosper and make returns to shareholders.

In this context it is no wonder that these companies and their stakeholders are so amenable to progressive political talk of the need for 'change' and 'transformation' in every corner of society. And with all the money sloshing around, it is no wonder that the promotional industries have adjusted to articulate this perspective and push it virtually everywhere we look.

This obsessive pursuit of change also naturally implies a rejection of existing reality, not just for being bad but for something that is being left behind, that is diseased and dying for lack of social support. As Christopher Lasch wrote back in 1979, 'In a simpler time, advertising merely called attention to the product and extolled its advantages. Now it manufactures a product of its own: the consumer perpetually unsatisfied, restless, anxious, and bored.'[22] For this consumer, the only hope resides in the future, in what new products and social transformation promise to deliver, in changing their current situation, rather than in the present moment.

The unsatisfied consumer is one who wants a change in their life, indeed perhaps to life itself. Encouraging dissatisfaction with existing reality therefore becomes a core aim of promotional techniques, to be contrasted with faith in *a future world* populated with new products and new habits. This is more or less what progressive politics wants to do as well. It wants to get to the promised land of the future by discarding the present and past. While the free market right fixates on self-interest and the economic benefits to be delivered by overturning existing social relations, the progressive left makes a deeper appeal to group interest and the general interest, to our desire to do good and be seen to do good, to our religious impulses and our sectarian instincts (fuelled, not mitigated by righteousness).

The aim of progressive left politics to 'change the world' in practice entails *changing people*. They need to be acted upon and changed into better examples of humanity. In practice this generally means making them more favourable towards progressive politics. Big business wants to achieve something similar: to make people align to their products and discard alternatives, seeing that process as one of improvement and progress. As Lasch identified, by embracing a politics of cultural revolution, progressives find themselves in a *de facto* alliance with corporations. And those corporations, E.J. Dionne has written, 'find it all too easy to exploit a radicalism that equates liberation with hedonistic self-indulgence and freedom from family ties'.[23]

One of the funny aspects of this is how *promotional work itself* is presented to us as a good in itself. It is sometimes called 'gesture politics' or 'virtue signalling'. The broadcaster pasting Black Lives Matter across sports fans' television screens, the politician taking the knee and the celebrity holding up a placard pledging them to the latest fashionable campaign: all see *the gesture* itself as an expression of goodness. By flogging trainers you can also be supporting Black History Month and contributing to ending racism. Progressive sociology is often lurking in the background, like in the Pepsi MAX slogan #PlayToInspire, the idea being that playing sport *inspires* good things to happen. It is a matter of causation, social science. And it leads naturally to political demands. For if sport can *do good*, then this is what it *must* do. The *purpose* of sport becomes a matter of inspiration, of making good things happen outside itself rather than the activity itself. The 2012 London Olympics slogan, 'Inspire a Generation', came from this place, befitting its origins in the New Labour government of Tony Blair. Simply by being there and claiming to be doing good, the messaging tells us, athletes *cause* good things to happen, having a positive impact beyond their individual achievements.

In this way sport becomes an activist occupation, as the arts and other occupations have, as a means for people to achieve political ends as well as commercial ones alongside their sporting successes. Kelly Hogarth, former publicist for footballer Marcus Rashford, has said of this, 'We're living in a world where we as consumers have a greater social conscience than we ever did before and I think it's given brands the opportunity to redefine what their values are.'[24] Brands have always looked to associate themselves with social popularity, but there is now a distinct political, activist bent to it, in the desire to be associated with certain 'values', gathering for the most part around a progressive political consensus which is sometimes highly ideological and radical, as with the support for BLM.

Through all of this, we might see how promotional activity is fundamentally political; even that promotion of one sort or another is the essence of politics. For, by pushing some people and one type of messaging forward, it also elbows others out of the way. It is the process by which some get to speak while others remain silent; the process by which some are rewarded and others are not. The promoted – and the promoting – appear more present in the world, more able to get at people and influence them, whether to buy a product or join a campaign or vote a certain way – or all of them merged into one.

## *The BBC as a promotional outfit*

The media appears as a vehicle for these promotional efforts: as a tool or ideally an ally with which to move in concert. The success of progressive identity politics in entrenching itself in both traditional and new media has been sensational: particularly its ability to capture those which are meant to be politically neutral like the BBC in Britain and its equivalents elsewhere. For the BBC under its former Director General Tony Hall (*in situ* from 2013 until 2020), aligning to progressive political activism seemed to become as much a priority as it was for key liberal-left institutions like the Labour Party and *Guardian* newspaper. In his resignation letter in January 2020, Hall wrote, 'In an era of fake news, we remain the gold standard of impartiality and truth.' And: 'Our values are timeless but the need for constant change is ever-present.'[25] The self-praise and marking of one's own homework is very much out of a promotional mindset, while talk of 'our values' and 'the need for constant change' could come straight out of a progressive political speech.

Anyone who has spent time on the *BBC News* website or with BBC television and radio in the 2010s and into the 2020s should be familiar with how this standpoint worked its way into output. In October 2019, the Corporation ran a self-titled campaign named *BBC 100 Women*, asking, 'What would the future look like if it were driven by women?' Explaining it on the *BBC News* website, campaign content writers wrote, 'From climate change activist Greta Thunberg, to trans woman Nisha Ayub who was put into a male prison aged 21, many on the list are driving change on behalf of women everywhere. They give us their vision of what life could look like in 2030.'[26]

This is what it means to give people *platforms*: places for people to promote themselves, in this case with the bonus that they will be curated to look good and not be interrogated as party political figures are. In this and other examples, the BBC has signed up to become a part of these individuals' promotional apparatus, with a huge platform to offer given a 38 per cent share of the British digital market according to data from Similarweb in 2021.[27]

During the time this campaign was going on, the main stories on the *BBC News* website had prominent links to campaign content. One had the title, 'On point: I know how powerful representation is' and led to a video of the American ballet dancer Precious Adams explaining how she joined the English National Ballet because it had a female director, talking about the significance of pink tights on her as a black woman and how, 'Representation has affected me and has inspired me so I know that other people need it too.' 'That's just what keeps me going and holds me in this position', she said.[28] It is a story of causation in which other people of her identity group have caused her to rise up in the world and given her the specialist knowledge of how she will do the same for others, just by being there. It is a story of pure promotion, indeed of pure politics in a sense. The role of ballet dancer appears primarily as a position of *power* and of beneficent power in her case. She shines with the modern, secular equivalent of a halo.

I think it is worth repeating that this *campaigning* 'content' was placed on BBC *News* pages. However, we have become used to finding this sort of promotional activity across the Corporation's output, including in Sports programming and the ubiquitous TV period dramas. With regard to the latter, the plots of works from very different times like H.G. Wells's *War of the Worlds* and Agatha Christie's *ABC Murders* have been rewritten to fit contemporary progressive ideology: the latter including an analogy between Brexit and fascism straight out of the most overwrought anti-Brexit campaigning.

The background to this is how, over many years, progressive identity politics was embedded into the fabric and organization of the BBC, with extensive personnel, leadership and output targets based around gender, skin colour, ethnicity and sexuality. The Corporation and its regulator Ofcom referred to this change agenda under the title 'representation and portrayal'. This is to say *promotion*, for it is about pushing some people forward, identifying them as *representatives* of others (a political role) and *portraying* them positively in this role. Promotion has sunk into wider organizational habits. Turn on BBC television or radio or visit the website nowadays and the chances are that it will subject you to some promotional activity: normally attempting to portray its presenters, guests, certain social policy ideas and political causes in a positive manner.

Alongside its commercial competitors and its counterparts in other countries, all of which appear to have been pushing in the same direction, the workings of the BBC took on an almost purely political quality during the 2010s: the purpose being to promote the right people internally, to push them forward and promote them as much as possible; treating seniority and power as the goal of activity rather than what the organization produces (except insofar as what it produces promotes more promotion). What used to be the means became the end. Tim Davie, the director general appointed by the Conservative government in 2020, has pushed back on this to an extent. But the approach is still embedded, especially in BBC staff networks that offer internal political representation to favoured identity groups and lobby senior management to reflect this in Corporation programming.

## *Effective technique*

The success of progressive promotion has perhaps shown itself most clearly on social media, through the sheer volume of on-message assertions that dwarfed and overwhelmed those of opposing forces.* Research from the campaign group More in Common found that 'Progressive Activists', who 'have strong views and take stances that sometimes put them at odds with the rest of society', were six times more likely to post about politics on Twitter/X and other social media platforms than any other group.[29] Peter Franklin wrote, 'In other words, an unrepresentative group with unrepresentative opinions on a controversial set of issues is having a disproportionate impact on the national conversation.'[30]

---

* As of autumn 2024, this seemed to have changed, at least on the Twitter/X platform under the management of Donald Trump supporter Elon Musk, with many progressives having left.

Another way to see it is that these people are able to put themselves out there in front of others more; and that this is an example of effective technique. It shows an ability to talk *effectively*, not just in talking a lot but having their talk listened to, approved of and passed on (the power of which Twitter's retweet function has revealed to us). Through sheer presence, the progressive activist's opinions have overwhelmed numerically much larger opposition forces and dictated the terms of political debate to a great extent – even with Conservative governments notionally in power. This domination of social media – just like that over mainstream media – is a form of promotional power; a function of presence rather than absence. It is a measure of confidence, certainty and entitlement: that the world and its future belong to you.

As we can often see from the remarkable success of Black Lives Matter and the daily waves of outrage that swirl around our public life, the politics of these activists is largely American in origin: arising out of universities and other institutions that have given themselves over to activists and their ideologies. As J.G. Ballard wrote, 'Publicity and promotion are the air that Americans breathe, and they take it for granted that in every minute of the day someone is trying to sell them something.'[31] The confident voiceovers on adverts telling us what is going on and how to fix it are also often American, as are the 'trainers' who are coming in and telling our companies and institutions how to run themselves, standardizing workers on how to relate to each other according to their identity categories. They speak with an absolute assurance and authority to which contradiction in the moment appears almost impossible.

These voices, as Mikhail Bakhtin put it, offer an illusion of unity. They express confidence. They are clear and well-articulated. They do not crack. The noises they make are familiar and even attractive to us. They project authority. There is a weight behind them, of something that might be wisdom but is maybe just power. They fit in with the fashions, having the look and accent of people who are favoured at the moment. Clearly, they are integrated into something much bigger than merely themselves. There is a unity to what they say: a *political* unity. And this appears to imbue the words they use with completeness. This is a form of seduction; and the only thing left for us to do is submit to it.

# 5

# *Eliminating opponents*

> For it is only criminals who presume to damage other people nowadays without the aid of philosophy.
>
> Robert Musil, *The Man Without Qualities*

Joseph Stalin said: 'Every Bolshevik under present conditions must have the ability to discern an enemy of the party and unmask him no matter how well disguised he may be.'[1] In other words the party member must be capable of identifying someone undesirable, even behind contrary appearances, judging them as an enemy and justifying their punishment. In Stalin's Soviet Union, what punishment entailed is well known: varying from execution to the gulag or merely excluded from society, as happened to composers like Dmitri Shostakovich and Sergey Prokofiev.

Stalin's Politburo colleague Nikolay Bukharin embraced this brutal logic to a seemingly crazy degree, accepting that it could rightly be used against him when he was tried for counter-revolutionary activities in 1938, found guilty and executed.

Martin Sixsmith writes,

> While Bukharin and the others had not committed the ludicrous anti-party crimes of which they were accused, they were no longer fully supportive of the direction the revolution had taken. So by the logic of the party, the logic by which they themselves had lived, their annihilation by the party was something that had to be accepted.[2]

The truth was the truth, the party was the sole authority and whoever it said was an enemy was the enemy, even if it was oneself. Once the experts, which is to say those in power, had identified an enemy, their judgement became absolute and punishment inevitable.

To try to defeat and remove opponents from power is of course a natural trait of politics. We have institutionalized it in democratic political systems. However, the process acquires an extra sheen of self-righteousness from the progressive story: the blessing of philosophy and knowledge. For progressives the elimination of opponents, preferably by conversion, is *necessary*. For right and good to prevail, those who are wrong and bad must be removed from contesting public life. This way, both the interests of progressives and the historical destiny of humanity are satisfied.

Under Khrushchev, the Soviet Union started to medicalize opposition as mental illness, using the authority of psychiatry to call it 'creeping schizophrenia'. As Sixsmith points out, 'it was impossible to disprove that you suffered from it and it allowed the state to confine sufferers in hospitals for "psychiatric treatment"'. 'It was never overtly stated, but the underlying assumption was that "if someone opposes the people's state, which is destined to bring happiness to all mankind, he or she must by definition be mad".'[3]

Of Communist China, Jung Chang and Jon Halliday write,

> In addition to execution and incarceration in prisons and camps, there was a third, and typically Maoist, form of punishment that was imposed on many tens of millions of people during Mao's reign. It was called being placed 'under surveillance' while the victim remained in society. . . . It meant one's whole family living like outcasts. The high-visibility stigma served as a warning to the general public never to cross the regime.[4]

In another precursor of our present times,* Mao even pushed for the elimination of horticulture: 'growing flowers is a hangover from the old society,' he said, 'a pastime for the feudal scholar class and other layabouts'. 'We must change it now', he ordered in July 1964. 'Get rid of most gardeners.'[5]

Imprisoning, starving and killing are just the crudest ways of removing your opponents from the scene. Claude Goëldhieux, a French prisoner of the Viet-Minh during the France–Vietnam war, wrote of how his Communist jailers used sophisticated techniques of indoctrination and manipulation on their captives. These included treating escapees not as escapees but as deserters and traitors to the Cause and to the truth.

---

* Cf. the idea that gardening and gardens are somehow racist and colonialist.

By attempting to escape, [the escapee] reneged his new-found faith and reaffirmed his former errors. By an individualistic, hence guilty, feeling, he had sabotaged the political action of the mass of prisoners. Thus, he ceased to exist. The sentencing to death was merely a concretization of this non-existence.[6]

The power to make someone's existence cease without killing them is a kind of power at which Communist regimes have excelled. The same techniques and justifications also proliferate in supposedly liberal, democratic Western societies like Britain, albeit without such totalizing control.

The battleground here is about reality itself. For it turns out that a great way to exterminate those things (and people) you dislike is to deny that they exist at all: to treat certain things as figments of imagination of inferior, backward beings – showing what Marxist terminology describes as 'false consciousness'. In order to eliminate that which provides existential support and identity to opponents, history becomes a particularly contested space. In the Soviet Union it was forbidden to publish any fact about the Second World War that was not in the official histories, with archives closed to further research.[7] Meanwhile the 'year zero' approach inherited from the French Revolution sought to eliminate signs of the past: including renaming cities and streets, recasting the alphabet and revising the calendar.

'In the case of England', the historian Robert Tombs writes of present-day Britain, 'some historians have come close to suggesting – sometimes with surprising vehemence – that it does not have, or should not have today, a meaningful history at all.' As he adds, 'it is unimaginable that the same argument could be made about Ireland, Scotland or France'.[8] However, it has been made about Ukraine. Vladimir Putin and other Russian nationalist ideologues have been seeking to eliminate an independent Ukrainian identity *by claiming it does not exist*; that it only *truly* exists as part of a greater Russian whole.

Given the context of Putin and Ukraine, this approach may seem extreme. However, saying something is true in order to make it true is so common in our own political life as to be almost universal. It is a habit. Virtually everyone seems to be at it. However, it only really works for those with high status and if it coheres with the agendas of others at that level: generating political pressure through concerted, collective presence, drowning out opposing voices and successfully laying a new covering over reality. Putin failed to achieve this in Ukraine, proving to be weaker than his propaganda led him to believe.

## *Victory already secured*

In the Anglophone West, progressive attempts to stop opponents from participating in public life used to be referred to as 'no-platforming'; nowadays more as part of something called 'cancel culture', which in turn is part of a 'culture war'. Of the latter, talk-show host James O'Brien says:

> There's no actual 'culture war', is there? It's just a new way of describing disagreements between people who hate racism & discrimination & people who love it. Meanwhile, 'woke' has just replaced 'politically correct' as the most pretentious way of saying 'not a massive bigot'.[9]

It is a curious argument, this. On one hand O'Brien denies that a metaphorical 'war' is taking place, referring to mere 'disagreements'. However he then describes his own side *hating* what the other side *loves*, so maximizing the emotion involved and framing the contest as one between good and evil; between those who reject racism and discrimination and those who embrace it. This is not the stuff of polite disagreement.

So how can there be no *actual* war in such a context? The answer seems to lie in the fact that it has already been won, by *us*. The *other* side talks about 'culture war' because *it* is fighting one, but *we* have already won. We have prevailed in the court of history and argument so have moved on from the field of political contest. In this framing, those who are right can present themselves strangely as *non-participants* in this metaphorical war. And doing so is one of their techniques to fight in it. You say you are peaceful in order to stop your opponents from fighting the war. By presenting yourself in this way, you score blows, appearing to be better and more virtuous than your opponents. You effectively present yourselves as the moral *winners* in order to win. You say something is true in order to make it true, to make your opponents feel like there is no point. It is a technique.

O'Brien also campaigns keenly to block opponents from appearing on television and radio – so once more showing the entitled sense of someone who believes *they have already won*. The columnist Martha Gill has used similar arguments against free speech campaigners, arguing that 'the scale of the problem' of preventing guest speakers from speaking in universities 'has been exaggerated'. She then makes the move of suggesting it is not a problem at all.

> Free speech advocates also misunderstand the motivation of those who might want to shut down a debate: they see this as a surefire mark of intolerance. But some debates should be shut down. For public dialogue to make any progress, it is important to recognise when a particular debate has been won and leave it there.
>
> Even the most passionate free speech advocate might not wish to reopen the debate into whether women should be tried for witchcraft, or whether ethnic minorities should be allowed to go to university, or whether the Earth is flat. No-platformers are not scared – they simply think certain debates are over. You may disagree, but it does not mean they are against free speech.[10]

As far as I am aware, there have been no cases of 'no-platformers' attempting to stop people from speaking on any of these subjects. Rather, they mostly consistently attempt to 'cancel' speakers with pretty normal conservative views plus people who reject biological men having access to women-only spaces. Gill suggests that no-platformers simply have a belief that 'certain debates are over'. That is to say that such things they campaign against are *of the past*: the issue has been decided in their favour and cannot be raised again. History has moved on.

This is a winner's position, of saying you have already won in order to win: not just claiming victory but permanent victory. The presumed entitlement to preside even over *what is discussed in society* is striking. It also shows off that habit of presenting our wishes as fact. In order to prevent something from being debated, we say the debate is already over and everyone has gone home. The real world of politics fades into the background, leaving us in a place where there is no conflict: a higher level of existence where everything has been resolved to the satisfaction of truth and right.

Before Elon Musk took over, Twitter executives used their actual power over public debate to turn this framing into reality: using 'shadow banning' or what they called 'visibility filtering' to reduce the visibility of undesirable individuals and institutions on the platform, but without letting their targets know. Bari Weiss, recipient of 'Part Two' of the 'Twitter Files' released by Musk, has written: 'The group that decided whether to limit the reach of certain users was the Strategic Response Team – Global Escalation Team, or SRT-GET. It often handled up to 200 "cases" a day.' Those placed on blacklists included conservative activist Charlie Kirk, Stanford University's Dr Jay Bhattacharya, who had argued that Covid lockdowns would harm children, and Chaya Raichik's 'Libs of TikTok' account, which shares videos of left-wing ideologues (often in positions of power, like in schools) propagating their ideological nonsense. 'Twitter repeatedly informed Raichik that she had been suspended for violating Twitter's policy against "hateful conduct"', Weiss says. However, in an internal memo after her seventh suspension, the Twitter committee responsible acknowledged that the account had 'not directly' violated its Hateful Conduct policy.[11] Raichik's crimes were political.

The 'safety' argument that Jack Dorsey's Twitter habitually used to justify blocking and suspending accounts has also appeared regularly in the more conventional 'no-platforming' episodes in universities and other places. This focus exploits John Stuart Mill's core liberal 'harm principle' to justify intervention – framing criticisms of themselves and allies as attacks that do 'harm' and endanger them. Progressive sociological ideas about how conservatives and others cause 'harm' simply by opening their mouths offer possibilities here, cuing the routine performances of exaggerated victimhood by activists, claiming maximal harm caused to them, notably to their 'mental health'. The natural pain of contradiction converts into harmful violation, requiring intervention and punishment; hence 'old' Twitter removing certain accounts and university authorities bowing to activist pressure to cancel certain speakers.

## *Transactivism: the limits of cancellation*

'For those wishing to bring about social change, gender is a good place to start', says Joanna Williams, director of the think-tank CIEO and a close follower of the higher education scene.[12] However, when that change involves nothing short of redefining what it is to be a man and a woman, you are going to be stepping on quite a few toes. And this is precisely where transgender activism has gone: attempting to liquefy these categories, to make transition from one to the other as easy as choosing what you want for dinner. Perhaps nothing demonstrates better the extent to which an ethic of change and transformation has consumed the Anglosphere than the remarkable success these activists initially had – securing legislative change and mass institutional support pretty much on the nod.

The right to choose your gender might sound lovely and liberating when presented in that way, until some of the implications become clear: of biological men being allowed into women's changing rooms and toilet facilities, to share women's prisons, to effectively abolish women's distinct identity. There are also the consequences for children being taught these beliefs as fact while they go through the travails of puberty and the natural questioning of identity that occurs during these years. All of this has been happening in our world, but questioning and criticizing it has often provoked a blizzard of condemnation, not just from transgender activists and their supporters but from celebrities and responsible authorities.

For the trans rights movement, assertions of victimhood and harm, of mental trauma and even death, have been central to their politics – offering a ground to their whole political approach. Their argument boils down to this: that anyone opposing them and their ideology, for example by arguing in favour of sex-based rights rather than chosen gender rights, is doing terrible damage to transgender people. In order to prevent this damage from taking place, opponents must be stopped from expressing themselves in public and from being heard in anything but a hostile light: essentially the same argument used by all totalitarian regimes to crush opposition.

A good example of this approach could be seen at a proposed screening of Deirdre O'Neill and Mike Wayne's documentary *Adult Human Female* at the University of Edinburgh in December 2022. A small group of transactivists first 'occupied' the lecture hall in which the film was to be shown, thereby raising crucial 'security' concerns for the authorities, which led to organizers switching the venue. However, the activists then, led by self-identified trans woman Robyn Woof, Edinburgh University Students' Association's Trans and Non-Binary Liberation Officer, physically blocked access to the new room – leading to a stand-off and the screening being cancelled altogether.

Their stance was in some ways counterproductive, gaining much attention and therefore publicity for the film and its feminist promoters. However the University and Colleges Union's Edinburgh branch, representing academics and other staff, supported efforts to get the film banned, demanding that university authorities cancel the 'transphobic' event.[13] On this occasion the authorities refused to comply, going back on their previous stance on such events, justified by ubiquitous 'safety' concerns, which acceded to transactivist demands, even though they created the safety risk.

The campaign of intimidation that feminist academic Kathleen Stock endured at the University of Sussex followed a similar trajectory, but with a substantial added threat level. Transactivists claimed that her gender-critical views had made many people unsafe both on campus and beyond. In the now-familiar language, she was denounced as a 'transphobe' and a 'terf' (a 'trans-exclusionary radical feminist'). Posters were put up on the route into campus repeating the accusations and demanding she be sacked from her job. In the women's toilets, she was confronted by stickers denouncing her for 'transphobic shit'. Masked figures appeared on site letting off flares and holding a sign reading 'Stock Out'. An Instagram account gained more than a thousand followers with the message, 'Our demand is simple: fire Kathleen Stock. Otherwise you'll see us around.'[14] The UCU Sussex branch and Students' Union both supported the protestors, in a sign of how crazy campus politics has become.

Stock understandably decided that she had had enough after all this and resigned her position. The protestors rejoiced in their success at removing an opponent from what they regarded as *their* safe space. However, in doing so they lost a more significant battle. The publicity Stock's case garnered and the measured way she responded to it ended up giving her a much bigger 'platform' for her apparently 'transphobic' views than she would have had otherwise.

Nevertheless, the ability to get rid of an opponent like this from what you treat as *your territory* is not to be sniffed at. It relies on a tried-and-tested formula which our authorities and media are used to giving way to: of maximizing the appearance of group and individual trauma and victimhood, accompanied with pleas for punishment to stop it. The reflexive giving-way to this approach by governing authorities is mercilessly exploited by activists, helping to nail down their influence within institutions, integrating them into the organizational fabric through various specialist positions, rules and procedures, helping to make the evidence base of victimhood they provide essential to ongoing activity.

*The Guardian* newspaper outsources authority to identity activists almost by rote, prioritizing their assertions in its news and opinion pages. The journalist Hadley Freeman says that while she was there, the newspaper refused to let her write about concerns about the campaigning LGBTQ+ charity Mermaids, which had been widely employed to 'train' public institutions including schools in gender ideology, despite how 'it was so obvious that something was very wrong here'.

She says:

> The answer, always, was no, but the reasons given were fuzzy: it wouldn't be right in that section, they couldn't see the news peg, it felt too niche. A more likely reason was one articulated to me with some passion on social media any time I tweeted anything sceptical about [Susie] Green or Mermaids: to question either was to wish trans children would die.[15]

When Freeman's colleague Suzanne Moore managed to get a gender-critical article past the *Guardian* editors in 2020, 338 members of staff and freelancers, including senior editorial staff, sent a letter to editor Katherine Viner (and external media) criticizing 'the pattern of publishing transphobic content'.[16] In doing so they were following the familiar pattern of not so much resisting *free speech* as treating the publication as *their* territory, with its boundaries to be defined by their beliefs.

On one level, for private organizations like *The Guardian*, this seems like little more than an old-fashioned power struggle, albeit with an ideological bent: of vital importance for the people involved but something for them to sort out among themselves. However there is an absolutism here which has proliferated across our public sphere. It contravenes the idea of the *liberal* institution (in the older British rather than contemporary American sense) which gives space – and a degree of respect – to those with whom it disagrees. Certainly, many institutions, led by *The Guardian* and *The New York Times*, and pressured by their employees, have pulled away from the old-style liberal stance in recent years. And so have wider institutions of public life, including universities and state-owned media. Here the approach of treating these places as *your territory*, to be defined by your beliefs and excluding those who do not share them, takes a more sinister form.

Joanna Williams says,

> The core demand from transgender activists is twofold. First, they demand the freedom to name themselves and the world as they see fit, even if it means overriding social and linguistic conventions. Second, they insist that other people obey these decrees and use the language that they prescribe. By policing language, a relatively small group of activists is able to shape, to a considerable extent, what can be said, written and even, ultimately, thought about gender. To police language is to get to the very heart of spontaneous social interaction between people, and to begin to shape our perceptions and understandings of the world.[17]

Policing means enforcement and inflicting punishment for the transgression of certain rules or even laws – in this case for not accepting the authority of transgender ideology on gender identity. This relates even to your own children – indeed maybe *especially* so, since the parent–child relationship is a primary site for potential resistance to gender liberation. Mothers and fathers are more likely to be bothered and more likely to be motivated to resist this ideology. For this reason they appear as potential enemies, possibly preventing vulnerable children from finding their true selves. The family appears as an enemy of personal liberation and the accompanying social progress.

The coalition that has gathered to fight against gender ideology has been impressively broad, but also potent, uniting parents with radical feminists and also with social conservatives, whose publications have offered places for gender-critical writers to publish their work after being turned away by their normal progressive outlets. Far from being eliminated, the much-denounced 'terfs' have if anything shown up more brightly than before – and with a greater sense of mission. As the Harry Potter author J.K. Rowling, a committed gender-critical feminist, says, 'The only time I've ever made reference to being cancelled, my book sales went up. . . . I do not consider myself cancelled.'[18] Stock says, 'Despite the best efforts of my critics, I survived my *annus horribilis* and have much to look forward to. It may be a cliché, but it still applies: sometimes speaking the truth really does set you free.'[19]

We can see here limits to the possibilities of eliminating opponents. A totalitarian ideology can only properly succeed in a totalitarian state system; and even then it is vulnerable in the longer term. Thankfully there are avenues for us to resist and for people to find meaning, purpose and solidarity in resistance. Having a part of the progressive coalition in the resistance against gender ideology has had a big impact here. Gender-critical feminists have brought energy and organization, split the progressive coalition and increased receptivity in places like the media and publishing which generally align to progressive causes.

However the ceding of state institutions (and other bodies) to gender and other identity ideologies has a relentless, grinding power of its own. The list of people who have one way or another been 'cancelled' for resisting this power grows by the day: from the schoolboy in Aberdeenshire who was suspended for insisting there are only two genders to the Christian doctor who was sacked as a disability claim assessor after saying he would not call transgender woman 'she' (with an employment tribunal confirming the justice of the decision).[20] Local councils have cancelled events held by gender-critical groups following complaints from transactivists. Instances have proliferated of police turning up on the doorsteps of people who have made gender-critical statements on social media, warning them to watch their language. Some, like Kate Scottow of Hitchin in Hertfordshire, have even been arrested and taken into police custody, in her case for 'harassment and malicious communications', in 'misgendering' a transgender woman.[21]

Hate crime is a crucial tool in the activist armoury and an established way to harass and intimidate opponents. Even if making a report fails to get them locked up, the way non-criminal speech *is talked about* as crime, and the fact that accusations are automatically recorded as fact, then spoken about publicly as 'crime', successfully criminalizes speech.* As there must be for bureaucracies like the police and local councils, there are rules and procedures at play here. In the case of hate and hate crime, these are somewhat opaque however, appearing more through the medium of internal *guidelines* and *policies* (often

---

* The rhetorical treatment of 'hate crime' by authorities and progressive politicians to describe activity which they dislike but is not legally criminal is Orwell's notion of 'thought-crime' made flesh.

prescribed by activist consultants) rather than in law set by legislators.

The work of categorization, determining what is acceptable and unacceptable speech, therefore becomes subject to the whim of bureaucrats. It must have a degree of formality in order to fit the bureaucratic order. However, when not codified in law, the bureaucrat in the police or local council gains considerable discretion over who and what to go after, given that pretty much anyone *could* count as being guilty at some time or other. Who is guilty and who is innocent therefore becomes more a matter of group-think: of general consensus. And of practical politics.* Defining it becomes more of a social skill, of alignment to generally accepted opinion within the organization and the wider social setting. It becomes a technique of aligning to informal rules.

And this is how the opponents of progressives are variously removed and barred from public service. Compliance with the informal rules of the game is rewarded, with well-paid, responsible positions, privileges and awards. Transgression is punished with removal and barring from responsible positions, public shaming and attempts to make life as difficult as possible for the transgressor: the same as in the Soviet Union and Maoist China. In this way, speech control becomes a key part of the technocratic toolkit: appearing as a rule of *law* but really counting as the expression of organized power within the bureaucracy and those who hang on to it.

The founder of sociology Auguste Comte believed that history has been governed by ideas; that 'the whole social mechanism is ultimately based on opinions'. 'Thus', as J.B. Bury explains it, 'man's history is essentially a history of his opinions.' And these are subject to 'the fundamental psychological law': progress.[22]

Comte is barely read these days, but his style of thinking is very much with us. From his standpoint, the guiding purpose of politics is to help history move through its progressive stages by gradually eliminating the wrong opinions from our minds and replacing them with the right opinions. It is not a process of consultation and participation, but a technical

---

* Witness the widespread anti-Semitic hate speech of Muslim imams in Britain recorded on video following 7 October 2023 which went unpunished, while individuals with little public profile were visited by police and arrested.

process of doing things to people, making them align to the world correctly, rather like placing a shelf on a wall. The social scientist-historian is in control here.

But, since people do not easily change their minds, attempts to discuss, debate and persuade devolve quickly into attempts to remove those with the wrong opinions from any positions where they might influence things: through marginalization, through policing and criminalization and also through extra-judicial violence and intimidation. On social media nowadays, we can see the profiles of those who believe in this approach – and it is remarkable how many are professional sociologists, economists and historians. These are experts *in us*. And, as they see it, they have the authority to decide who among us can be admitted to society and who must be kept out.

In this way, to be on the right or wrong side of history is a moral position for progressives. To be on the right side of history is to be blessed, to be an agent of goodness, bound to succeed in the future; while to be on the wrong side of history is to be earmarked for marginalization and elimination (at least existential elimination, but sometimes material elimination too). History decrees that the wrong type of people with the wrong type of opinions will cease to exist. These sorts of people will no longer prosper, will no longer share in power and indeed will eventually die off altogether like a tribe or species that has gone extinct. Morality becomes a variation of sociology, of apparent fact and of actual power.

For those who believe in history as a righteous power like this, a role naturally appears of *doing* the work of history just as Christians or Muslims might see themselves doing the work of God. The role of the believer is to carry out the virtuous work of extinguishing those whom history has earmarked for destruction.

As the sociologist Zygmunt Bauman has written:

> With one stone of rationality, modernity killed two birds. It managed to recast as inferior and doomed all those forms of life which did not harness their own pains to the chariot of Reason. And it obtained a safe conduct for the pains it was about to inflict itself. Both achievements gave it the confidence and the courage to proceed which otherwise it would have sorely lacked. They also made the rule-governed house which modernity built hospitable to cruelty which presented itself as a superior ethics.[23]

When integrated into a system of identity politics, the reordering mechanism of modernity works to reorder people according to their racial profile, their sex and gender status and other such identity characteristics. It works to judge, promote and punish, manufacturing and reproducing a social hierarchy wherever it holds sway. This is all based in superior knowledge. The elimination of opponents is rational and moral, for ensuring historical progress.

# 6

## *The politics of expertise*

Progressives in public life like to compare themselves to pilots or surgeons. They point out how you would not want any old person to fly you somewhere or conduct surgery on you, so why would you want someone who does not understand how society works to rule over you? They see themselves as people to whom we should defer on all important matters: as experts in society and history – in *the whole*. As they see it, we should leave them alone to deploy their expertise on how things work, returning only to thank them at the end of their work.

In this perspective there is a classically modern way of generating political authority: of claiming to be *above politics*, independent of it. It is a way of exerting power, separate from the futile contentions of politics. It is a matter of technical expertise which the expert can judge as right or wrong without anyone else's input. This style is now so common in our public life as to be almost ubiquitous. The technique of attaining political authority by invoking technical expertise has become so habitual as to be almost unconscious.

### *The 'independent expert'*

In June 2015, during the run-up to the United Kingdom's EU referendum, the state-sponsored Economic and Social Research Council (ESRC) set up a new organization called UK in a Changing Europe (UKICE) to replicate its Future of Scotland initiative for the Scottish independence referendum in 2014. As UKICE said of its mission, 'The primary objective is to disseminate academic research in an accessible format to inform public and political debates on the UK's place in the EU.' Anand Menon, a professor of European politics at King's College, London, was appointed as director; and so the organization began its work, coordinating debates, producing research materials and serving as a source of information for those looking to know more about the European Union and the UK's membership of it.

After the referendum was fought and lost by the Remain side and its state sponsors, UKICE changed tack to examining the consequences of the vote and considering different options for the UK as it embarked on a future outside the EU bloc. In 2019 it raised a further £7.5 million from the ESRC in order to continue providing 'a strong evidence base to inform what is the most critical issue facing not just the immediate, but also the longer term, future of the UK', as ESRC deputy director of research Jeremy Neathey put it.[1] After the ESRC was incorporated into a new body called UK Research and Innovation (UKRI) in 2018, UKICE was left operating at three removes from government oversight as a quango reporting to another quango reporting to another quango which itself operates at arm's length to government. You do not get much more insulated from government influence than this while still remaining within the government system.

The organization described itself as 'the authoritative source for independent research on UK–EU relations' and 'an award-winning, impartial academic think tank', providing 'evidence grounded in research'. In these and other words in which UKICE described itself, we can see the nature of expertise as a source of political authority. It exists to *inform* (so to provide *information* or *evidence*); it is *independent* and *impartial* (which is to say it is apolitical); it wins awards (so is admired); and crucially is authoritative (so wields authority, a political trait).

In January 2023, UKICE published a joint report with the Centre for European Reform (CER) co-written by its Senior Fellow Professor Jonathan Portes and the CER's deputy director John Springford.\* Entitled *The impact of the post-Brexit migration system on the UK labour market*, it drew widespread publicity for the claim that, as a Bloomberg headline boomed, 'Brexit rules cost Britain 333,000 workers'. The report claimed that, by June 2022, 'there was a significant shortfall of around 460,000 EU-origin workers, partly but not wholly compensated for by an increase of about 130,000 non-EU workers' under the liberalized regime

---

\* The CER describes itself as 'an award winning independent think-tank devoted to making the EU work better, and strengthening its role in the world'. It is therefore explicitly aimed at increasing EU power, not just within the borders of the EU but outside too.

implemented by Boris Johnson's government, that had resulted in an estimated immigration figure of 1.1 million during that year – a record high.[2] The pair's longer working paper admitted that it was difficult to disentangle issues of supply and demand as well as the impact of the Covid pandemic, but that it was nevertheless 'a useful thought experiment'.[3]

Notwithstanding the veracity of conclusions grounded in guesswork and supposition, the report made a number of assumptions. For a start, in referring to 'very large shortfalls of EU-origin workers', it assigned shortages specifically to national groups, as if certain, mostly low-skilled, low-wage jobs could only be done by people of EU origin. In doing this it treated EU free movement as a sort of default position from which any change is a loss. The mention of 'Lost EU Workers' in capital letters to emphasize their importance seemed telling. All the talk of shortfalls, shortages and losses painted a picture of a declining working population, when in fact it continued to grow in the eighteen-month period which they were addressing. They were really talking about shortfalls compared to a 'counterfactual' (i.e. theoretical) situation in which the number of EU workers continued to grow at the same rates as they had done before – i.e. very strongly – despite many having gone home during the Covid lockdowns.

This raises some fundamental questions. For a start, it appears that, for the authors, growth in the working population – and of the population as a whole – is necessary and inevitable: a good in itself. Any situation in which an employer cannot find a worker at the wage rate they are offering is a market breakdown and must be met with further liberalization of immigration rules. EU free movement serves as a gold standard in this respect especially for its role in allowing low-wage, low-skilled vacancies to be filled. From these assumptions it is evident that people are merely economic units who are either viable at current wage rates, like EU Workers are, or count as irrelevant and a burden on society. Portes and Springford did not consider how better wages and working conditions for groups like lorry drivers might be something to be welcomed. Rather, they sided with the Next boss Lord Wolfson in saying that what was by any standards a liberal immigration system, further liberalized by the Boris Johnson government, was 'crippling growth'.

Portes, as the UKICE contributor, has been an outspoken opponent of Brexit and its proponents. He is also one of the most committed public advocates of mass immigration, having played a major role in the New Labour governments' quiet embrace of it as policy from his place in the Cabinet Office's Performance and Innovation Unit (PIU). He obviously has extensive experience and genuine technical expertise in the area he is writing about. However, this expertise appears within a certain framing which converts open questions of political decision-making into closed matters of economic logic and self-evident moral righteousness. His paper here, published in alliance with what is in some respects a lobbying organization for the EU, gives a specific and quite narrow purpose to public policy. It closes off alternative ways of framing, for example the priorities of maintaining national sovereignty and democracy, protecting the wages, working conditions and housing costs of the existing working population; also preserving the countryside from relentless urban sprawl that results from high population growth. In his work, sponsored by UKICE, Portes is effectively defending his own policy and legacy. He is almost the opposite of someone who is 'impartial' and 'independent' – as his regular, ferocious denunciations of those who oppose his agenda in articles and social media posts show only too well.

In a blogpost written with senior research fellow Jill Rutter, Anand Menon as UKICE director admitted that 'the UKICE experience has shown that many academics are not as aware as they should be of the implicit biases in their work'.[4] However Menon's own articles and social media have shown obvious commitment to the EU and its goals, not least free movement. He has also sided with the EU on the United Kingdom maintaining checks on goods passing between Northern Ireland and the rest of the UK. And he formerly worked for the European Commission.

In fact, in most UKICE-headlined output, the EU has appeared as a reference point of solidity, goodwill and rationality – in contrast to a hostile, irrational, Conservative pro-Brexit administration. This matched precisely the EU's messaging on Brexit. The organization even produced a friendly fifty-page report on the EU aimed at schoolchildren, referring to the bloc merely as 'an economic and political partnership', failing to mention the constitutional goal of 'ever closer union' and the reduction in national democratic possibilities, let alone the explicit imperial ambitions of many leading EU figures.[5]

In practice, these much-trumpeted ideas of being 'impartial' and 'independent' are promotional tools: a more sophisticated way of being partial, a way of *justifying* partiality and protecting it from challenge – and successful in that too.

This practice of being partial via the language of impartiality gathers around the assumption that all political opinions are based on either correct or incorrect information and must be guided towards correct sources, otherwise they are illegitimate and wrong. However, as Christopher Lasch wrote back in 1998:

> Unless information is generated by sustained public debate, most of it will be irrelevant at best, misleading and manipulative at worst. Increasingly information is generated by those who wish to promote something or someone – a product, a cause, a political candidate or officeholder – without arguing their case on its merits or explicitly advertising it as self-interested material either.[6]

This is what seems to have happened with UKICE and other similar organizations. Indeed, these traits have become a default for public discourse across the Western world. Rather than arguing a case, the supposedly independent expert is teed up as a deciding force, asserting authority over a situation through their command of *information*. As Lasch put it, the press 'embraced a misguided ideal of objectivity and defined their goal as the circulation of reliable information – the kind of information, that is, that tends not to promote debate but to circumvent it'.[7] By placing certain blocks of information into the public sphere, you can direct debate away from other sources of information and from matters which are more political or existential in character.

For UKICE, this concern with informing people from a position of authority formed part of a broader strategy of maximizing the organization's *impact* in the public sphere.* As Menon has explained it, the priority was to 'get us on the front pages all the time'.[8] The purpose of maximizing media exposure is to *move* public opinion, the assumption being that the *information* they provide will have certain effects that will

---

* A couple of months after Keir Starmer's Labour government came into power in July 2024, Menon revealed that the ESRC was not advancing funding to support UKICE beyond when its existing grant expired in March 2025. It had had its impact, it seemed. It had been successful. Ironically, this was a moment at which Europe was changing quite fast, with right-leaning parties, determined to reduce illegal migration, getting elected across the bloc, putting the old institutional consensus under question.

by definition be good. This is a technocratic approach to public opinion, seeking to engineer opinion in a way that the organization does not articulate explicitly, but is nevertheless clear. This approach is sometimes described as 'policy laundering': using government money to fund organizations that attempt to influence government policy. Operating via a chain of arm's-length organizations helps to get around requirements for civil service impartiality in a similar way to how corporations use networks of shell companies to hide certain commitments and liabilities. Through this laundering process, the 'impartial', 'independent' expert view appears as if out of nowhere, cleansed of its origins and motivations.

From outside government, others regularly attempt the same ruse. There was 'Independent SAGE', set up to oppose the government on Covid policy, suggesting it was being negligent in not clamping down harder on people's freedoms – and founded by the anti-Brexit, anti-Tory activist-journalist Carole Cadwalladr. On Brexit itself, the *Financial Times*'s former editor Lionel Barber, given a Légion d'Honneur by President Macron of France a few months after the referendum, his citation crediting 'the Financial Times' positive role in the European debate', set up a body called the 'Independent Commission on UK–EU Relations'. In announcing it, Barber tweeted the mantra, 'Brexit isn't working!' But then almost the opposite: 'We want to promote informed debate and find solutions – NOT refight the referendum.' Lord Kerr, author of Article 50 of the EU's Lisbon Treaty and a fervent opponent of Brexit, was one of those brought on board. Another was the academic Helena Farrand Carrapico, beneficiary of a Jean Monnet Chair funded by the European Commission.

These sorts of organizations, both from outside government and inside it through 'arm's-length' quangos like the Office for Budget Responsibility (OBR) and National Infrastructure Commission (both founded by George Osborne), effectively work to protect certain established political ambitions, laundering them into impartial, objective 'needs' of the government system. The point is not so much to participate in debates as end them.

The expert's privileged position is precisely to be above politics, overseeing the public sphere as an authority figure who is beyond question for having no apparent interest or bias or prejudice. He or she appears in those coveted 'expert' slots in the media to express the correct view and correct the wrong ones. And it seems that these self-styled 'independent experts' sometimes even fool themselves into believing they are not committed politically. This serves as an excuse to commit even more politically, assured by the knowledge that they are just being factual and apolitical: the perfect authority figure for a modern, rationalist, secular order.

## *Identity politics as expertise*

When the PR man and Conservative Party donor Iain Anderson defected to Keir Starmer's Labour Party in 2023, he did so, he said, partly to help 'end the culture wars'.[9] A former 'LGBT business champion' under Boris Johnson, Anderson had grown disillusioned with the Tories' growing resistance to the gender reform lobby. His assumption that his own position, and that fundamental changes in what it means to be a man and a woman, are in no way part of 'the culture wars' (but that those who disagree with him *are*) evokes a common assumption that progressive identity politics does not count as political at all. In the mainstream media, this is reflected in the way identity activists are often pushed forward not as lobbyists but as experts: as specialists in the situation of their identity group. This puts them into positions where their authority appears as unquestionable and is not questioned: those 'expert' slots where they are protected from opposition on the matters they are concerned with.

Actor Daniel Radcliffe was one of several Harry Potter film cast members who took issue with J.K. Rowling, author of the original books, for opposing gender self-identification. In a statement published by the American LGBT support organization The Trevor Project, Radcliffe started off with the standard slogan in supporting his position, then continued:

> Transgender women are women. Any statement to the contrary erases the identity and dignity of transgender people and goes against all advice given by professional health care associations who have far more expertise on this subject matter than either Jo or I. According to *The Trevor Project*, 78% of transgender and nonbinary youth reported being the subject of discrimination due to their gender identity. It's clear that we need to do more to support transgender and nonbinary people, not invalidate their identities, and not cause further harm.[10]

Here we can see the submission to authority: to 'experts' in *professional* bodies who get to decide fundamental issues of identity and dignity. These exalted people all apparently offer the same advice on transgender issues: that if a biological man says he is a woman for example, then he is. To disagree is to discriminate and to do harm. Radcliffe's fellow cast members like Emma Watson said much the same, with Watson suggesting that others follow her in donating to trans-supporting charities Mermaids and Mama Cash.

For a while this mobilizing of expertise to support gender self-identification was astonishingly successful in Western Anglophone countries, even under supposedly 'conservative' governments like that in Britain. Global Butterflies, which provides training on trans and non-binary gender inclusion, got to provide modules for the UK Ministry of Defence under the title 'Expert Insight Series'. The BBC used the activist group Stonewall as 'the experts in workplace equality for LGBTQ+ people' as part of its 'BBC Allies' scheme.* Similar institutional capture occurred in the Government Equalities Office and the House of Commons' Women and Equalities Select Committee.

However, the expertise that these bodies and individuals were deferring to was not so much grounded in objective knowledge as ideology combined with acute political skill, exploiting the willingness of elites to give way to identity activists claiming oppression. In conducting a review on the Tavistock Gender and Identity Development Service (GIDS) in London, the paediatrician Dr Hilary Cass said, 'The evidence base on which it prescribed major hormonal interventions such as puberty blockers was close to non-existent, and many clinicians had expressed concerns about poor diagnosis and record-keeping, and a culture of shutting down criticism.'[11] Activist ideology had found its way even into medical services within the National Health Service (NHS). Children from Ireland were also referred there to help them transition, contributing to an explosion in 'patient' numbers.

Across the identity politics world, independence, expertise and authority are deployed as weapons to delegitimize political opponents.

---

* I think it is worth emphasizing that an 'ally' is an explicitly political role, its use just one example of how the BBC has institutionalized identity politics into its organization, creating wider implicit alliances to political parties that embrace the same ideologies.

The Runnymede Trust, one of the most vociferous race lobbying groups in Britain, describes what it does as 'authoritative, evidence-based interventions to overcome racial inequality'.[12] In 2022, the National Police Chiefs' Council (NPCC) and the College of Policing set up what they called an 'Independent Scrutiny and Oversight Board' (ISOB), as part of a new action plan to tackle racism and racial disparity in the police. The new body was stuffed with race activists, with three of the six initial members being public Labour Party supporters. Barrister Abimbola Johnson was appointed as chair, having been on record advocating for crime being 'reclassified' so that we 'no longer need to fund a police force'.[13] This aligns to the Black Lives Matter ideal of 'defunding' the police and also to the old Marxist idea that the state will naturally wither away following the revolution. This sort of politics now widely appears under the label of 'independent', making it sound somehow impartial, distanced and objective: an illusion of illusions.

The money in identity politics is to be made largely by providing training: convincing bosses that they and their staff need to be re-educated to deal with their respective victim groups in the correct way. This normally involves placing a protective cordon around favoured groups, removing the possibility of criticism and dispensing with disciplinary functions in addressing them, deferring to the activist ideology that sees them as victims by definition, as never *guilty*.

Like many organizations, the media company Sky (now owned by American juggernaut Comcast) has implemented the system of diversity as an organizing principle: including by restricting recruitment of correspondents in London to non-white, minority ethnic and women.[14] In 2021, Sky employed the race ideologue lawyer Shola Mos-Shogbamimu (who perhaps significantly includes 'Dr' in her Twitter profile) to lecture staff on 'Allyship & Psychological Safety', buying up a batch of her books to distribute among staff.[15] Around this time, 'Doctor Shola', as she is widely known, claimed that anyone offended by footballers 'taking the knee' was 'subhuman', called journalist Dan Hodges 'a Racist Apologist epitomising the inferiority complex of white supremacy' and denounced Conservative Home Secretary Priti Patel as a 'Racial Gatekeeper Extraordinaire'.[16] We must assume that the 'psychological safety' of each of these people does not matter.

Psychology and mental health have become a crucial source of authority in this space, offering an evidence base grounded in authority to justify the punishment and suppression of alternative viewpoints.

Joanna Williams says:

> Transgender activists see words as a conduit of distress. In the 1990s, the definition of violence expanded – and the corresponding group of victims increased – with the idea that language can inflict not just psychic harm on people, but physical harm, too. The opening lines of *Words That Wound* [a 1993 book on hate speech that proposed widening definitions of such things as racism] explore the impact of what its authors describe as 'assaultive speech'. They describe how words are used 'as weapons to ambush, terrorise, wound, humiliate and degrade'. This 'assaultive speech' is supposedly not just psychologically damaging but also physically harmful.[17]

In the transgender movement as elsewhere on the progressive identity politics scene, activists often claim to be having physical symptoms caused by opposition to their demands which they then recategorize as 'abuse'. Susie Green, the energetic (now former) boss of charity Mermaids, was appointed series lead consultant for the 2018 ITV drama *Butterfly*. From this position she persuaded producers to quote a statistic that 48 per cent of trans young people had attempted suicide. This figure was based on a small and self-selecting group of volunteers, so nowhere near meeting statistical standards, but was nevertheless presented by the programme as established truth.[18] Indeed it appeared across the public sphere with barely a question, proving dramatically effective at winning support for transgender activism. It was almost perfect in fitting liberal-left prejudices about how social causation works, with oppressor groups (like white people, men and 'cisgender' individuals) causing bad things to happen among victim groups (non-whites, women and transgender).

Such generalized stories presume a blending of different types of expert knowledge: sociological, psychological and physiological, resolving itself into a simple schema of cause and effect in which oppressive people cause pain and trauma in their victims, directly and also indirectly by influencing others. Words pass from oppressive speaker to listener-as-victim, causing pain in the body and mind. And so words become a form of violence.

This is politically useful, for it achieves a breach of John Stuart Mill's classic liberal 'harm principle', which decrees whether something is worth intervening against in a liberal society, justifying punishment of whoever originally said the words in question.

This is the political positioning of activists. Yet these ideas have also been progressively accommodated by the mental health industry in recent times. The American Psychological Association's 'Guidelines for Psychological Practice With Transgender and Gender Nonconforming People' show a complete embrace of them, emphasizing that psychologists and other mental health professionals require training in 'trans-affirmative' practice in order to avoid doing harm to transgender people. The guidelines state, 'Transgender and gender nonconforming (TGNC) people are those who have a gender identity that is not fully aligned with their sex assigned at birth', thereby accepting the reality of self-defined gender identity, while casting doubt over sex identity, which is merely 'assigned at birth' and therefore wholly provisional.[19]

The APA is quite open about the involvement of what it calls 'the TGNC community', which is to say transgender advocacy organizations, in putting together these guidelines.

This story of advocacy merging into academic psychology and therapeutic practice is by no means unique. In his book *Crazy Like Us*, Ethan Watters has written of how Western notions of mental health have been 'homogenizing the way the world goes mad'.[20] Public concentration on conditions like anorexia and depression as health emergencies has, through the power of suggestion, helped them to proliferate in populations. Watters refers to 'a pervasive and mistaken assumption in the mental-health profession: that mental illnesses exist apart from and unaffected by professional and public beliefs and the cultural currents of the time'.[21] Writers presenting conditions as the consequence of certain societal ills have glamorized those conditions and elevated the social role of sufferers: encouraging others to present the relevant symptoms, which then increases the sense of crisis around them.

Those who do not accept such crises as decreed by Western academics and researchers appear as backward. Watters writes of how Western 'experts' confidently predicted an epidemic of post-traumatic stress disorder (PTSD) and depression in response to the 2004 tsunami in Sri Lanka. 'As part of its billion-dollar pledge of assistance', he writes, 'Australia sent multiple teams of counsellors with the intent to bring the mental-health services in the region "into the modern era".'[22] Few of the traumatologists sent over from Australia and other places had the slightest understanding of the people they were meant to be delivering 'psychological first aid' or 'critical incident debriefing' to, nor of how local cultures already had their own ways of dealing with such disasters. Sri Lankans, Watters says, 'conceived of the damage done by tsunami as occurring not inside their mind but outside the self, in the social environment'.[23] Western professionals often saw this as a form of denial of ultimate psychological reality and the need for their services.

The promotion of often vaguely-defined mental illness as a variant of conventional medical illness, as has become fashionable in the West and increasingly beyond, imposes a model which demands *treatment* by *professionals*, often assisted by the pharmaceutical industry. This in turn demands significant spending. It also places mental health practitioners on a pedestal like conventional doctors, according them a role to administer *cures* to *disease* in the population. However, given that you plainly cannot achieve this just by talking to individual sufferers one-to-one through the 'talking cure', it opens up possibilities for a much greater social role than the normal doctor: one that aligns nicely with political ideology.

In 2020, the APA president Sandra L. Shullman seized on the killing of George Floyd and other examples of apparently racist killings to say:

> We are living in a racism pandemic, which is taking a heavy psychological toll on our African American citizens. The health consequences are dire. Racism is associated with a host of psychological consequences, including depression, anxiety and other serious, sometimes debilitating conditions, including post-traumatic stress disorder and substance use disorders. Moreover, the stress caused by racism can contribute to the development of cardiovascular and other physical diseases.[24]

Similar examples proliferate across American medical practice and have started to appear in Britain and elsewhere. It reflects a wider trend which Christopher Lasch has again identified. 'In order to justify the expansion of therapeutic authority over the family, the school, and large areas of public policy', he said, the helping professions 'made extravagant claims for their expertise. They set themselves up as doctors not only to sick patients but to a sick society.'[25] This just happens to match the agendas of progressive left-wing politics in seeing society as a patient that needs their enlightened administration to cure. '"Social justice," as liberals have come to define it', Lasch said, 'now refers to political therapies . . . [and is] concerned, above all, to expand their professional jurisdiction.'[26] Expertise appears as a new and fruitful way of doing social justice politics in a different idiom that is more effectively insulated from criticism. For politicians and activists adopting the style, it promises almost boundless authority, protected from immediate questioning. For the psychological industry and activist charities, burgeoning income streams beckon, both from the state and from wealthy clientele indoctrinated into this fashionable style which simultaneously knows what is going on and what to do about it.

Merging into the 'independent' expert role, those adopting the activist style are now teed up as a deciding force, asserting authority over the situations they are interested in. They appear to have command over what is going on. They express boundless confidence in themselves and their knowledge, in the facts and evidence which they have to hand and which prove they are right. In this way they successfully launder interest group politics into expertise. Politics is converted into knowledge and authority. In the process, politics itself is neutered; with opposition effectively quarantined as lacking the necessary authority or tolerated as an essentially irrelevant reactionary echo.

## *The nature of expertise*

Thinking about the nature of expertise itself, I think we can identify two levels. The first is the basic meaning: of proficiency in a technique or skill like flying a plane or performing surgery. Then there is the second sense, the social sense of being *recognized* as an expert, having *the status* of someone with superior powers in a certain area. The pilot and the surgeon combine the two. They have genuine proficiency in their field and society recognizes this proficiency, assigning them to the task where they can put it to use: a domain that is strictly limited.

Flying a plane and conducting surgery are complex skills. However, in each of them there are relatively narrow goals that the expert is meant to achieve and a relatively narrow set of means to achieve it with. Moving from this situation to the notion of expertise in society is a quantum leap. The ends you seek and the means you use to achieve them are both potentially much greater, to the extent of no discernible boundaries existing on either. Anyone claiming to be able to negotiate these possibilities in the same way that a pilot would fly a plane or a surgeon conduct surgery is assigning to themselves the sort of powers and wisdom that a God would have.

In contrast, the Danish physicist Niels Bohr once said, 'An expert is a man who has made all the mistakes, which can be made, in a very narrow field.'[27] For Bohr, expertise was something strictly bounded, within 'a very narrow field'. However progressives tend to take it the other way: generally treating their authority as expandable, without borders and boundaries except that between themselves and their opponents; between their own rightness and their opponents' wrongness. This rightness is something which can cover the whole world and history, uniting the universality of the Christian religious style with the appearance of intellectual rigour. It is an intoxicating prospect for anyone with pretensions to social power.

Rather than encouraging humility, the wide and seemingly unbounded vistas of expert authority offer constant possibilities for shifting one's focus and throwing opponents off course. While maintaining the whole world as the sphere of their expertise, the expert as the initiator of activity can also compress what is *relevant* by only including aspects in which they do have specialist knowledge, the field of economics being a common example. However any discipline with large amounts of impenetrable jargon serves well. After all, part of the point is to maintain that demarcation between yourself as expert and those who must defer to your authority – and this is done largely through the use of specialist language.

In this way the expert imposes a certain type of framing on the world, of what matters and what can be done – but also of who is qualified to speak about it (only those who speak the specialized language). This all works to narrow down the possibilities of politics, placing alternative forms – and other people – out of sight. The field where intervention is justified stretches well beyond the horizon, but what shows up within it is pared down so it can be confidently handled. This process treats the world as an instrument for the expert to manipulate and deploy. It fits the technocrat's style of seeing society as a means to achieve their own goals: goals which are meant to benefit society but whose content is either left vague and inexplicit or converted into narrow technical measurements like GDP.

There is genuine technical expertise in all of this. There is genuine skill in generating *the appearance* of expertise, of being accepted as an expert. Even if the nature of the expertise is questionable, success in pressing it upon us (for example every time we turn on the radio) cannot help but have an effect. By taking on the role of expert and using the power of suggestion and repetition, the social expert succeeds in making others recognize their authority, or at least not opposing it. This is a form of expertise in itself. It is just not that which is claimed.

The most potent weapon in the armoury is not the ability to fly the plane of society or conduct surgery on it but to make us accept that *they* can and should be doing it. It is a form of *knowhow* which only makes sense if the person concerned is integrated into a system of power where they can control some of the levers, or are confident of how they will be controlled. Many, attracted by the aura of authority around the role, talk the same expert's talk from a position of little power and get nowhere with it. Wherever you find a recognized expert, you will also find a network of interest and power which confers the recognition. Experts in society are the people modern technocratic power pays to justify itself. Indeed, in a sense they *are* modern technocratic power: a preferred means to get around the constraints of democratic government and accountability.

## *The role of predictions*

A crucial tool in the kit is the prediction: something that creates truth before reality shows us the evidence.

Just before the 2024 American Presidential Election, the podcaster and former Conservative MP Rory Stewart made a bold one in response to the veteran journalist and broadcaster Andrew Neil. 'Journalists would like the US race to seem as close as possible', he said, 'it suits their appetite for suspense and @afneil's desire to prod the establishment. But this won't be a close race decided by a "couple of thousand votes". He [Neil] is wrong. And Kamala Harris will win.' He supplied reasons for his confidence, including that 'Trump's lost ground since 2016', concluding, 'The polls are "herding" at 50:50 to protect themselves after past misses – ignore.'[28]

When the extent of his wrongness emerged during a live broadcast a couple of nights later, Stewart seemed to be admirably frank in confronting it. However the explanation he came up with skilfully turned his wrongness into a form of rightness.

As he explained:

> I think I was wrong because I'm an optimist; and I hate the idea of being right pessimistically. I think you can be a false prophet and right. . . . My bet on Kamala Harris was a bet on the American people. It was a bet on liberal democracy. It was a bet against populism. It was a bet on hope.[29]

This explanation almost exemplified the progressive mindset. Stewart's starting point was that he was right, in political, moral and rational terms. For him, his mistake was merely technical in misunderstanding how far the American people had progressed towards his point of view. He was effectively placing himself in the future, expecting the American people to catch up. As it turned out, they were not as wise as he had assumed. And so his startlingly wrong assertions on the facts ended up vindicating him as a human being, distinguishing himself from the mass, once more asserting his superiority.

Predictions like Stewart's effectively stand ahead, in front, waiting for everyone else to arrive. They get to the place they are talking about before the rest of us do, curating the scene before we have had the chance to see it for ourselves. According to this perspective, if we do not end up in the same place in time, then *we* have failed.

This assumption of superior authority can make predictions a potent political weapon. They help to justify our desires, turning them into necessities and making alternative approaches appear impossible for the rational and/or moral self. Predictions tell us that the path we want to take will inevitably succeed, while that of our opponents will inevitably fail. They turn 'want' into 'should' and even 'must'. As Stewart said later: 'We were wrong to believe Kamala Harris would win. We were not wrong to believe that she should have won. Or that the values + vision that she represents can win again.'[30] In effect predictions are a form of the praxis that Marxists employ: uniting theory and practice, making practice a mere consequence of theory and closing off alternative approaches as by definition wrong.

The prediction sets the scene for political battles, offering guidance to the group of what to look for and highlight – and therefore also what to pass over. The prediction suggests how opponents will fail, offering a suite of things to look out for and highlight. It offers clarity and helps guide future activities. It therefore helps to facilitate the thing it predicts – at least in the minds of the people who gather around it. This phenomenon can be illustrated through the old transport industry doctrine of Predict and Provide, whereby you predict future demand for a mode of travel and then provide new infrastructure like roads and runways to meet that demand. However, by building new roads you make road travel easier, thereby generating the demand you predicted and maybe more. So Predict and Provide ends up amplifying the problems you were apparently trying to resolve. The only people to gain are the contractors, the car-makers and the oil companies who sponsored the predictions in the first place.

Predictions seduce us into acting, sometimes in the interests of others. In Vietnam, the American military leadership constantly talked up the ability of the South Vietnamese and their own forces to prevail, damning journalists who doubted them as uninformed and irresponsible. One of the American slogans of the Second World War, 'We can win; we must win; we will win', perhaps expresses it best.[31]* Here, the prediction asserts will and confidence more than predictive power. It inserts a stake in a piece of existential territory, making a commitment that must then be followed through and defended. It is an inherently progressive tool: always confident of improvement *for us* and with that, for the world or the universe, just as long as we defend our reputation.

The plethora of predictions about the disastrous consequences of Brexit take a similar form. Once made, they had to be fulfilled – largely by more predictions anticipating disaster to confirm the previous ones. Many, for example from the supposedly 'independent' Office for Budget Responsibility (OBR), proved much too pessimistic. However, whether or not they come true seems almost beside the point. For all the

---

* The chant 'I believe that we will win!' employed by American sports teams continues this tradition today.

predictions of disaster, given sufficient publicity, *themselves* added up to an appearance of continuous disaster, which made it a real disaster. As with the American chant, the main effect of these predictions was not to create an intellectual test in the future but to create an event in the present moment, one which has an impact on the people who hear it, gathering them around a vision of destiny. Predictions are inherently progressive. They put forward a belief about the future: that we know what will happen there, that we know what will work and that we are right. They are progressive social science made flesh.

PART TWO

# THE PROGRESSIVE SOCIETY

# 7

## *From art to activism*

'In fifty years, people will find my music obvious; children will understand and sing it.'[1] So said the Austrian composer Anton von Webern, perhaps the most serious exponent of the serialist strand of music composition in the early twentieth century. Needless to say, Webern was wrong. His music is as obtuse as it ever was for normal music listeners and children do not sing it, let alone understand it.

Webern however did become a hero in intellectual music circles, among post-WWII academic composers and musicologists who spend their time pontificating about music and issuing decrees about what is good and bad; about what music is sufficiently advanced and what is behind the times. The serialist approach which Webern's teacher Arnold Schoenberg had come up with, according equal status to each note (rather than having a tonal centre like B flat or C for example), had been a genuinely new departure in music. It followed Schoenberg's earlier discarding of tonality and conjured up for many – especially after the Second World War – heady visions of a new music, overthrowing Western traditions and bringing in a new dawn, without associations to a dreadfully tainted past.

Webern's rigorous approach to serial composition led to him being accorded hero status by Pierre Boulez, a French composer of the post-WWII era known more for his outspoken utterances and for his wider role in music culture than for his music. Calling himself a '300 percent Leninist', Boulez dismissed any music from before 1900 as mere 'nostalgia' and even denounced Schoenberg and his rival modernist Igor Stravinsky as stuck in the past and insufficiently revolutionary.[2] He upheld the prematurely deceased (and decidedly unrevolutionary) Webern as a sort of God-like figure, saying that composers who failed to submit to his twelve-note disciplines had no right to call themselves composers. As the music critic Norman Lebrecht has described it, 'anyone who had not felt "the necessity of the 12-tone language" was, in his view, "superfluous".'[3]

Schoenberg was an Austrian Jew who, as Lebrecht presents it, 'believed he had found a "method of composition that will assure the supremacy of German music for 1,000 years"'. He adds, 'though this dream was confounded by public resistance and political reverses, his 12-note technique became the basis for what was perceived as musical progress for the rest of the century'.[4]

The American writer Harold Schonberg (not a relation), writes:

> Schoenberg felt himself to be a man with a mission. . . . He conceived of music as an art that conveyed 'a prophetic message revealing a higher form of life toward which mankind evolves.' Schoenberg, of course, was the prophet bearing the message. A higher force was directing him.[5]

He told his friends of how, 'The Supreme Commander had ordered me on a higher road.' Schonberg (Harold) says, 'His letters are full of an insistence on the unalterable rightness of his music. Schoenberg's egomania approached Wagner's. "I believe what I do and do only what I believe; and woe to anybody who lays hands on my faith. Such a man I regard as an enemy, and no quarter given! You cannot be with me if you are also with my opponents."'[6]

Like Webern, Schoenberg believed his music would inevitably prevail, though made the schoolboy error of predicting when.

Schonberg again quotes him:

> 'In ten years,' [Schoenberg] wrote in 1910, 'every talented composer will be writing this way, regardless of whether he has learned it directly from me or only from my works.' Later he was not so confident. 'Today,' he wrote in 1924, 'I realize that I cannot be understood, and I am content to make do with respect.' Several years before his death he was resigned to his fate. In a letter written in 1947 he said that 'I am quite conscious of the fact that a full understanding of my works cannot be expected before some decades. The minds of the musicians, and of the audiences, have to mature ere they can comprehend my music. I know this, I have personally renounced an early success, and I know that – success or not – it is my historic duty to write what my destiny orders me to write.'[7]

Schoenberg and many of his compatriots took these sorts of attitudes with them to Britain and America after fleeing the Nazis. Ralph Vaughan

Williams, who worked to get some of them released from British internment camps, was struck by how strident and domineering they could be, writing in 1942, 'The Austrians have a great musical tradition, and they are apt to think that it is the only musical tradition and that everything which is <u>different</u> must be <u>wrong</u> or <u>ignorant</u>; they think moreover that they have a mission to impose their culture wherever they go as being the only one worth having.'[8]

The revolutionary and theoretical aspects of the serialist project were anticipated by Richard Wagner, who alongside his giant operas wrote a series of tracts including *Art and Revolution* (1849), *The Art Work of the Future* (1850) and *Jewry in Music* (1850). He supported European revolution. 'I will destroy the existing order of things', he said. 'So up, ye peoples of the earth! Up ye mourners, ye oppressed, ye poor!'[9] However he later started condemning 'the vulgar egotism of the masses' and expressed a fierce anti-Semitism, demanding Aryan racial purity. Hitler said of him: 'Whoever wants to understand National Socialistic Germany must know Wagner.'[10]

Hannah Arendt famously said, 'It is well known that the most radical revolutionary will become a conservative the day after the revolution.'[11] In the Soviet Union, the exciting artistic and intellectual ferments of the 1910s and 1920s were increasingly frowned upon and suppressed after the Revolution. Schonberg writes of how, 'A dreadful pall of uniformity fell over Russian art, literature, and music; and critics – all of them official spokesmen of government doctrine – developed a weird jargon in which music was evaluated not on its own merits but on its doctrinal purity.'[12] The aim shifted from usurping established power to protecting it.

Serialism has something quite significant in common with this. For in Schoenberg's hands it represented a closing down: the imposition of a new order of rules after his previous *liberation* of music from the *domination* of tonal centres in music. And the schemas he, Webern and others came up with served as tools for a form of political organization: for dividing the right people from the wrong people, with the right ones deserving favour and the wrong ones meriting marginalization.

Some of the music they composed is interesting, not just intellectually but aurally as well. The serialists' lingering musical instincts did sometimes push through the mathematical constraints of their theories.

They did achieve new and valuable things in music, albeit their project exhausted itself after a brief burst in the 1950s and 1960s. Their main legacy lies in the theoretical disciplines: in academic musicology, where music is talked about, theorized about and judged. In this domain the serialists provided tools to help intellectuals distinguish themselves from the masses, to assert themselves as more advanced than the rest.

The words and theories have provided a language for academics to promote their authority as *experts* in music and indeed the wider society, dictating what are greater and lesser forms of culture. By achieving dominance in the universities, this language has become a shared language for a group which is constantly working to police its boundaries as simultaneously those between acceptable and unacceptable culture. For this group of musicologists, those who do not share the group's rules and customs must be excluded for the sake of music and culture. Outsiders' opinions on music appear as illegitimate for being founded on insufficient, out-of-date knowledge. Through this process, the ideas of serialists have endured within the judgemental Western intellectual-political tradition, even as the music seems to have exhausted its possibilities long ago.

### *Useful art*

Between October 2018 and February 2019, the Tate Modern gallery in London gave parts of its space to a self-styled Cuban-American 'artivist' called Tania Bruguera for 'a series of subtle interventions' under the rubric 'Hyundai Commission: Tania Bruguera – 10,148,451'. One of the effects Bruguera curated for visitors was to provoke 'forced empathy' for the projected image of a refugee to London from Syria, using an organic compound in the air to induce tears: so literally forcing visitors to cry.

Bruguera, described as 'a key player within the fields of performance, interdisciplinary practice and activism' with 'a unique concept for her political approach to art – Arte Util (useful art)', was also appointed Lead Artist for the community outreach programme Tate Exchange as part of her residency.

For her own 'programme' in this role, Bruguera convened a group of local people called Tate Neighbours, the purpose being 'to explore how the Tate could be a better institution and also to inspire people to take action'. Translated into simpler English, she was training them to be political activists. Appearing in the programme literature as representatives of 'the community', the Neighbours turned out to be handpicked by Bruguera with the assistance of an organization called Counterpoints, which advocates for migrants, refugees and 'social change' in the arts sector. The first discussion with them she initiated was on the topic 'How do we DISRUPT the INSTITUTION?' In a video promoting this initiative, one participant, described as a 'Retired Local Resident', appeared wearing a Che Guevara beret and recited how, 'now, I do feel that I am an activist, actively concerned and actively expressing myself in sorts of new ways'. Indeed, the video focused almost exclusively on assertion, written and verbal, in the forming of slogans like those to be chanted at a protest or put on a placard. Those highlighted included:

I'm committed to acting
WHERE I COME FROM,
WHERE I NOW LIVE
WHERE I AM AT THIS MOMENT

WHEN THE
RIGTHS [sic] OF
MIGRANTS ARE
DENIED, THE
RIGHTS OF
CITIZENS ARE AT
RISK

And

LOVE
PEOPLE
YOU DON'T
KNOW

We might see how Bruguera's 'useful art' deploys *the world of* art (famous galleries, the audiences who flock to them and corporate sponsorship) in an instrumental manner, directing them to achieve specific effects in the world. In the Neighbours initiative and slogans which emerged from it, neighbourhood and community appear as things which are curated by *the artist* as a political actor, not as things that evolve organically over time as people get to know each other in a local area. In this case it gathers around shared political activity and messaging associated with Bruguera's concern with migration and borders. From her Tate video, the slogans kept on coming, including the simple 'migrants', 'WE ARE ALL FROM MIGRANTS', 'Migration enriches cultures' and 'Dismantling White Superiority': so injecting a racialist angle into the mix. At one point she brought in the spectre of conspiracy, referring to how 'nationalistic ideological tendencies are infiltrating the world . . . separating people between "us" and "them"' (as if she was not doing precisely that herself). As well as conspiratorial, her stance was defensive: as if an already-achieved revolution is under threat from reactionary, nationalist forces. She presented a situation in which the right people (like artists, migrants and handpicked 'community' activists) are being threatened by the wrong people, whose wrongness is partly defined by them distinguishing 'us' from 'them'. The perspective takes a colonialist attitude to settled populations, seeing them as a group whose thoughts need to be suppressed if they do not match the correct slogans; the borders that separate them from outsiders must be removed so destroying their citizenship, making it *de facto* a redundant category.

In the upper echelons of the visual arts world, the assumption that artistic activity should have a specific purpose beyond itself, making things happen beyond itself, sometimes appears almost universal. The causes to which artists (or 'artivists' in Bruguera's terminology) devote themselves are also remarkably uniform, to the extent that the arts, progressive political activity and indeed corporate publicity often seem to be enmeshed with each other. Art is appearing more as event or gathering on the lines of political campaigning than as an autonomous sphere of activity, shining lights on these other worlds.

The Turner Prize of 2019 certainly went that way. The biggest and most prestigious prize in the British art world, that year the four nominees effectively took it over, writing a joint letter to the jury insisting that they should share the award, noting how the social and political issues they made their art about were of great importance and urgency and should not be divided from each other.

> The politics we deal with differ greatly, and for us it would feel problematic if they were pitted against each other, with the implication that one was more important, significant or more worthy of attention than the others.
>
> At this time of political crisis in Britain and much of the world, when there is already so much that divides and isolates people and communities, we feel strongly motivated to use the occasion of the prize to make a collective statement in the name of commonality, multiplicity and solidarity – in art as in society.[13]

As *The Guardian* put it, 'This year's Turner prize has been one of the most political in its history with work exploring themes of migration, patriarchy, torture and civil rights. The artists asked judges not to pit those subjects against each other.'[14]

In making such a pitch, the four reduced their work to subject matter: to what it was *about* rather than what it *was*. They pre-empted the judges by applying their own, political, standards of importance to what they had produced. And, rather than tell the artists to bugger off, the jury issued a statement echoing the artists' messaging and saying they were 'honoured' to do as they were told: thereby playing their own role in breaking down borders between judge and judged, winners and losers, art and politics.

In the middle of the 2019 General Election campaign, the artists used their platform to issue another statement.

> We each seek to use art to push at the edges of issues, mapping the bleed of one into another, across time, across sectionalities, across the realm of the real and the imagined and through walls and borders.
>
> This year as it has often done in the past, the prize has sought to expand what it means to be 'British'.
>
> We find this significant in an era marked by the rise of the Right, and the renewal of fascism in an era of the Conservatives' hostile environment, that has paradoxically made each of us and many of our friends and family again increasingly unwelcome in Britain.[15]

As Tate director Maria Balshaw gushed, 'This year's #TurnerPrize artists are fearlessly committed to the creation of positive change.'[16] One wore a Tories Out badge and seemingly everyone felt good about themselves.

In doing so they formed a strong, united group: a political entity for which historical sociology plays a crucial, authoritative role. Talking of the Turner four, Tate Britain director Alex Farquharson emphasized how 'their work seeks to foreground the voices of those who have been marginalised by dominant historical accounts or accounts of society today'.[17]

Getting ready for a run of her production of Shakespeare's *Henry V* at London's tourist hot-spot The Globe, Holly Race Roughan, artistic director of Headlong Theatre, said:

> When I read Henry V, I thought: 'Fucking hell, this is the pinnacle of English mythologising, and white supremacy, and toxic masculinity.' I felt like I'd discovered the dirty, murky roots of English nationalism. I wanted to pull the play out of the ground and look at those roots and start asking questions about them. What is Englishness? What social and political purpose does it serve?[18]

A committed political activist and organizer, Race Roughan's framing of specifically *English* nationalism as *dirty* (and therefore in need of being cleansed) might raise an eyebrow given her company secured £680,000 from Arts Council England, England's national arts subsidy organization, during the period 2018–22. However such attitudes and the dubious history behind them do not appear to be a deterrent.\* In fact Headlong managed to secure four months at The Globe to showcase her reimagining of *Henry V*, trading off the name of one of the greatest playwrights in history in order to display her generic political views of the moment.

During the Covid lockdown in 2020, a BAME-only 'anti-establishment' group called Rising Arts Agency won help from Bristol City Council to place its political messaging onto more than 370 advertising billboards in the city area. One of the slogans on these billboards read, 'The blood is on your hands' repeated three times accompanied with the message 'So, Mr White Man . . . What are your plans?'

Euella Jackson, Engagement Officer for Rising Arts, told Arts Council England, which provided development funding to the organization, that the project allowed them 'to radically reimagine public space and we did

---

\* Anyone looking for the roots of English nationalism should probably start with the Norman Conquest and resentment at the 'Norman Yoke' that imposed itself on the country.

our best to turn Bristol into our radical gallery space'. 'We were really driven by the killing of George Floyd and wanted to help our community turn to creativity in times of crisis and to tell the sector and the city – that we are TIRED.'[19]

Here we see an extension to the appropriation of space, from private galleries where people visit voluntarily to public space where the messaging is forced on those passing by. In this case the messaging promotes an idea of the white-skinned man as a killer that needs to atone for his killing: a scapegoat figure deserving of denunciation and punishment, similar to how the bourgeois, kulak or rich peasant featured in the Soviet Union and Maoist China.

Taking names like 'Creative Producer', the people promoting this messaging are primarily advocates and ideologues. They work for what is really a hybrid political advertising agency. And they are gaining help both from local government and the national state arts subsidy body, Arts Council England.

## *Transforming the nation*

In its strategy paper for 2020–30, entitled *Let's Create*, Arts Council England ('ACE' for short) sheds light on why a political organization like Rising Arts might receive the taxpayers' money it doles out (£446 million a year in 2023–6), explaining how, 'Many people are uncomfortable with the label "the arts" and associate it only with either the visual arts or "high art", such as ballet or opera.'[20]

> We also recognise that the traditional boundaries between and around cultural activities are disappearing as new technologies and other societal changes alter the ways in which many artists, curators, librarians and other practitioners work, as well as how culture is made and shared. We're excited by these changes, which we expect to accelerate over the next decade – and in response, we will become more flexible about the range and type of cultural activities that we support over the years to come.[21]

As a result, ACE says, 'we have used "creative practitioners" rather than "artists" as an umbrella term for all those who work to create new, or reshape existing, cultural content'.[22]

The argument here is basically sociological: that something is happening in society that the overseeing organization must adjust to in order to avoid becoming irrelevant. And this justifies it breaking down the barriers between artistic and non-artistic activity so that the latter might receive money previously reserved for the former. The role of artist merges with the non-artist, forming different parts of a wider soup of 'culture' or 'creative' activity which can incorporate such things as fashion, advertising and political messaging. It means a greater range of existing activity can be supported, just as long as it can satisfy the ACE's sprawling bureaucratic demands.

For organizations which devote themselves to artistic activity rather than agitprop and social engineering, ACE's perspective is distinctly unfriendly. A 2020 paper, 'Diversity in classical music', from ACE's director for music, begins sternly: 'The workforce of our orchestras and ensembles is not fully reflective of the diverse society in which we live.' She talks of how 'barriers' of disability, race and gender need to be broken down, of a need for 'relevance' and social purpose and how 'the pace of change is too slow'. Then in even stranger, more ominous prose: 'We believe that a key marker of the classical sector's ability to fully demonstrate its power as a relevant and powerful force for good within our society is its inclusivity.' And then the sociological clincher: 'Classical music benefits significantly from the innovation and energy which comes from more inclusivity.'[23]

The tangible results of this commitment were revealed in ACE's 2022 funding round, with Welsh National Opera losing a third of its funding, the English National Opera initially losing the whole of its £12.6 million annual grant* and the Britten Sinfonia having its entire £406,000 grant removed. Meanwhile the London-based Chineke! Orchestra, marketed as 'Europe's first majority-BAME orchestra', won a first grant of £700,000, rising to £2.1 million over three years. According to ACE, Chineke! and Paraorchestra, the world's only large-scale ensemble for professional disabled musicians, 'have shattered preconceptions about the talent and creativity of such musicians'.[24] Details about this shattering and of the preconceptions which have been shattered are thin on the ground. It just

---

* ACE later restored funding after the reaction to this news and further negotiations.

stands as a sociological fact – and as a *good thing* which an arts funding body should obviously prioritize.

The appearance is of a circular self-justification: that classical music will become more inclusive by imposing administrative standards of inclusivity. Good will be achieved by being good; good *is* achieved by being good. Quality of composition and performance, ability, technique and training appear as afterthoughts, if that.

All of this activity comes under one overriding purpose: the need for 'change', that defining progressive principle. *Let's Create* features the word and its derivations thirty-one times in its sixty-seven pages. The document includes a chapter entitled 'The case for change', a page given to promoting 'Theatre that changes the world' and repeated talk of how 'Arts Council England must change'. In the latter exhortation, we might see an echo of Bruguera's activist group 'disrupting' the Tate *as an initiative of the Tate*. The purpose of the institution is to disband itself as something irredeemably tainted and therefore illegitimate. It is like an evangelical conversion.

The fundamentally revolutionary character of this approach is reinforced by the absence of variations of 'preserve' and 'conserve' in *Let's Create*. Meanwhile, there are just four mentions of 'tradition' and its derivations, all negative in framing. To England's rich artistic traditions, ACE is holding up two fingers, couching its rejection as a mere consequence of social change.

Chief executive Darren Henley's final words to *Let's Create* are: 'Together, let's create better lives.' This reflects how the document is effectively a manifesto for social improvement, with arts and culture serving as an instrument to *make society* – and us – *better*. And it does this by funding activities, not necessarily artistic in any meaningful sense, that seek to suppress the longstanding population of England and any culture which persists that might be associated with them, in the name of culture.

We might call this a *progressive imperialism*: imposed by elite institutions on certain unfavoured non-elite populations in order to erase their presence in the world, which they have judged is holding back social progress. The revolution or colonizing process here is ongoing. It treats migrant populations (including people with several generations of presence in the country) as a revolutionary subject to be thrown against longer-standing, backward groups in order to improve society. It reproduces similar relations to those imposed in revolutionary societies like the Soviet Union and Cambodia (as Kampuchea) but perhaps more closely those which prevailed under colonial rule in places like South Africa, Australia, Canada and South America, where immigrants (in this case from Europe) formed the vanguard of social change and improvement.

*Let's Create* itself has a 'What we want to achieve' section, opening with another statement: 'By 2030, we envisage a country transformed by its culture and at the same time constantly transforming it: a truly creative nation in which every one of us can play a part.'[25] The role of creativity is to *transform* the nation, it seems, in a sociological sense. And this is something that *everyone* can take part in. This transformation achieves 'positive change' (a catchphrase that proliferated around the time of Brexit and Trump to distinguish the change that progressives want from that which actually happened during this time). 'Good governance and leadership will be critical in inspiring positive change', we read, 'and growing teams that are happy, inclusive and able to draw on the widest possible range of ideas and experiences in order to build successful businesses over the next decade.'[26] This is utopian, dream-worthy stuff: a melange of lovely-sounding things almost without limit, all happening at the same time to everyone touched by the magic touch of *creativity*. It is a wet dream of an organization that appears to see itself as a sort of alternative government, bravely attempting to change the country in spite of the actual government of the time.

The way ACE marks its own homework is instructive. Towards the beginning of the document, it tells us that it is beginning the 2020s 'with a far clearer understanding of the role that culture can play in building the identity and prosperity of places, creating stronger communities, and inspiring change'.[27] This is a claim about sociological knowledge. Effectively this organization which hands out 'arts' subsidies is claiming to understand how social causation works in order to change it: not just in minor ways but by building *identities, prosperity, strong communities* and *inspiring people* to make change happen (i.e. to become effective political activists). And this social scientific approach helps to ringfence its authority.

This quasi-imperial, change-making role is certified in mountains of bureaucracy. For ACE expects the organizations and artists it subsidizes to show the same sort of superpowers that it claims to have: micromanaging not just themselves but the audiences who attend their shows so that they *reflect* the people living nearby. One of its four 'Investment Principles' is Inclusivity & Relevance. Of this it says that it will confer targets on funding recipients based on how their governance, leadership, employees, participants, audiences and the work they make 'reflect the communities in which they work'. Coming straight out of the Public Sector Equality Duty (PSED), these targets will cover 'both protected characteristics (including disability, sex, and race) and socioeconomic background'.*  [28]

The intersectional cookie-cutting required tells us where this is leading. To negotiate your way to funding success, people and organizations have to remake themselves in the image of progressive bureaucracy. For many, this means employing consultants who are familiar with this world, who have the right connections into progressive identity politics, so siphoning off money to pay them. It is a form of legalized corruption, going through the state, largely 'independent' of government. And it leads to a relentless standardization, through employment of the same people to fill in the forms and set the policies; with statements everywhere designed to impress the bureaucrats rather than entice the paying public. And this is reflected in the artistic or 'cultural' output of organizations and people who get through the process, all but eliminating the distinctiveness of who they are and what they do. It all merges into the same mush of appearance and assertion.

The writer J.G. Ballard had some words to say about the Arts Council in his memoir *Miracles of Life*, observing that the funds it disperses 'have created a dependent client class of poets, novelists and weekend publishers whose chief mission in life is to get their grants renewed'. 'I assume that the patronage of the arts by the state serves a political role by performing a castration ceremony, neutering any revolutionary impulse and reducing the "arts community" to a docile herd.'[29] That 'docile herd' however now expresses its docility by playing up how *revolutionary* it is: how committed to change, transformation, overturning and disruption,

---

* This seems like a virtually impossible task, not least in highly transitory urban areas. However there is a possible shortcut if you manage to get some local 'community' activists on board, increasing the political content of what you are doing, aligning to local political power and thereby reducing artistic autonomy.

all to remain in the sway of the cultural establishment and the status quo it maintains. Just like in the Soviet Union, anyone with any sort of official status must desperately assert their fealty to the state and its rulers in order to preserve their position in the power structure: and art is just another tool for that purpose.

# 8
# *Progressive capitalism*

Back in the 1990s and early 2000s in Houston, Texas, a company originally formed around the unglamorous business of natural gas pipelines was making a big splash: growing rapidly based on a business model that it claimed had created 'a new kind of energy company'. Stock market analysts and journalists lapped up the story, helping the shares to soar higher and higher. *Fortune* magazine named the company, rebranded as Enron, 'America's most innovative company' six years running. Financial analysts said it had 'redefined the worldwide energy marketplace with its vision', praising its 'ground-breaking strategy'. Bethany McLean and Peter Elkind later wrote of Enron's chairman Kenneth Lay, 'He was acclaimed as a business sage, a man of transcendent ideas who had harnessed change in an industry instinctively opposed to it.'[1]

Enron executives described themselves in religious and utopian terms. They talked of how they brought 'missionary zeal' and were 'spreading the privatization gospel in countries that desperately need this kind of thinking'.[2] President and chief executive Jeffrey Skilling said, 'We were doing something special. *Magical.*' He saw his position at Enron as not just a job but a mission. 'We were changing the world. We were doing God's work', he said.[3]

A big part of the Enron story was claiming that the existing energy sector was out-of-date and desperately needed deregulation – from which the company with its banks of traders also stood to benefit. Lay wrote to George W. Bush, then Texas Governor: 'We can't afford to wait. Delay is dangerous. . . . It's time to let the forces of the market work their magic. . . . The nation's new energy system is being installed now.'[4]

McLean and Elkind write:

> They believed that free markets made the world a fairer place, one where price dictated deals, rather than relationships or other 'noneconomic' factors. To them, the lines were clearly drawn: it was visionaries versus Neanderthals.

'Enron,' says a former trader, 'was all about changing the world, showing up every day to be a pain in the ass to every incumbent.'[5]

Enron acted like its model and its business were incontestable, with Skilling labelling other companies as 'dinosaurs' and asserting that Enron was going to 'bury' competitors given its more advanced stage of development. To demonstrate its superiority, Enron delivered Wall Street the desired steady increase in earnings, manufactured through dodgy accounting and rigged financial transactions. This fitted the progressive profile of continual improvement, known in advance, with those responsible being in a sense blessed and righteous. Doubters were instantly dismissed as stupid and 'not getting it'. Any internal and external critics were removed from positions of influence, in the latter case via threats to withdraw lucrative contracts from counterparties: allowing the company to largely dictate what others were saying about it.

We know what happened to Enron. In order to show continual progress to the world, the self-styled World's Leading Company was squirrelling away debt and losses using special purpose entities (SPEs) and other complex financial transactions. When its share price started to fall, it had nowhere near enough genuine cash-flow to support its commitments, leading to a dramatic collapse and eventual indictment of several of its executives plus the fall of accountancy giant Arthur Andersen.

Enron might seem like a world away from 'the modern left' and its progressive capturing of institutions. However, there are similarities: not least in the habit of promoting its authority as unquestionable based on apparent understanding of social and economic change. Like the progressive left now, Enron used words and theories to dazzle onlookers and pre-empt any challenge (or even examination) in the moment. Executives presented their authority in moral terms, as conferred by a combination of God and history (ironically a habit that goes back at least to the eighteenth century). They projected a strong sense of destiny, wrapping up the company's story with that of the world: the idea being that, as it and its ideas prevailed, so would truth and right in the world. And all the while, they relied on very earthly carrot and stick incentives and threats to variously seduce opinion formers and marginalize those who did not play along.

At the centre of the Enron story was an idea of progress: of a rotten world that needs fixing, *by us*. The company demanded totalized, systemic change in its areas of operation, which it expanded ambitiously with characteristic *chutzpah*. It saw itself as more advanced in historical terms than the world it was denouncing and presented the changes it demanded as essential and *necessary*. Its superior knowledge also gave Enron executives the authority to make it happen and to benefit from it through huge bonuses and share options.

## *How capitalism is progressive*

The capitalism that Skilling, Lay and colleagues believed in so fervently is an inherently progressive force. It delivers change, growth, expansion and also often technological improvement. It does this through competition, by creating winners who thrive and losers who are left behind. While the winners effectively appear as being on the right side of history, aligned to it and benefitting from it, the losers appear, in the market at least, as irrelevant, backward and out-of-date.

The processes that deliver these results have a natural inevitability about them, appearing largely separate from the choices of any single individual and impervious to external forces. Capitalism generates history in its own way, through market forces, rushing us all headlong into the future whether we like it or not. It brings verifiable improvements, not least to the convenience of everyday life through time-saving, productivity-enhancing devices like the washing machine, personal computer, bank card recognition technology and smartphone.

Competition and the market economy have spurred industrialization and created higher living standards. This seems incontrovertible. As such, capitalism is perhaps the most tangible force of Progress in our world. Whether this progress is absolute will always be a matter of debate given the costs, for example on deskilled, casualized workers, on the environment and non-human species, but the improvements are undeniable.

This is how it has been conceived almost since the generally-recognized beginning of modern capitalism in Britain at the end of the eighteenth century. Adam Smith's *The Wealth of Nations* (1776), the most influential economic book of that time and indeed perhaps of any time, combines an idea of Christian-style Providence with a scientific account of nature as a harmonious whole existing under natural laws. This applied to human life too, Smith thought. As he wrote, 'Human society, when we contemplate it in a certain abstract and philosophical light, appears like a great, an immense machine whose regular and harmonious movements produce a thousand agreeable effects.'[6] This is where the idea of the 'invisible hand' comes from, converting the collected actions of human self-interest into more general societal well-being, like a machine. As Jacob Bronowski and Bruce Mazlish say, 'Man's task, therefore, was to understand the nature or structure of things and to adjust himself harmoniously to the necessary results of this structure.'[7] With Providence integrated into this conception, becoming part of the science, we are presented with the conventional progressive outlook on the world: of a relentless, inevitable march into the future which is knowable and therefore scientific; but also providential, so blessed by God. Massive social change was indeed in the air as Smith was writing, with the American Revolution getting underway, the Industrial Revolution taking off around him in Britain and France heading towards its own Revolution.

Robert Nisbet writes: 'There was very close affinity between faith in progress and faith in what today we call economic growth.'[8] For early progressives and enlighteners like Smith and Voltaire, it was blindingly obvious that commerce, liberty and progress were inseparable, that growth in economic activity was tied up with general social improvement. Making money was a good in itself, not just for the individual concerned but for society.

This faith continues to be widely held in the economic engines of government, in the think-tank world and in business circles today, where pretty much anything can be justified if it delivers 'growth'. The approach typically does not direct itself to average wealth of the population (via GDP per capita) but GDP itself, which measures the sheer size of an economy. In other words, it considers *more* as better by definition: a core plank of economic progressivism.

## *Territorial colonization*

This approach of maximizing wealth generation infers a particular role for land, territory and nature, seeing them as *resources* that need to be put to work. This conception was explained by the English philosopher

John Locke, who had a major influence on the Americans in their revolt to set up the United States and subsequent expansion West.

In his *Two Treatises of Government* of 1689, Locke did not just offer a justification for resisting and revolting against colonial power, in this case from distant London. His theory of natural rights also had an account of property which justified *appropriating* territory: thereby opening the way to a different form of colonization.

As Locke put it:

> The Law Man was under, was . . . for *appropriating*. God Commanded, and his Wants forced him to *labour*. That was his *Property* which could not be taken from him where-ever he had fixed it. And hence subduing or cultivating the Earth, and having Dominion, we see are joined together. The one gave Title to the other. So that God, by commanding to subdue, gave Authority so far to *appropriate*.[9]

'Subduing' or 'cultivating' the Earth' created an implicit, God-given right to possess and own it, under Locke's theory. This arose as a consequence of creating *value* out of it. Effectively applying the Puritan work ethic, this theory saw right, value, meaning and ownership as vested specifically in *working the land*, in combining land with labour. Those who did not treat land in this way forfeited any right to it. It was God's Command, Locke said, which would make it a truth universal to the whole world.

There is a ready-made idea of progress to be found here. As Locke said:

> Land that is left wholly to Nature, that hath no improvement of Pasturage, Tillage, or Planting, is called, as indeed it is, *wast*; and we shall find the benefit of it amount to little more than nothing. This shews, how much numbers of men are to be preferd to largeness of dominions, and that the increase of lands and the right imploying of them is the great art of government.[10]

Land is improved by being worked and developed. The more land government can allocate to being worked and developed, the better. And the more people on it, working it, also the better.

Here we can find one origin of the American legend of the poor immigrant family which struggles its way out west, establishing a homestead and working the land hard, not just to better themselves but to fulfil the manifest destiny of their country, continent – and even humankind. Secondly, we can find the origins of a specific kind of conflict over land, whereby this justification of ownership *de facto* trumps any rights of others (in this case native Americans) who regard land as something held in common and which cannot be traded.

Thirdly, we can find a typically modern, contemporary account of the meaning of land. For, while Locke's account justifies a transfer of land from the common ownership of one people to the individual ownership of another, this individualism cannot endure except under a wider legal framework with accompanying enforcement mechanisms. And this has a universal justification: it is supported by an idea of right and justice, ordained by God and independent of any consent from those who have a different sort of relationship to the land.

For Locke, regarding the vast expanses of North America, recently discovered and relatively empty, available land seemed to be limitless. The existing occupants – estimated nowadays to have been around a million mostly nomadic 'Indians' – were failing to make use of the bounteous natural resources on offer, thereby creating a massive opportunity for others. It seemed that there was enough land to spare for everyone who wanted a piece of it. In a sense, it therefore appeared rather like any other goods whose supply could be increased at any time to meet demand; like a limitless commodity. Locke admitted that his ideal was incompatible with the rule of money, but nevertheless it attained huge influence precisely in a world of money, and does so to this day.

Today, land appears in liberal political discourse in line with Locke's theory, as a *resource* that, above all, needs to be used and exploited. The more land that is worked, the harder it is worked and the more people living and working on it, the better – never mind what they are doing or how it relates to local communities or nature. The point is to generate more production, more trade, more wealth and more taxable income for the modern state to use to dispense its largesse. In that sense the development of land and increasing concentrations of people working on it appear as goods without limit. Population itself appears as an unlimited good, aligning to Locke's humanist belief in man as a rational animal.

Locke's primary concern was agriculture, but modern liberals tend to ignore this in favour of bricks and mortar, steel and concrete. They privilege *building* in order to accommodate more and more people as workers, thereby making the land more productive and the territory as a whole richer. Their promotional talk exists in a sort of End of History paradigm in which a country like Britain no longer counts as an island nation, long reliant on food imports and therefore vulnerable when supplies become stressed (as in the two world wars of the twentieth century). Rather its land is just another available resource to be expanded into, built on and filled with as many worker bees as possible. These worker bees generate wealth, which can then be exchanged into food and other goods from the global marketplace. From this perspective, land is merely another commodity employed to generate wealth in the most efficient way possible.

And so today's 'policy community' broadly see the land of Britain in a similar way to how Locke saw America in the late eighteenth century: as something without limit which we need to fill up and put to work. While Housing Secretary, the Conservative Sajid Javid said: 'Only around 11 per cent of land in England has been built on', reflecting a widespread assumption that we can and should keep on expanding into our environment pretty much indefinitely.[11]

This attitude appears to arise originally from the Protestant ethic, grounded in work as the primary meaning of life and applied to land. It pushes us always to more activity, more development, more exploitation, more population and more wealth generation: initially to fulfil God's will but now to satisfy the need for progress, *for more*. To fulfil our destiny, it seems, we must expand continually into the environment. Other, relational, meanings to land, like the love of it, as it is, effectively become illegitimate if they interfere with this process of expansion and the progress that it reflects.

The economic progressive agenda of expansion into our environment generally exists in concert with advocacy for more or less unlimited immigration: cramming as many people into a space as possible without heed for the consequences. In 2022, official net migration for 'the UK' as it is now known reached an unprecedented 745,000 people, with 1.23 million new immigrants entering the country. Following two decades of record incomings, the population of the UK had reached an estimated 67 million people by mid-2021, 8 million higher than in 2001: an increase of 400,000 per year on average.[12]

As the Conservative minister Chris Heaton-Harris explained in March 2023, 'We accept a huge amount of migration because we like it, because it's really good for the country's economy and social fabric in general.'[13] In order to compensate employers for the end of EU free movement after Brexit, successive Conservative governments hacked away at other restrictions on immigration. Minimum salaries for new immigrants were slashed to £21,000 a year, well below the national average. The idea of implementing a requirement for British employers to advertise jobs in Britain first was also quietly dropped; the same goes for serious action to deal with mushrooming illegal migration via the English Channel.

For business, even as United Kingdom immigration records were successively blown out of the water in 2022–3, bosses and lobbying groups were demanding more, intensively lobbying the Conservative government for regulations to be loosened even further to meet apparent skill shortages. As eBay UK boss Murray Lambell said, 'We need more people in the country.'[14] There are no limits and no possible limits to this outlook: to expand the economy, the population must be increased, indefinitely. The negative consequences on things like housing availability, transport infrastructure, healthcare capacity and biodiversity are left for another day and other people to confront.

The motives for business are quite transparent. Talk of 'staff shortages' refers to the inability of business to fill vacancies at their desired wages and conditions. Economist Alan Manning writes of this:

> If we had a firm that says, 'I'm struggling to sell my product', we'd be inclined to say, 'Well, perhaps your product is priced wrongly. Or it's not a very good product.' But somehow when employers complain that 'nobody wants to take my jobs', they expect us to say, 'Oh well, we'll provide you with some workers who will do it under the terms and conditions you view as appropriate'.
>
> And there may be reasons why sometimes you say, well, okay, this sector just can't compete for workers in the open labour market, but we think this sector is really important, so we're going to give them a dedicated ringfenced supply of workers – migrant workers, almost certainly. But just be very clear that that's what you're doing. You will cause that sector to become totally dependent on that source of labour.[15]

This seems to be what has happened in the United Kingdom. Employers have become more or less totally reliant on importing labour at all levels of the job market, in the process losing any sense of commitment to the country and its people. Their relationship is rather with the national government, whose role (which was widely accepted by Conservative ministers) becomes effectively that of *producing* a constant stream of pliable workers willing to accept the wages offered to them, without regard for any negative consequences and how the population feel about it. From this perspective, people are just another form of commodity, more or less economically viable under present market conditions and therefore either to be picked up or discarded as convenient. The government here is playing a role in the supply chain as, in effect, *a manufacturer of people* (as well as land, as we have already seen), rather than as an entity whose role is to represent the people or the electorate.

Such a role for government is implied in Adam Smith's *The Wealth of Nations*. Bronowski and Mazlish write:

> Unfortunately, Adam Smith often treated labour as a commodity rather than an activity; very much like the things one buys and sells. For example, he writes: 'It is in this manner that the demand for men, *like that for any other commodity* [our italics], necessarily regulates the production of men; quickens it when it goes on too slowly, and stops it when it advances too fast.' In this respect, what he said had quite a disastrous effect during the next thirty or forty years [the early years of the Industrial Revolution]. When one propounds a labour theory of wealth in which labour is treated mainly in terms of supply and demand, a very inhuman kind of civilization is implied; and the implication became reality in the years after Smith's death.[16]

By treating people as commodities, you treat them as something that can be reproduced in a market, without limit; as something you are entitled to transport and deploy as you wish. But while people can now be provided almost without limit from abroad by liberal immigration policies, the extra land to house them is not so easily provided – demanding more punitive measures to coerce the existing population into making space. A free market in land means pressing long-term residents to cede what control they have over their surroundings in order to satisfy the 'needs' of the economy, business and the new people they have brought in.*

---

* Hence the present 'war on nimbys' being prosecuted by many in the British policy community from both left and right.

Along these sorts of lines, the economic historian Karl Polanyi referred to both land and labour as 'fictitious commodities', pointing out that, 'Laissez-faire was planned'.[17] It requires coercion to prevail: existential colonization by values and law rather than by forces of invasion.

While successive Conservative governments liberalized the immigration system principally out of a sort of economic faith, the left tends to see open borders as more about showing 'compassion' to all migrants as a favoured category (similar to how Christian leaders like former Archbishop of Canterbury Justin Welby see it). However, acting in this way appears to have other positive effects from the perspective of the modern left: specifically in helping to create a more diverse society which will politically overwhelm those who they denounce as 'racist' and 'xenophobic', including the Conservative Party as an institution.

Nevertheless, the business lobby and the neoliberal right, including wide swathes of the Conservative Party, has formed a remarkable *de facto* alliance with the progressive left and its associated interest groups over immigration, conclusively winning the political battle on this issue against the electorate. The merging of moralistic left and neoliberal positions on immigration was a major feature of the anti-Brexit reaction from 2016 onwards, with people even on the far left inadvertently embracing free market ideology to support their positioning, while business lobbies and believers in free markets on the right utilized some of the moralistic language of the left.

## *Woke capitalism*

In the years following the Brexit vote, banking giant HSBC's advertising and marketing for audiences in Britain went heavy on messaging focused on breaking down borders. On its behalf, New York-based ad agency Wunderman Thompson rolled out a campaign entitled 'We are not an island', outlining how Britain was existentially anything and everything but British. They followed this up the next year, using the Cambridge-educated comedian Richard Ayoade, to 'explore the topic of national identity, pondering whether home is "where your parents were born", "where you find yourself" or simply "where your heart is"', concluding that people 'hail from wherever they feel most at home'.[18]

This advocacy for what we might call a sort of *national self-identification* makes the country where you come from, the place where you were born, raised and have lived, a matter of *choice* rather than of fact. This seems like a pretty transparent come-on to wealthy liberals who had felt themselves alienated from their country by Brexit. You may have been born, raised and continue to live in Britain, the messaging goes, but if your heart rejects its people for the way they voted, then HSBC will happily celebrate you renouncing your nationality and choosing a European identity for yourself.

Capitalists have understandably embraced progressive left politics to confer a moral element onto their lobbying. And this has merged into a wider 'woke capitalism' in which corporations have widely embraced left-wing activism and progressive identity politics, not merely for self-interested or public relations purposes but in order to transform themselves: out of conversion and belief.

Alessandro Manfredi, executive vice-president for the 'hygiene' products brand Dove at the conglomerate Unilever, tells us:

> It's not enough to focus on individual interventions – we need to influence the entire social ecosystem to foster change. We want to change beauty by disarming the threats it presents to girls' self-esteem, breaking down toxic beauty practices and stereotypes through education.[19]

These words could easily be those of a feminist academic or perhaps a Labour MP outlining her party's approach to women's issues. This 'actionist' approach as he described it means 'driving representation in advertising'; also 'investing in education', plus the obligatory support of Black Lives Matter in order 'to make the beauty industry more equitable'. Manfredi explains: 'Actions speak louder than words. Brands and companies should have a purpose, because all businesses should be built responsibly.'[20]

Here we can find the contemporary progressive corporation giving itself the role of holding our hands as we pass into a more equitable, more conscious and just future. The profit motive has found a way *inside* that process, creating a beautiful utopian aura in which everything appears to be aligned.

We probably encounter this vision of shiny, politically-correct multinationals most often from Big Tech behemoths like Google and Microsoft. These giant corporations are literally and self-consciously *reshaping the world* with their products and services, not just using black and transgender activists in adverts in order to sell moisturizer.

Before he sold Twitter to Elon Musk, then-chief executive Jack Dorsey appeared at a major conference wearing a #StayWoke T-shirt. His personal commitment was reflected in his company's increasingly active 'content moderation' practices, which always seemed to target views and people seen as *anti-woke* or inconvenient to progressive politics. The suppression of a *New York Post* story about Joe Biden's son Hunter just before the 2020 election was a particularly egregious example. However, at a lower level this activity went on relentlessly, suppressing the access of dissident voices to Twitter's public sphere, particularly those who maintained that trans women were still biologically male, often with little if any due process.

Musk's takeover made the social media site something of a political outlier in how it handled information and assertion in the US-dominated Big Tech sector. Other companies like Google, Apple, Amazon and Microsoft have been explicit at various levels in their support for progressive causes, notably identity-related – and Bill Gates even gave a million dollars to an organization, Equitable Math, whose purpose was 'to dismantle the culture of white supremacy that exists within the math classroom'.[21]

Before Donald Trump's return, there was a widespread habit among large companies, not just US-dominated multinationals, to outsource certain corporate policies and functions to race, gender and other activists. LGBT+ organization Stonewall especially achieved great success in getting companies to recite its messaging through use of the Stonewall UK Workplace Equality Index, which awards rankings to organizations based on how much they align to its goals. Private as well as public organizations fell over themselves to get the apparent public relations coup that this represented, leading some to call the Index one of the most effective instruments of social control ever devised.*

---

* It certainly showed how many organizations in the progressive identity politics space have learned how to leverage the routine 'liberal-left' outsourcing of authority to them that I identified in my previous book, *The Tribe*.

In 2022, home improvement giant Wickes won accreditation as a 'Stonewall Gold Employer'. In August that year it sponsored a stage at the Brighton Pride festival featuring its branding alongside slogans such as 'Ban Conversion Therapy for ALL' and 'No LGB without the T', the latter a dig at the new LGB Alliance organization, which had been highly critical of Stonewall for its insistence that transgender women should have all the same rights as biological women. The next year, Wickes's chief operating officer Fraser Longden appeared at the Pink News Trans Summit, sponsored by EY (the rebranded Ernst & Young) and the advertising giant Publicis, telling participants that 'bigots' who did not agree with his company's 'trans-inclusive policies' are 'not welcome in our stores anymore'.[22]

This habit of big corporations telling customers where to go if they do not like their political commitments has become quite a trend. Sainsburys did it in 2020, putting out a statement celebrating Black History Month and saying that 'anyone who does not want to shop with an inclusive retailer is welcome to shop elsewhere'.[23]* In 2022, Halifax Bank tweeted out the slogan 'Pronouns matter #ItsAPeopleThing', featuring an employee badge with the line 'she/her/hers'. When criticized for the move, which facilitates full employee self-identification by gender, one Halifax Twitter account manager tweeted out, 'We strive for inclusion, equality and quite simply, in doing what's right. If you disagree with our values, you're welcome to close your account.'[24] Some financial services providers have even seen fit to jump the gun in this respect: deploying a sort of *financial* moderation of those people whose opinions do not match their values. Nigel Farage gained most attention when targeted by Coutts on this basis, but there were many previous examples. PayPal suddenly shut down the personal and organizational accounts managed by Free Speech Union founder Toby Young in 2022. In 2023 Tide Bank notified the podcasters at Triggernometry that their account was to be closed without giving a reason, before hastily backtracking after Konstantin Kisin made it public (Kisin and partner Francis Foster had previously had problems with YouTube, owned by Google, 'demonetizing' their videos, so reducing their platform and cutting their income).

---

* The supermarket chain also created 'a safe space for our black colleagues to gather in response to the Black Lives Matter movement' that year.

Where there is a stick, there is also a carrot. On the recruitment site Neuroworx, an article appears entitled 'Why diversity in the workplace is a must'. It explains to employers, in true utopian fashion,

> As long as you showcase how progressive your company is, people will resonate with it and the diversity will grow naturally. Now, more than ever, equality and diversity in the workforce is something that people value and seek out when looking for new jobs.[25]

Here, people who are not progressive do not count as diverse; nor indeed as people, while equality and diversity are treated as allied rather than competing concepts. It shows off how the politics of diversity treats its opponents as if they are not part of society; as if progressives do actually own the world. There is an assumption that progressive pre-eminence is *natural*, as if this is just the nature of historical progress. At the Pink News Trans Summit mentioned above, the director of 'Trans in the City' Emily Hamilton said of 'gender critical' beliefs that *'there is no room for those views in the new world'*.[26]

We can see here a pervading existential colonization of the world, claiming ownership of it and the right to decide what happens; but also the levers of power being exercised to properly make life difficult for political opponents.

In many American-dominated multinationals in recent times, you could be forgiven for believing that Hamilton's statement is true, with infrastructures of control deployed to try and keep employees and executives in line with progressive identity politics. 'Representation', a political concept (in this case related to identity categories like 'Black' and 'LGBT+'), has become a ruling principle in many of these settings, turning human resources decisions into political minefields in which the right sort of people must be favoured at least in proportion to their *representation*, which is to say their relative presence either in the organization or the community or wider society. Mandatory training is provided to embed the ideology and 'reverse mentoring' of senior managers by young activists to drive it in further. Activist writers are brought in to lecture staff on how to behave, their books promoted and corporate messaging tailored to reflect the brave new world of dogma. Anyone who disagrees with any of it has the unfalsifiable accusation of 'unconscious bias' thrown at them: the ultimate trump card for an authoritarian politics wielded on the workforce, appearing as incontrovertible knowledge. And all the while the capitalist bosses play along, at least for now.*

The regime of progressive capitalism has come a long way. Its task of overturning and bringing in new ways has always made old customs, techniques and people redundant. But now, through the twin tracks of HR and PR – human resources (covering appointments and workforce discipline) and public relations (self-presentation, promotion, messaging) – corporations have taken on the methods of totalitarian dictatorships in order to manage their workforces and to mould public discourse. Business managers, lobbyists and left-wing activists have found themselves on the same page, working with each other and saying interchangeable things about diversity and equality, how the modern workplace should be governed and about the need to break down boundaries of identity and of national borders.

On borders, the capitalist tendency towards commodification of everything leaves a person's economic value or cost-effectiveness as the only respectable way of differentiating them from others: so notions like citizenship as well as 'man' or 'woman' become obstacles or 'barriers' that need to be removed. The nation-state becomes just another part of the production line, manufacturing the conditions and the people to maximize profits and economic growth. The state, as expressed in numerous utterances by former and serving British civil servants, detaches itself from the existential relations it might have had with a territorially-bounded population or electorate, indeed from any sense of community or belonging defined by territory. The runaway train of change careers its way on to a destination unknown, but known to be better than before, to be freer and more equal, more just and fair, while also hopefully being more profitable. It delivers the state more *growth*. And this ties in with Adam Smith's notion of the *wealth* of nations. Any other meanings to the nation may be removed, except the state and its wealth: an agenda that globalized corporations can fully embrace in parallel with their own.

---

* There are signs of the situation changing, with the business case for diversity and representation appearing to collapse and some corporations declaring that they'll stop making divisive political statements. Trump 2 has been an obvious catalyst for this process.

## *Manufacturing the consumer*

Notwithstanding talk of 'Go Woke, Go Broke', the commitments of large corporations to social and political causes often align with money-making, forming bonds with wealthy consumers who want to appear not just as rich but as *good*; also to those identity groups seen to be needing favour, who conveniently also appear as growing demographic markets in Western countries.

Consumers must always to be courted and convinced in order to buy products. However, in a sense we might say the consumer needs to be created or *curated* too. The philosopher John Gray has said of this:

> Where affluence is the rule, the chief threat is the loss of desire. With wants so quickly sated, the economy soon comes to depend on the manufacture of ever more exotic needs.
>
> What is new is not that prosperity depends on stimulating demand. It is that it cannot continue without inventing new vices. The economy is driven by an imperative of perpetual novelty, and its health has come to depend on the manufacture of transgression.[27]

Young people play an important role here, as a group that is constantly renewing and reproducing itself through new generations: a group that promises perpetual *newness*, inherently aligned to a progressive view of the world. For corporations over the years, the young have appeared as agents (or subjects) of a permanent revolution in consumer fashion: constantly overturning the world they have inherited, overthrowing traditions as a permanent disrupting force. They appear to be aligned to a politics of change but also to a throwaway, disposable, fluid lifestyle with no permanent commitments; antagonistic to family ties and therefore more open to capitalistic influence and messaging, often in the guise of left-wing rebellion.

New products often need to generate new habits in order to establish themselves. Young people are naturally more receptive to this, since their habits are in the process of being formed. They can therefore be used to help both the process of breaking old habits and the adoption of new ones based around new products, especially new technology. We might see here a natural alignment between the capitalistic drive to create new markets and the progressive way of being, with its instinct for change and the destruction of old ways (and marginalization of older generations). Capitalists and progressives are in many ways natural allies; the progressive way of being privileges disruption and change that capitalism constantly delivers in practice.*

The self-definition of the progressive as an expert on society is also attractive for corporations seeking to give reasons for people to consume their products. The expert offers authority, guidance and clarity, pushing people towards certain likes, dislikes, hopes and fears which can then be indulged in the marketplace. The consumption of media is an obvious example, but this goes much further, especially where scientific authority can be mobilized.

In his book *Crazy Like Us: The Globalization of the Western Mind*, Ethan Watters titles one chapter 'The mega-marketing of depression in Japan'. The chapter details how UK-headquartered GlaxoSmithKline (GSK) and other pharmaceutical giants set about converting Japan to Western ideas about mental ill-health and the benefits of SSRI (selective serotonin reuptake inhibitor) antidepressants in dealing with it.

Melancholia had been traditionally regarded in a positive light by the Japanese, so entreaties about the dangers of depression initially had little impact, until GSK marketers hit on the concept of 'a cold of the soul', which helped to change attitudes. As Dr Laurence Kirmayer, director of Social and Transcultural Psychiatry at McGill University in Montreal, told Watters, 'What I was witnessing was a multinational pharmaceutical corporation working hard to redefine narratives about mental health. . . . These [pharma] companies are upending long-held cultural beliefs about the meaning of illness and healing.'[28]

One of the most striking elements of the story is how the marketing people fully believed in the story they were trying to convert the Japanese with. It was not a mere cynical marketing effort but really a sort of conversion they were attempting, to what they saw as a new and better way of seeing the world. Anthropologist Kalman Applbaum at the

---

* Alongside this, we might say that the 'built-in obsolescence of products' developed for the modern economy also applies to cultures and societies. New technologies and fashions create new cultures and societies which then have to give way in turn. In effect our societies are in the process of permanent self-destruction, permanently generating morbid symptoms.

University of Wisconsin made a research project out of how Western pharma companies were trying to do this – gaining 'remarkable access to the inner workings of these companies', Watters writes.

> It is important to note that the drug-company executives whom Applbaum interviewed didn't present themselves as people driven only by profits. Rather these men and women saw themselves as acting with the best of intentions, motivated by the belief that their drugs represented the proud march of scientific progress around the world.[29]

Moreover:

> During his talks with the executives, consultants and marketers for the drug companies, Applbaum heard a repeated theme. These men and women kept talking about different cultures as if they were at different stages of a pre-determined evolution. The American market, with its brand recognition, high rates of prescriptions (by specialists and non-specialists alike), and free-market pricing, was seen as the most modern and advanced. Japan was fifteen years behind the United States, executives would say.[30]

As Christopher Lasch has written, 'Capitalism has gradually substituted the free market for direct forms of domination.' As part of that process, it has refashioned colonial relations so that 'Instead of imposing military rule on their colonies, industrial nations now govern through client states, ostensibly sovereign, which keep order in their stead.'[31] I would reframe Lasch's point to increase the role of markets and capital and reduce that of nations, so that most states and international bodies are effectively serving as clients to international capital. Capitalism is the colonizing force more than the nation-state (whose power of action is now substantially reduced by international agreements and institutions).

As I see it, this is how the working class in nations like the United Kingdom has been largely subdued, defeated and pushed out of the centres of power in the inner cities: by the operation of market forces, supported by an inattentive, indifferent state which is fixated on GDP numbers.

By keeping its property market open to the whole world, the technocratic rulers of Britain have allowed a steady squeezing of its longstanding population out of property ownership, to be replaced by wealthier people and more motivated groups from elsewhere. The 'UK' state has effectively played the role of client state on behalf of global capital. At least indirectly, it takes an antagonistic relation towards its own citizens who cannot afford property of their own, assuaging their marginalization and displacement with benefit payments. In a capitalist society like this, you will generally not be turfed out of your home and community by a direct invasion of hostile outsiders, but rather by your inability to afford market rents, mortgage rates and house prices which others from outside can afford. But the end-result is pretty much the same.

This just one of the ways in which processes of colonization have been turned back on to Western liberal countries by their rulers in concert with the global rich and powerful. The spirit of progressivism colonizes our institutions with progressive identity politics; it colonizes our land by appropriating it, cordoning it off and selling it off to people from elsewhere; and it colonizes our minds with consumerism, so that we do not notice or do not care.

# 9

## *The technocratic state*

Jacob Bronowski and Bruce Mazlish write that, in John Locke's view, a government 'ought to be ... a research establishment run by political scientists', whose business it is to discover what the natural laws of society are and to govern accordingly.[1] And this account of government, they say, 'laid the permanent foundations of the liberal movement'.[2]

Locke was a major influence on the formation and Constitution of the United States. His account of property rights justified the appropriation of the North American continent by *individuals* supported by state power rather than the traditional mode of conquering *by a state* or other collective body. And, nowadays, Locke's ideal of government, *a research establishment run by political scientists*, looks uncannily like how modern liberal technocracy sees itself. In our world, the administration of experts does not just relate to compartmentalized areas like transport and agriculture but treats the whole of politics, the economy, the world, history and the future as a compartment requiring specialist attention (and from which other sources of power must be excluded).

The idea of *discovering* laws of society like Newton discovered laws of gravity aligns closely to the progressive practice of claiming authority from the understanding of history and the future. However, as with the world of science after Newton, it appears to contemporary elites that the discovering has already occurred. Authority, from a progressive and technocratic perspective, has already been established, based on a form of legitimacy linked to *knowledge*. You govern *accordingly*, as Locke put it, based on a superior understanding of how society works. This understanding is of social causation: knowing how one action generates a certain reaction, consistently and reliably, like clockwork. And since you know how social causation works, you know what will and what will not *work*. You are working *with* the laws rather than against them. You are on the right side of them rather than the wrong side. In this way, modern technocracy keeps on discovering what it already knows. It keeps on discovering that it is right.

This word 'technocracy' gets thrown around quite a lot these days. My *Oxford English Dictionary* refers to it as 'a social and political system in which scientific or technical experts hold a great deal of power'.[3] Etymologically, the word combines the Greek terms 'techne', meaning technique, with 'kratos', meaning a form of rule. So, when someone moans about 'technocrats', they are really complaining about government as technique, government that considers means but does not pay much attention to a wider purpose. As a style, technocracy treats ends as already decided and not up for debate, which has the effect of significantly reducing the space of politics. A technocratic mindset typically uses the words 'politics' and 'political' as negative signifiers, normally delivered with a sneer.

This makes the technocratic state a certain type of political state. It operates in tension with democratic government, pushing back at the possibility that alternative forms of politics might arise and prevail. Its hostility to democracy and democratic participation appears as part of a more general resistance to opposition of any kind, which it treats as dangerous and illegitimate, indeed as against 'democracy', whose meaning it appropriates and redeploys. While old-style absolute monarchies had the 'Divine Right of Kings', in technocracies senior bureaucrats see themselves as rational custodians of all that is good and right: quietly keeping the state going in defiance of politics rather than because of it.

Needless to say, this stance is itself highly political. The rejection of politics is a political stance. It speaks either of submission to power from ordinary citizens, who recognize there is little point in voting, or of power itself, which rejects competing forces. As an exertion of power, technocracy treats the distribution of power as already completed. It promotes the assumption that there is only one proper way to govern: the way it governs. It reflexively delegitimizes alternatives to its rule, for example by criticizing them for not being 'evidence-based', where only carefully-selected, convenient evidence is considered (including from campaign groups funded by the state).

Ordinary people are denigrated as unqualified and too ignorant to participate in such processes and in major affairs of state: hence the widespread contempt for the Brexit referendum and result, not just in

Whitehall but in Brussels, Paris and Washington too. A technocracy acts in the people's interest, knowing better than them what is good for them. As such it is not as far away from one-party Communist states as we might think. It also promotes itself as democratic of course.

In the progressive sense the technocracy appears as *post*-political. It is more advanced and has successfully eliminated unnecessary contention. For technocracy, 'politics' looks like an unhealthy relic of a tainted past: a dirty word. In this way, modern technocracy is a form of authoritarianism, but one that does not recognize itself as authoritarian since it sees its authority as right and justified. For the technocrat, authoritarianism describes *competing* and therefore *flawed* sources of potential authority. The public challenger is authoritarian, while the existing power is neutral and impartial.

## *The British Civil Service*

There is a moment in HBO's *The Wire* in which out-of-favour police commissioner Ervin Burrell attempts to retrieve his position with Baltimore's new mayor Tommy Carcetti. 'The ministers' of the city's black churches are demanding punishment for an aggressive and mistaken car stop on one of their number led by a gormless white detective. Burrell walks into the mayor's office and plonks down the police department's General Orders onto his desk. '600 pages of rules, regulations, directives, orders. You fire a white police[man] for a bad car stop on a black minister, you'll lose the rank and file. It's not *cause* enough. But if a commander cannot find the grounds for firing a saint in here . . . .'[4] He motions to the huge folder sitting on the desk.

The more rules and laws you have as a bureaucracy, the more control the bosses and the owners of the rules (looking at you, human resources professionals) have over staff and anyone else who comes under their purview (for example contractors and guest speakers). The stunning success of left-progressives in capturing the institutions of the British and other Western states without necessarily being in government has been largely down to capturing this part of the system: the rules and regulations dictating how and why people are employed in the state apparatus, how they are favoured and disciplined while at work and how they are removed.

Anna Thomas, a work coach for the Department for Work and Pensions (DWP) at a Portsmouth Job Centre, felt the force of the rule-book when she started to question racialist favouritism and indoctrination promoted by her employer. In January 2021, she was asked to promote a job-seeking event for unemployed female, BAME and LGBT candidates who might be interested in working for London's Metropolitan Police, specifically excluding straight white-skinned men, who she says made up the majority of her clients. After discussing her concerns that the event was discriminatory and unlawful with colleagues on a Teams chat, a superior made an official complaint about her. An investigation was launched and in November she was dismissed, apparently based on her comments causing 'upset', 'distress' and 'offence'.

Thomas had already been investigated for misconduct after complaining about an 'anti-racism hub' and 'learning resources' on the staff intranet promoting among other things the work of American racialist writers Ibram X. Kendi and Robin DiAngelo as well as Black Lives Matter and LGBTQ+ charity Stonewall. Peter Schofield, DWP's permanent secretary, introduced the hub with a statement telling staff they were 'responsible for being actively anti-racist' and asking them to 'make DWP an anti-racist organisation', Thomas says. On the hub, civil servants were encouraged to treat racism like Covid-19 and to 'assume that you have it' in the wake of the murder of George Floyd and the Black Lives Matter protests. In this case her complaint was upheld, the hub being obviously political in character. Schofield was advised he should not have contributed in this way and the content was removed. Later on Thomas secured a £100,000 payout from the DWP in a claim for improper dismissal.

Thomas told *The Telegraph* that the politicization of the Civil Service 'only seems to trend or be popular when it [affects] the politicians at the top, but it does happen to everyday normal civil servants that are just trying to do their job, but notice that something's wrong. I was punished for whistleblowing.'[5] The sort of highly political activity she complained about was rife across the UK Civil Service and other government agencies (including schools, the health service and justice system) for more than a decade of Conservative-led government. At the Department for Levelling Up, Housing and Communities (DLUHC), staff were shown a video about 'allyship' encouraging white people to become 'allies' of ethnic minority colleagues, to listen and not contradict and 'give them time to heal and recover from a fight they've been having for their entire lives, often for generations'. As it said, 'When we become an ally, this primarily means acknowledging that we, ourselves, are part of a society, norm, culture or a system that is racist.'[6]

The standard racialist ideology promoted by the Civil Service and enforced by managers prescribes that harm can only go in one direction: being inflicted by those who resist progressive identity politics onto those who embrace it or are seen to be protected by it. The latter are seen to suffer from distress and require restorative action, including against the former. The likes of Anna Thomas are effectively treated as enemies of the state: to be disciplined, punished and removed from places where their damaging beliefs would do further harm.

The proliferation of rules in a state or private bureaucracy creates multiple possible infractions for which punishment can be handed out: not just to the rank-and-file, but also to a state's notional political bosses. In recent years, we have seen how ministers of government in the United Kingdom are highly vulnerable, especially to 'bullying' allegations being slapped all over newspaper front pages and news bulletins, based on off-the-record briefings from officials. Even without the complaints being upheld, the reputational damage and intimidation meted out make such actions more than worth it if you have an agenda. In Britain, the targets of such allegations in recent years, almost without exception, have been ministers and appointees whose political approach does not match the liberal-left progressive one. David Davis, Jacob Rees-Mogg, Boris Johnson, Kemi Badenoch, Nick Timothy, Dominic Cummings, Dominic Raab, Priti Patel and Suella Braverman to name but a few: all have variously been committed Brexiteers, sceptics of progressive identity politics, immigration restrictionists and/or proponents of reform, to the Civil Service itself and to the 1998 Human Rights Act (which enshrines the European Convention on Human Rights in British law). More conforming, acquiescent types like Rishi Sunak, Jeremy Hunt and Penny Mordaunt were by contrast left largely alone.

The Home Office, the department responsible for immigration and asylum in Britain, went into open revolt against Conservative ministers who sought to increase restrictions. On the policy to ship the mushrooming number of 'small boats' Channel migrants to Rwanda, Civil Service unions threatened mass walkouts while postings appeared on online staff noticeboards accusing the government of being immoral and Nazi. Permanent Secretary Matthew Rycroft initially refused to carry out his instructions from Home Secretary Priti Patel with a classic piece of technocratic obfuscation: 'I do not believe sufficient evidence can be obtained to demonstrate that the policy will have a deterrent effect significant enough to make the policy value for money.'[7] One of his predecessors, Sir David Normington, did not hold back: 'My assessment: well, first of all it's inhumane, it's morally reprehensible, it's probably unlawful and it may well be unworkable.'[8] He seemed to be proved right at least on the latter points when the European Court of Human Rights in Strasbourg ruled that flights could not proceed on account of a 'real risk of inhuman and degrading treatment' in Rwanda – a judgement backed up by British courts.

The objections of technocrats, activist staff and judges to the policy matched those of the Church of England and indeed the new King Charles III. In his Easter sermon in 2022 the then-Archbishop of Canterbury Justin Welby added that the policy 'cannot stand up to the judgement of God'. He elaborated on this later in a speech to the House of Lords:

> The book of Genesis tells us 'God created mankind in his own image'. In Matthew 25 in the parable of the sheep and the goats, Jesus tells his followers, about those who are strangers 'whatever you did for one of the least of these brothers and sisters of mine, you did for me'.
>
> Care for the stranger has long been embedded in societies of Christian and Jewish roots and of other faiths right round the world. The welcome arrival in the UK of other religious faiths has deepened those traditions of compassion.[9]

Except for his repeated references to God, Jesus and the Bible, Welby's language about this issue were almost identical to that of the technocrats and also of secular progressive commentators, including liberals, socialists and many Conservatives. *The Times* columnist David Aaronovitch called the Rwanda policy 'shaming', to which *BBC Newsnight* presenter Emily Maitlis added, 'It just feels deeply deeply "unBritish". We used to be great at compassion.'[10] Some compared the proposal to Nazi policies like deporting Jews to Madagascar. Ben and Jerry's Ice Cream teamed up with a migrant charity to issue its own statement: 'Most people are kind and compassionate, right? Yet our Government's plan to forcibly send people to a country thousands of miles away, simply for seeking refuge in the UK, is cruel and morally bankrupt. Under these racist and abhorrent plans, people who only "hoped for safety" and "a show of humanity" instead face "further trauma, further danger".'[11]

Clergy, commentariat, campaigners and public servants all emphasized values of compassion, kindness, humanity and morality in contrast to the Conservative government's inhumanity, immorality, unkindness and even racism.* Progressives, Christians and technocrats were united in a moral, political stance, dividing society into groups of good and evil. The good follow the example of Jesus or codes of human rights, while the evil discriminate against and punish others just for being others.

I think the state's stance on mass migration shows off the moral underpinnings of the technocratic state as something that integrates rationality and morality in an overall great goodness. John Locke's conception of government as 'a research establishment run by political scientists' is, I think, more or less how the higher echelons of the modern Civil Service see themselves: with the science incorporating morality. It frames good government as an intellectual endeavour of *understanding*, in a scientific sense, but also displaying moral values that dissolve the difference between citizen and non-citizen. This is fundamentally opposed to a democratic conception of government as an activity grounded in commitment to a limited population, its traditions and to the programme of those people elected by the population to rule. I do not think it is beyond the bounds of possibility for the former tendency to accommodate itself to the latter with reasonable moderation and realism. However, the more that technocrats take their scientific, 'evidence-based', *expert* status as non-negotiable, and the more the moralistic forces of high society gather together in concert, the more difficult it becomes. The widespread penetration of progressive identity ideology and activism into the state apparatus (not just in Britain but in other, allied Anglosphere countries) adds a whole new layer to these difficulties. Adopting critical race theory in particular actively turns the state against the majority of the population

---

* This is despite the policy being pursued by two ministers of South Asian ethnic background, Priti Patel and Suella Braverman.

in quite an aggressive way, seeing the people as an oppressive force that needs to be either re-educated or actively opposed and suppressed: rather like an imperial power would stamp down on native revolts.

The traditional technocratic approach used to be more about knowing than doing, for example producing *reports* about what is going on and what should be done rather than intervening on the ground to make things better. In that sense it has been closely aligned to academic practice, especially generalist academic practice. But now that academia has swung strongly towards progressive identity ideology, the Civil Service has clearly been emboldened to do the same, giving way to the authority of a certain type of activist *as a truth-teller* in the same manner that explicitly liberal-left institutions have been doing for a while. This has helped to cushion and justify the grubby, everyday activity of trying to remove opponents from positions in the power apparatus.

John Nott, a former Conservative government minister, said back in the 1980s, 'Whitehall is the ultimate monster to stop governments changing things.'[12] Nowadays, the Civil Service widely trumpets its commitment to 'change and transformation', to the extent that this seems to be its defining purpose. The deployment of progressive identity politics (favouritism linked to 'protected' identity characteristics) as a set of organizing principles adds a more dynamic, moralistic source of authority to the state's role, but also a more specific and narrow one. It confers on the state the role of antagonist and participant in political life, while claiming to be above politics: rejecting even the possibility of alternative pathways in a much more overt way than before. Internally, it is backed up with a proliferation of staff roles (the ubiquitous Diversity, Equity and Inclusion or DEI infrastructure), playing a role not unlike Communist Party commissars did in the institutions of the Soviet Union: to enforce compliance and orthodoxy.

The historian Peter Hennessey once described the Civil Service as 'the hardest target in British journalism'. The journalist and academic Anthony Verrier, quoted by Hennessey, called it the 'permanent government'.[13] Yet this great behemoth of bureaucracy operating at the heart of our system of power is largely protected from scrutiny and accountability in the way that the elected governments it is meant to serve are. Up until now it has been a virtually invisible force at the heart of the state, protected by an unrivalled rhetorical infrastructure that asserts its authority based on apparent neutrality, impartiality and evidence. In recent years, especially in the wake of the Brexit referendum of 2016, we have been exposed to precisely the same language gathering around another source of bureaucratic, political authority: the European Union.

## *The EU: a technocratic empire*

The EU's rulebook is the *acquis communitaire*, 'impenetrable to its citizens', Perry Anderson writes, 'but inescapable for its states'.

> Originally put together as a codification of EEC regulations to which the UK, Denmark and Ireland would have to adapt on entry into the Community in 1973, when it already came to 2800 pages, the *acquis* now runs to 90,000 pages, the longest and most formidable written monument of bureaucratic expansion in human history (the notorious US tax code is a mere 6500). Foucault's overblown identification of knowledge with power here finds literal embodiment.[14]

Anderson quotes Joseph Weiler on how this behemoth makes Europe's 'constitutional operating system . . . axiomatic, beyond discussion, above debate, like the rules of democratic discourse, or even the very rules of rationality themselves, which seem to condition debate but not be part of it'.[15]

As the EU's executive body, responsible for 'instigating and implementing the EU's policies', the European Commission presides over the *acquis*. However, Anderson follows the EU's house historian and intellectual Luuk van Middelaar in suggesting the European Council as the centre of EU power: the place where member state representatives come to meet, in private. Then there is the European Parliament – an institution of 'elite consolidation', as Italian scholar Stefano Bartolini puts it (and quoted by Anderson). On top of a hefty salary, at the time of writing MEPs received a tax-free 'general expenditure allowance' worth €57,336 per year to pay for their offices outside the Parliament's own buildings. They got a daily 'subsistence' allowance of €338, again tax-free, just for signing in to the Parliament building, whether it is sitting or not. Then there is the €320,808 they received every year to pay for their staff. As *The Times*'s Brussels correspondent Bruno Waterfield has written, 'The money is a powerful tool of patronage and nepotism within political parties.'[16] For those parties and their leading figures, often struggling for funds, the money and the opportunity to dole out jobs to party hacks, associates and dependants buy a lot of goodwill.

Then there is the secretive European Court of Justice (ECJ) and European Central Bank (ECB), with their sweeping powers to respectively decide what is lawful and unlawful (not necessarily in conformity to the *acquis*, making this an explicitly political court) and to intervene in the economy of the EU, with virtually no oversight and accountability.

At the very least, some of this might be worrying to anyone concerned with democracy and nation-state power. However, added up, it also offers significant attractions, not least in squirrelling away a lot of the boring, technical, regulatory work required for a hyper-globalized capitalist world to keep itself going and not spiral out of control. The attractions are not just technical and interest-based however. As the German sociologist Wolfgang Streeck has written, specifically of Britain:

> For the Euro-idealists on the liberal left the EU was a preview of a political future without the blemishes of a political past, a constitutively virtuous state if only because it was not yet a state at all, uniquely desirable for people who saw their own post-imperial country in need of a moral refounding from above.[17]

The passionate yearnings of defeated 'Remainers' towards the EU since the British Brexit referendum only go to show how potent such dreams are. They can seem totally out of all proportion to the largely transactional daily reality of the EU with its Single Market, Customs Union, its booming bureaucracy and what many observers describe as a fundamentally neoliberal nature. However the Remainers, now Rejoiners, are not alone in their vision of the EU as an embodiment of progress. Like nation-states have done over the years, the EU nurtures its own (supra-national) myths. The Commission is in the vanguard of this process, once tweeting that the EU, 'is peace', 'is freedom', 'is solidarity', 'is diversity', 'is human rights', 'is opportunities', 'is Erasmus', 'is research', 'is protection', 'is equality' and, lastly, 'is the future'. For many in and around the EU system, the EU is a utopian project, existing on a higher plane of reality to the tainted, troubled Earth.

In Anderson's words, the EU presents its actions as 'the last word in an up-to-date polity'.[18] The certainty and authority, the appearance of knowledge and the feeling of having consigned large swathes of political activity *to the past* – all this clearly has a powerful appeal to progressives. It confers a sense of movement into the future as well as a dismissal of the past. This is perhaps the only way that such a union as the EU could work, representing a sort of mutual acceptance among member state elites that they should narrow down the possibilities of political activity in order to effectively coordinate their affairs and march into the future together.

All of this contributes to a relentless pressing towards further unity, 'ever closer union', defined by the transition of nation-states under the EU umbrella into 'member states': something explored by the academic Chris Bickerton. Bickerton writes, as quoted by Anderson, 'The concept of member state expresses a fundamental change in the political structure of the state, with horizontal ties between national executives taking precedence over vertical ties between governments and their own societies.'[19]

This is why European Council might be conceived as the centre of EU power: for it joins the constituent governments together, binding them to each other under the physical and existential infrastructure of the EU. The assimilation of horizontal accountability as an assumption among leading EU figures and supporters is quite striking in this context. In relation to Brexit, it could be seen by constant appeals to the importance of being 'in the room' and sitting 'at the top table': conceptions designed to appeal to British elites who might actually be doing the sitting in the relevant rooms. This is the level at which almost all EU discourse takes place: not vertically down to individual citizens but horizontally towards those with a more tangible interest in power.

In the European Union, we can see many of the traits of the UK Civil Service but on a much grander scale: the politicization of the bureaucracy and legal functions; the sense of distance from citizens to power; indeed, the sense that the operations of government are – and must be – beyond scrutiny and beyond contention; and that governments contesting this must be put back in their place.

The EU appears to us not so much as a technocratic state as an example of how technocracy has transcended the nation-state and subjected it to a great imperial power, presiding over nations, quelling any nascent rebellions: for example with controls on free expression. The EU is a technocratic *system*, an empire of rules and regulations that presents itself as absolutely rational. In this way it appears as powerfully attractive to many progressives and indeed to national technocrats: like a wet dream of promotional, assertive power that, it appears, cannot ultimately be contradicted. Celebrating the EU is really celebrating a certain kind of power.

# 10

## *Nationalisms, good and bad*

In 1912, the composer Ralph Vaughan Williams wrote a short article for the Royal College of Music magazine entitled 'Who wants the English composer?' In it he commented, 'Nobody wants the young English composer; he is unappreciated at home and unknown abroad. Indeed, the composer who is not wanted in England can hardly desire to be known abroad, for though his appeal should be in the long run universal, art, like charity, should begin at home.'[1]

In the article, as the late David Manning put it, Vaughan Williams 'expresses frustration with contemporary music and musical culture in England, complaining that established and popular continental composers are dominating the tastes of audiences, and unduly influencing the musical style of native composers. To write genuinely original music, he explains, the English composer should focus on his own country and its culture, rather than attempt an imitation of the "great" composers."[2]

Vaughan Williams asked:

> the lilt of the chorus at a music-hall joining in a popular song, the children dancing to a barrel organ, the rousing fervour of a Salvation Army hymn, . . . the Welshmen striking up one of their own hymns whenever they win a goal at the international football match, the cries of the street pedlars, the factory girls singing their sentimental songs? Have these nothing to say to us?[3]

It seems significant how, even around the apex of British Empire and power in the world, British elites themselves (often spoken of as 'English' during this time) widely regarded their own culture as inferior to that of others in Europe. Also, how this expressed itself in a widespread prejudice *against* their own composers and musicians; indeed, against the very idea that it was possible or desirable to make high quality music grounded in Britain as a place. From abroad, this attitude appeared to attract corroboration, finding a slogan in the polemic *Das*

*Land Ohne Musik* (*The Land Without Music*) published in Germany in 1904.*

Despite his best efforts, these notions continued both in Britain and abroad during Vaughan Williams's life and have lingered to the present day. Indeed, the stand he took and the efforts he made to write music with a base in English folk song made him a particular target of them – in Britain as well as in Continental Europe and the United States. One of the main charges made along these lines is of apparent *insularity*, sometimes associated with a lack of *technique*. This accusation has gathered for the most part around his apparent failure to follow musical developments abroad, particularly the various modernist, avant-garde movements which often looked to strip music of any emotional, local and sometimes tuneful content.†

The German critic Jan Brachmann says that Vaughan Williams 'is often belittled by the British as the good-natured teddy bear of their tradition and by the rest of Europe as the insular oddity of a pastoral musician'.[4] The second image matches what Vaughan Williams himself said back in 1941, that 'the attitude of foreign to English musicians is unsympathetic, self-opinionated and pedantic. They believe that their tradition is the only one (this is specially true of the Viennese) and that anything that is not in accordance with that tradition is "wrong" and arises from insular ignorance.'[5]

These sorts of attitudes have had a strong presence in British musical life, with an intellectual elite that is more interested in musicology than music. They attempt to reserve music as a specialist occupation which is only for the right people like themselves, deploying political ideas and ideologies as a gatekeeping device to keep the wrong people out. Indeed, under the guise of a global 'openness', attitudes to music and contemporary politics have sometimes appeared to merge in recent times, the music

---

* The author, Oskar Adolf Hermann Schmitz, said in this tome, 'The English are the only cultured nation without its own music (except street music)', a statement that actually fits Vaughan Williams's ideas rather well. However, politically Schmitz's polemic fitted into the growing jingoistic and anti-British movement in Germany in the lead-up to the First World War. The attitude it expressed was longstanding, having been expressed by Heinrich Heine among others beforehand.

† In fact, Vaughan Williams *was* following them, in the sense of noticing and thinking about them. He hardly had a choice. However he did not follow them in the sense of following their example in his own music, except perhaps in a sarcastic form in the Symphony No. 4.

serving as an alternative channel to express the solidarity of the right people and their antagonism to others. For this intellectual and assertively cosmopolitan overclass, Vaughan Williams for a while served as a prime target, not least given his self-professed nationalism and the immense popularity of his piece *The Lark Ascending* with ordinary people.

A lot of the antagonism on display has gathered around nationality and national affiliation more than the music itself. Music journalist Hugh Morris taps into this rich seam in saying:

> The residual spectre of British (read: English) exceptionalism that characterizes our politics, governance, and musical life runs strong in Vaughan Williams; this highly-stylized idea of him is regularly aired on the permanently-halcyon airwaves of Classic FM. It's no surprise that he now represents a highly middlebrow attitude to music in the UK.[6]

Many claim they *hate* Vaughan Williams's music on a similar basis. Of *The Lark Ascending*, the sports journalist Elizabeth Botcherby has written, 'I hate it', referring to it as 'Middle England radio fodder that I actively switch stations to avoid'.[7] Associations with things other than the music keep recurring in such commentary. Padraig Reidy, editor of the website *Little Atoms*, brought immigration into the mix in tweeting, 'I hate The Lark Ascending. There. I said it. Deport me.' *Guardian* columnist Rafael Behr concurred, calling the piece 'Massively overrated', thereby moving it away from the love that normally characterizes people's appreciation into a linear, judgemental framing – akin to the Viennese attitude that Vaughan Williams criticized above.[8]

Clearly, much of this sort of talk has been given an extra edge by Brexit. Philip Clark in *The Guardian* compared what he called 'the bucolic tonality' of Vaughan Williams and contemporaries with 'the experimental instincts of Europe', so drawing a contrast between a *backward* Britain (especially England) and a *forward-looking* Europe. He also mobilized William Glock, a BBC Controller of Music in the 1970s, as someone who 'attempted to redress Euroscepticism' by placing modernist composers at the heart of his programmes (alongside this he implausibly claims that Glock was not *discriminating* against others in this policy).[9]

The message here is that modern is good and modern is European. Britons who embraced modernism are Europeans and those who did not are parochial, British and bad.* The former Labour minister and technocrat Andrew Adonis jokingly offered a simpler interpretation but from a similar perspective, tweeting, 'Elgar adored Germany & dedicated "Nimrod" to a German. Holst will be banned or have his name changed to Harris. Handel will be sent back to guess where. Delius has big pro-European problems. So we are left with Vaughan Williams & Greensleeves!'[10]

## *Englishness as a disease*

For J.G. Ballard, docking at Southampton in the winter of 1946, England certainly appeared to be the very opposite of modern. He has written of how, 'Small, putty-faced people moved around, shabbily dressed and with a haunted air.'[11]

> A steady drizzle fell for most of the time, and the sky was slate-grey with soot lifting over the streets from tens of thousands of chimneys. Everything was dirty, and the interiors of railways carriages and buses were black with grime.
>
> Looking at the English people around me, it was impossible to believe that they had won the war. They behaved like a defeated population. I wrote in *The Kindness of Women* that the English talked as if they had won the war, but acted as if they had lost it. They were clearly exhausted by the war, and expected little of the future. . . . Everything was poorly designed – my grandparents' three-storey house was heated by one or two single-bar electric fires and an open coal fire.[12]

As Ballard pointed out, he was by no means alone in having such thoughts among visitors to Britain in this time. The masses of foreign servicemen and women who had passed through during the war felt largely the same. Refugees from Nazi Europe were shocked at the lack of central heating in the respectable middle-class houses to which they were assigned. The

---

* Vaughan Williams was an English nationalist in cultural terms, but supported the idea of a Federal Union or a sort of United States of Europe later in life – seeing it contrarily as a way to preserve national particularities while keeping the peace. Nevertheless, it is impossible not to notice how the barbs and denunciations thrown at him over the years merge almost exactly into those thrown at Brexit voters, from ignorance and insularity to backwardness and nostalgia for something that never existed.

performance of British armed forces was often notably poorer than war propaganda made out, with equipment and tactics often badly inferior to their German opponents and their American allies later on. Ballard himself was struck by the optimism and modernity of America, of its people and its technology, like the sleek, silvery P-51 Mustang fighter plane.

Of his 'home' country, he suggested, 'With its ancestor worship and standing to attention for "God Save the King", England needed to be freed from itself and from the delusions that people in all walks of life clung to about Britain's place in the world.'[13] Looking back from 2008 he spoke of how 'the system of self-delusions that underpinned almost everything' in the lives of the English 'fed into my troubled sense of who I was, and encouraged me to think of myself as a lifelong outsider and maverick. It probably steered me towards becoming a writer devoted to predicting and, if possible, provoking change. Change, I felt, was what England desperately needed, and I still feel it.'[14]

Ballard's narrative of post-war England or Britain more or less matches the one which predominates today, albeit ossified by constant repetition. Talk of imperial nostalgia, misplaced obsession with the Second World War and the need to abolish outdated social codes has become a narrative of accepted opinion: of reflex and cliché, thereby merging into promotional and campaigning activity, which after all depends on constant repetition. Ballard wrote of how 'Middle-class people in the late 1940s and 1950s saw the working class as almost another species, and fenced themselves off behind a complex system of social codes.'[15] This remains the case now, but his own ideas have been assimilated into the narrative: a way of distinguishing yourself from the plebs, placing that which is disapproved of outside the self. An image of Britain stuck in the past has become a favoured narrative of our globalizing overclass, used to fence itself off from ordinary people. The image offers a way for elites to wipe their hands of responsibility for and connection to others while at the same time asserting their superiority and virtue. Effectively it is a recalibration. The class system that Ballard hated has found new life through the ideas of change that he promoted: putting a renewed distance between the overseers and those they oversee, based on apparently superior knowledge and understanding.

British elites wiping their hands of their compatriots have formed a grand alliance with others abroad who are also keen to denigrate and undermine the country and its people. EU officials and the elites of major member states have been particularly keen allies, as have Irish and Scottish nationalists and the powerful American progressive establishment with its important links to mainstream and new media tycoons.

Some of the language used towards the British and English by writers and commentators following the Brexit referendum was startling in its brutality and hostility, often grounded in ludicrous claims that Britons – and Tory English Britons in particular – remain obsessed by Empire. In the years following Brexit, *The New York Times*, once a serious paper of record, ran a succession of high-profile articles denouncing Britain and its people along these lines. One, appearing just hours after the death of Queen Elizabeth II, featured a professor of history at Harvard saying that 'the Queen helped obscure a bloody history of decolonization whose proportions and legacies have yet to be adequately acknowledged'.[16] The author, Maya Jasanoff, wrote of the 'karmic' assassination of Lord Mountbatten by the IRA in 1979 and how the government of Boris Johnson 'leaned into a vision of "Global Britain" steeped in half-truths and imperial nostalgia'.

From Continental Europe, Brexit provoked exultant denunciations, with the Empire often mobilized to suggest a long and continuing lineage of national guilt. During Theresa May's time as Prime Minister, the German newspaper *Der Spiegel* ran an article entitled 'Watching a country make a fool of itself', with the sub-heading: 'No country in the world has cultivated arrogance the way Britain has'. It presented a cartoonish vision of the country based on the most overwrought fantasies of anti-Brexit journalists and campaigners:

> There has been no shortage of articles about what the golden future will look like that London has promised British citizens. First, the trucks will back up all the way to Wales because the borders are back. Then the petrol stations will run out of petrol and there will be a scarcity of drugs in the hospitals. Meanwhile, once all the Polish plumbers have gone back home, there will nobody to call when the toilet clogs up.
>
> They'll be left in their water-damaged homes with no heating oil and no aspirin – and their Russian neighbours will be in extremely bad moods.

The combination of wild assertions with a preening seriousness and superiority is a regular feature of these denunciations. Having blasted the British for arrogance, this particular writer says, 'The disadvantage of being intelligent is that it hurts to watch someone act dumb. . . . It is also worth noting that at a certain point in every country's history, decay becomes unavoidable.'[17]

As these attacks have passed backwards and forwards between elites in different countries, they have snowballed, gathering momentum and credence like a more sophisticated version of village gossip. However, the origin of them appears to have been largely in Britain itself: in the Brexit campaign and its aftermath – not least in the accusations of racism and xenophobia made by Remain supporters against the Brexit side. The mobilization of dubious hate crime statistics played a crucial role here, helping to nail down the narrative as fact. As Jasanoff wrote in her *New York Times* article, 'We may never learn what the queen did or didn't know about the crimes committed in her name, but xenophobia and racism have been rising, fueled by the toxic politics of Brexit.'[18]

*Der Spiegel*'s reference to Polish plumbers indicates what a significant role immigration plays in this story, backing up the narrative among the progressives of the Western world that Britain could not survive without that which is distinctively not British, or at least not English. As Carl Bildt, the former Prime Minister of Sweden, put it, 'Where would Britain be without people from other countries? Poor, boring and declining. But few dare to say so.'[19] On the contrary, it is received wisdom – and there are plenty in Britain who are keen to indulge the same thoughts.\* Appearing on a 'Horrible Histories Brexit special' on BBC children's programming, the comedian Nish Kumar presented an excruciating clip of Queen Victoria's butler explaining to her how 'British things' are all imported and the product of war, slavery and Empire, concluding that 'British things. . . turns out there's hardly any'.[20] Here we find the national broadcaster using a compulsory levy on the population to educate its children that the nation they live in, its people and culture are variously worthless, illusory and the result of crime. This sort of talk understandably encourages a sense of superiority in people who are not

---

\* There is clearly some truth to Bildt's words, but the intention to denigrate and demean those who do not count as immigrants in Britain is clear I think.

British but have an interest in the country. It also emboldens those who have laid down roots in Britain to renounce any affiliation to the place as a place and to its people as a people: encouraging them to see themselves purely as products of elsewhere or something else, as a higher class, with a destiny to prevail over the inferior others they live amongst – similar to the old colonial attitude to 'natives'. There is a distinct imperialist aspect to it: a reverse progressive imperialism led by the post-imperial elite, imposed on the non-elite populations of the old imperial centre.

Daniela Nadj, a London-based law academic and popular progressive tweeter, spends much of her time online lecturing the country in which she lives on how it is inferior and needs to follow her instructions, like a school teacher from times past laying down the law to her errant pupils. In one tweet she said, 'Great Britain, it's time to arrive in the 21st Century. That means three things: 1) Get rid of the Royal Family 2) Rejoin the EU and 3) please, please change your electoral system.'[21] In another, having received quite a lot of reaction for her widely broadcasted words, she redirected her scorn to England specifically, saying: 'I love living in London and Britain has been amazing to me in many ways. It's my home. But boy, England, you have a big, big problem with racism, xenophobia and misogyny combined with a disdain for intellectuals. You need to have an open national debate about it asap.'[22]

It may seem somewhat impolite to be speaking this way, not least when the evidence for such attacks is mixed at best. However when senior British people and British media are embracing the same messaging; when *The Guardian*'s Zoe Williams repeats a common view that English patriotism stands for 'idiotic exceptionalism' and 'excruciating jingoism'; when the actress Emma Thompson backs the Remain side by calling Britain, 'A tiny little cloud-bolted, rainy corner of sort-of Europe, a cake-filled, misery-laden grey old island'; when the TV scientist Professor Brian Cox responds to an ethnic Asian minister's mention of 'the British people' by saying the phrase is 'inflammatory and divisive and also errant vacuous nonsense with no meaning in a multi-party democracy'; when the famous evolutionary biologist Richard Dawkins says, 'if I were Scottish today I'd want to leave the nasty little backwater that England is becoming' and 'I'd be proud to be Scottish or Irish. Just not English', is this not just normal conformity and integration into a society you claim to despise?[23]

Does this not appear as a *continuation* of something as well? As someone living and writing in the years when Britain actually gave up its Empire, V.S. Naipaul knew a thing or two about the British overseeing class and its foibles. In the 1970s, he wrote:

> They grumbled, journalists, politicians, businessmen, responding week by week to the latest newspaper crisis and television issue; they echoed one another; they could become hysterical with visions of the country's decay. But the little crises always passed, the whispered political plots and business schemes evaporated; everything that was said was stale, and people no longer believed what they said. And failure always lay with someone else: the people who spoke of crisis were themselves placid, content with their functions, existing within their functions, trapped, part of what they railed against.[24]

Attacking Britain, the English, the voters (otherwise known as the stupid, ignorant masses), and doing so from an assertively liberal or left-wing point of view, is this not an expression of status, of belonging? Does it not represent *integration* with a British ruling class that is used to getting its way and outraged at the population for its own failure to control them adequately? And is this not itself one of the foundations of a genuine English or British disease, of the characteristic problems that the country has, not least of exalting people who *say* things (the right things) over those who *do* things?

## *Ireland: a properly progressive nation*

After a fraught few weeks of debate in Ireland about transgender issues in which the Dublin Pride organization terminated national broadcaster RTÉ's 'media partner' status, Irish premier Micheál Martin used an old and neat political trick to show his support for the trans lobby. Speaking to an LGBT+ group, the Taoiseach said, 'I'd be very concerned about that and I've watched it in the UK and we certainly don't need that kind of debate in Ireland.' He added, 'First of all, acceptance is the key for trans persons and I think we need a debate that creates a space for understanding and from an informed perspective, and sometimes we don't get that in a highly charged forum.'[25]

Paul Hosford, 2021 Irish Journalist of the Year, concurred, writing of how, 'In the UK, the discussion around trans rights and treatment has ... taken on many of the characteristics of a moral panic, about which many faceless Twitter profiles care suspiciously deeply.' He cited comments by the Green Party's Marc Ó Cathasaigh: '"We're beginning to see an importation of culture wars that are being waged elsewhere where debates around these issues are becoming weaponised and are being used to stoke fears and to sow division."'[26]

You can see in each of these assertions calls for Irish civil society to come together by *not being like them*, so not being like the British in having *toxic* debates on trans issues. It is a call to the group: to stay united by rejecting the other and their ways, which is to say not allowing contentious political debate on such matters.

By framing the issue in this way, the Taoiseach and others were tapping into a strong current of national feeling in the years following the United Kingdom's Brexit vote in 2016, characterized by widespread contempt for the neighbours and self-satisfaction over Ireland's contrasting commitment to the EU.

This current has expressed itself in a number of ways, including in apparently growing public support for the historic role of the IRA and its 'armed struggle' against British rule. This sometimes appears in a remarkably casual fashion, as when the Irish Women's Football Team celebrated a win in 2022 by chanting 'ooh ah, up the ra'. The Irish journalist John McGuirk said of this that,

> these ladies did not express, in their chant, anything that we genuinely, as a nation, believe it unacceptable to feel. From the ground up, through various degrees of politeness and refinement, Anglophobia is Ireland's tribal national religion. Nothing we do, nothing we say, nothing we believe, can compare to eight hundred years of oppression. That story is drummed into us from our first day at school, to our last. It is repeated through the respectable media outlets. It is expressed in sporting rivalry, and not voting for England in the Eurovision, and the outbursts of maniacal national outrage any time an Irish person we're proud of is mistakenly described as 'British' by the villainous UK media.[27]

This sort of sentiment can be baffling from a British perspective given how well Irish people have settled into British society, to the extent that we – and also others from abroad – may indeed *not* notice a difference sometimes. However, perhaps that high degree of integration has in fact aided the gathering hostility, by bringing ethnically Irish people in large numbers into elite strata of society in Britain, where they have found that expressions of British and English national identity are widely scorned and expressions of hostility welcomed. Indeed, we might say that an anti-British Irish identity paradoxically serves as a form of integration into British civil society.

The commentator Fintan O'Toole has served like something of a production line for this strangely *integrated* hostility, churning out countless articles featuring remarkably frenzied denunciations of Brexit Britain and its major figures. He also penned a book entitled *Heroic Failure: Brexit and the Politics of Pain*, which psychologizes Brexit as 'essentially an English phenomenon', a fantasy of the 'English reactionary imagination' and a consequence of 'imperial nostalgia': interpretations that have become truisms in the progressive firmament of the West.[28]

In an enjoyable review of what he calls 'this entertaining and infuriating book', the Northern Irish academic Professor John Wilson Foster writes, 'the restriction of Brexit to its English essence allows the author to view it as a phenomenon that defines the truest England: "Brexit is at heart an English nationalist project"'. He adds, 'England is anthropomorphised as a patient on a couch whom the author diagnoses in order, supposedly, to effect a cure. Any English history adduced in the book is evidence of behaviour betraying a national disorder.' And, 'Brexit is never analysed as the Exit of Great Britain and Northern Ireland from the European Union but instead . . . as a man (a white man, a middle-aged or elderly man, an angry man, a racist man, an arrogant man and, I'm afraid, a straw man).'[29]

O'Toole's analysis is psychological, but with that also sociological: finding in English identity the original root cause of *really bad things*, just as Communists found it in the bourgeoisie and landowners and Nazis found it in Jews, Slavs and Communists. However Wilson Foster suggests that O'Toole's ferocious and unrelenting analysis 'hints at a fixation' that has another source – in closeness, in shared identity of a sort, and in a sense of personal betrayal. As he puts it:

The educated Irish have for decades lived what I call two-passport lives, culturally inhabiting Ireland and England without incongruity – or challenge. One thinks of all those Irish entertainers, sportsmen, professors and lecturers, BBC reporters and correspondents who live and work at the heart of British culture, and help that heart pump the blood of the culture, yet oddly have nothing good to say on the intimate Irish–British relationship. O'Toole has rightly given himself permission to explain mockingly the English to themselves because like Wilde and Shaw he not only stands among them but, at the level of educated culture, to flip Byron, is of them.[30]

The Irish reaction towards Britain and England over Brexit has certainly shown us something that is very different from mere detached judgement: often expressing itself in visceral, personalized hostility. There has been an extra edge to this for those with positions at an EU level. On troubles with the Northern Ireland Protocol, Brigid Laffan, as a former director of an EU research body, exclaimed at one point in 2022, 'The view in Dublin is that relations are worse than at any time since pre-Thatcher. Concern about the lack of expertise on Ireland & EU for that matter in the system. Cannot do business with Truss or Johnson the mantra. Public consensus on perfidious Albion. A pirate state!!'[31]

With their affiliation to this state, the unionist people of Northern Ireland find themselves right in the firing line for such a perspective. In various tweets that he later deleted, Daniel Keohane, a Dublin academic and associate fellow of the Centre for European Reform, wrote, 'Sooner NI Unionists realise their cause is lost, esp because of Brexit, better. A majority on this island will vote to join an Irish republic, not to stay in a sectarian British monarchical Union. No one in Republic cares for Unionists. You are done, how done is up to you.' And then: 'Someday British friends might realise what their state really represents: imperialism. Until that state is long gone, as our American cousins know, there is no peace.' Also: '@TheActofUnion is violent construct that should never have happened, and destroyed most lives on this island.'[32]

The violent, hostile sentiment – from someone widely deployed as an independent expert on UK–Irish relations – could hardly be clearer. Like Laffan's words, they also claim a much wider authority. While her words were claiming to express the Irish state view, Keohane's were claiming to represent Irish society. Notably, both individuals are also tied into the EU system, where recognition of Northern Irish unionists has been virtually non-existent.

Amidst all this raging, the insults, threats and ominous warnings of violence, it has been striking how much Irish participants in these affairs have appeared to be *enjoying themselves*. There has been a considerable performative aspect to it, featuring a lot of back-slapping between the Irish establishment, those in and around the EU system and also Democrats in America, keen to emphasize their Irish affiliations. The air of smugness on all sides has sometimes been overpowering, the impression being that the Irish are very much *in the room*, on the side of power.

In this sense we might see that Irish nationalism – including the uglier sides of it – has found a home in the wider world. It has found a role in its alignment to pan-national progressive goals and institutions, in its embrace of globalization and vocal rejection of 'taking back control' in Britain. Official Ireland and its media supporters have taken on fashionable causes from the Anglophone world like gender self-ID, mass immigration and Black Lives Matter, while using pockets of opposition to them in England as a further reason for their own support. There has been a serious air of *demonstration* about it. *Look at us: we're on the right of history. Unlike that horrible lot over there.*

The principal centres of power for these causes are abroad however, mostly in America, but also in Britain. Ireland tends to pick up each of them as a *follower*. The Dublin-based blogger Conor Fitzgerald links this almost reflexive adoption of such causes to a trait he calls 'goodboyism'.

'Goodboyism', he says, is,

> the tendency in the Irish establishment to ostentatiously direct themselves towards external sources of cultural authority over and before the Irish populace or the interests of Irish people. The closer those authorities are aligned to the values of the global managerial class, the greater the Irish tendency to seek their approval. So for instance deference can be paid to Barack Obama but not to Donald Trump; toward the EU but not the UK government.[33]

We might again see a sort of paradox to aggressive anti-Britishness in Ireland here. For the dominant narratives to be found in the Republic – the causes embraced, the language of politicians and the bureaucracy – are almost identical to those that pervade British public life, the commitments of the British Establishment. Indeed, the promoting of a single Irish position on many issues like Brexit plays an important role in British public life, often appearing as something that is beyond criticism: as mere truth, pure and unsullied – something the Irish elite appears to exploit as much as they can. By their trenchant attacks on Brexit Britain and the English, and by making life difficult for Britain's post-Brexit governments, the likes of Micheál Martin, O'Toole and Laffan placed themselves firmly *alongside* Britain's own overseeing class, playing a role on their behalf as well as for the EU. Through this they have elevated Ireland's status as a suitably progressive nation that does all the right things, viewed not just from Brussels, Berlin and Washington but from London. As Fitzgerald points out, the perspective has little interest in the Irish people; it is more interested in the approval of ruling elites elsewhere.

Ireland's self-identity has shifted considerably in recent decades, becoming self-consciously progressive and modern. Progressive identity plays an important role in offering a release from the troubles of history through the promise of change and novelty. This comes with a habit of treating the past as something to be fought against and defeated, which in turn means fighting against the past's apparent representatives in the present, not least the British or English.

Sometimes, I get the impression of a looming tragedy associated with this oppositional identity, which has been largely neglected amidst the self-congratulation in the Republic as well as in Continental Europe. For a start, by embracing Anglophobia and anti-unionist feeling so fully, the Irish establishment played straight into the hands of Sinn Féin, for whom these narratives of hostility are the meat and drink of politics. If you were seeking to promote peace and reconciliation on the island of Ireland, empowering the inheritors of a ruthless tradition of political murder and organized crime is probably the last thing you should be doing. Nevertheless, when the same sort of hostility has established itself as high-status opinion in Britain and the EU too, the easy thing is to go along with it and enjoy the acclaim.

In such a context on national identity, Ralph Vaughan Williams may as well have placed a big target on his back. As someone who looked to the English past, whose music is widely regarded as quintessentially English, and whose *Lark Ascending* used to annually win a poll run by that most unfashionable of radio stations, Classic FM, he has sometimes appeared as a lightning rod for anti-English and anti-Brexit sentiment.

It has been noticeable to see how readily this arises particularly from nationalist Irish and Scots – the latter of whom are keen to replicate the Irish model of a self-consciously progressive new state within the EU. The popular Scottish nationalist journalist and broadcaster Ruth Wishart for example tweeted of *The Lark Ascending* winning the Classic FM poll again, 'Who are the people voting for this tediously twee piece? Of all the composers in all the world?'[34] And, 'The Lark is just dreich in my ears. I doubt it would rate Classic FM's top spot on this side of the border.'[35]

Here, we see that contrast again between the good nation and the bad one. England and English people appear as something negative and twee, associated with insularity and 'dreich' music, while the Scots are imagined as having much better taste, preferring that which comes from the wider world rather than England.

Such notions may seem mundane and trivial. However they show us the everyday thoughts through which politics works itself out, forming groups not so much around who we are but who we are not – the negative other. In national terms, this process is sometimes referred to as 'xenophobia'; and clearly those pointing the finger at apparent xenophobes are often guilty of it themselves.

For progressives, the thing that distinguishes them from real xenophobes is that they are *right*. Their contempt and hostility appear to be grounded in a solid foundation of knowledge; that the other *really is* a bad type of person, one who is holding back the march of history (otherwise known as their will).

In this way, Scottish and Irish nationalism transcend the normal progressive antagonism to nationalism, not just by their relative freshness and embrace of victimhood, but by their more general rejection of the past and its continuation in the present, however harmless that may be. They appear to be on the right side of history and of politics: seeking change and embracing the most modern attitudes like on transgender rights and immigration, while attacking the bad people who remain attached to an oppressive, white-dominated, male, imperial and anti-trans past.

# 11

# *Playing Jesus: The activist as narcissist*

'I'm, like, so excited to *talk*', said the Duchess of Sussex, Meghan Markle, in an interview for a New York-based website dedicated to women. The journalist doing the interview said of Meghan, 'She's flinging open the proverbial doors to her life; as any millennial woman whose feminism was forged in the girlboss era would understand, she has taken a hardship and turned it into content.'[1]

In the interview, the Duchess's words kept reverting back to two narratives of redemption. One concerned her and her husband, Prince Harry, making a new life away from an oppressive Royal Family. The second concerned others who they were now blessing through their work and presence. She quoted words she apparently said at their wedding, about her 'resounding knowing that, above all, love wins'. And she told the interviewer, 'I hope that is the sentiment that people feel when they see any of the content or the projects that we are working on.' This matches the stated aim of their company Archewell's 'nonprofit' division to put 'compassion into action'.[2]

Confronting these narratives, Meghan's critics have gathered around the idea that she is a 'narcissist', employing a psychological concept based on the Greek legend of Narcissus, who fell in love with his own reflection. The description does seem to fit Meghan as someone who is constantly pushing herself forward, genuflecting on her role in the world; someone who married into royalty then sought to transform the institution fundamentally according to her own ideas; someone who then exploited her and her husband's conflict with the family to make money, speaking all the while as a fount of goodness in the world.

There is a strong controlling aspect to the whole affair, as when Meghan says in the interview that she and Harry are 'like salt and pepper. We always move together.'[3] Especially for old-style British tastes, it is all a bit much. Indeed, it sometimes appears as if the whole world exists as an accessory to the Duchess's personal ambition: drawing credence to the labelling of her as a narcissist.

## *Narcissism as culture*

'Narcissism', according to the *Encyclopaedia Britannica*, consists of,

> pathological self-absorption, first identified as a mental disorder by the British essayist and physician Havelock Ellis in 1898. Narcissism is characterized by an inflated self-image and addiction to fantasy, by an unusual coolness and composure shaken only when the narcissistic confidence is threatened, and by the tendency to take others for granted or to exploit them.[4]

In 1979, Christopher Lasch had a book published called *The Culture of Narcissism*, which identifies narcissism as a core part of Western, especially American, consumerist culture. Based on this perspective, you could say that narcissism is not just a property of the individual but something that is in the existential air we breathe. Lasch refers to 'the emergence of the narcissistic personality as the dominant type of personality structure in contemporary society'.[5] To participate in our culture is to participate in a culture of narcissism.

This sort of perspective might be a little fairer on Meghan for one thing, in recognizing that she is not an outlier in her relentless self-promotion and the way she discards those who do not fall into line with it. Rather, she is the norm – at least in public life, at least in the West and particularly in America. In this sense the common psychological identification of narcissism as a *disorder* is not wholly accurate. To a large extent, being Meghan means *fitting into* our social order and pressing into the possibilities it offers for upward mobility. Could someone like Donald Trump really become President of the United States in anything but a culture of narcissism? And without the promotional support that such a culture provides, could Meghan get away with her self-presentation as a potential world-saviour despite leaving a trail of destroyed relationships in her wake?

The interview with the Duchess of Sussex featured above reveals that she is a close friend of the American feminist Gloria Steinem, who Lasch has criticized for treating politics and therapy as indistinguishable. By treating politics as therapy and therapy as politics, you naturally go down a route in which society appears as a means to satisfy the therapeutic goals of the individual, all individuals. The notion of therapy is widened to cover anyone deemed to be suffering, while the role of the therapist is expanded to cover anyone who seeks to *treat* them in a sense: specifically politicians and activists with an interest in social justice. When society or an institution fails to play along with the attempts of the politician- or activist-as-therapist to heal the world, this appears as an injustice, for interrupting the healing process.

Lasch identified the origins of this style in the 'social gospel' of early twentieth-century American Protestantism, which started to see society as a patient that needed be treated by 'specialists in the cure of souls'.[6] For the late twentieth- and early twenty-first-century iterations of this style, the therapist appears as an 'expert' in society, who understands the fundamental causes of suffering and instructs us all on how we should behave to end it. This generally focuses on what we can and cannot say in order to avoid harming others.

Of Steinem's book *Revolution from Within*, Lasch writes:

> It is completely consistent with the dominant brand of liberalism, a liberalism obsessed with the rights of women and minorities, with gay rights and unlimited abortion rights, with the allegedly epidemic spread of child abuse and sexual harassment, with the need for regulations against offensive speech, and with curricular reforms designed to end the cultural hegemony of 'dead white European males.'[7]

This matches closely Meghan's agenda, which vests significant authority in people like herself who think they understand the core sicknesses that society passes on to the individual – and how to cure them. The merging of politics and therapy opens up the world as a field of play for this sort of activism: giving activist-knowers a heady sense of power and entitlement. Their idea of therapy bursts beyond the confines of the consulting room and the constraints of professional standards onto society as a whole. The talking cure becomes universal. Whole new disciplines of surveillance and regulation are introduced to control talk, making sure that it benefits society and in particular those groups deemed to have particularly intense therapeutic needs as a result of psychological trauma going back generations. There no longer needs to be any direct contact between patient and therapist. Interventions are rather targeted at public figures and the masses, bringing the therapeutic mindset into all corners of existence, from parliamentary speeches to social media postings and everyday conversations in the workplace.

For the narcissist, this role of activist-knower indulges a fantasy in which the self should imprint itself everywhere, preventing the non-self from appearing wherever possible. Many activists come to treat the world almost as an extension of themselves, its purpose being to meet their desires, framed as therapeutic needs of marginalized groups and of society.

This is almost a definition of narcissistic behaviour. However it is now indulged at almost every turn by our major institutions, encouraging more of the same behaviour, and then invariably ending up in disappointment and denunciation as impossible goals of social redemption are not achieved. The cry goes out, 'more must be done' – and the process goes on with even more intensity and gathering hysteria.

Lasch writes, 'therapeutic morality encourages a permanent suspension of the moral sense'. It deprives people of their agency, infantilizing them as objects to be cared for by a mobilized professional class.

> Therapy legitimates deviance as sickness, but it simultaneously pronounces the patient unfit to manage his life and delivers him into the hands of a specialist. As therapeutic points of view and practice gain general acceptance, more and more people find themselves disqualified, in effect, from the performance of adult responsibilities and become dependent on some form of medical authority.[8]

This 'new therapeutic culture of narcissism' stretches from the entertainment industry to schools, academia and the justice system, where courts widely treat offenders as patients of the state, to be cared for and sympathized with for their backgrounds rather than punished for breaking the law.[9] It is administered by what Lasch calls, 'A new ruling class of administrators, bureaucrats, technicians, and experts', whose 'existence as a class often goes unnoticed'.[10]

Lasch maybe pushes the medical authority point too far. However, ponder how often we condemn others using medical and psychiatric terminology, including the term 'narcissist'. By damning others as narcissistic, we may in fact be showing narcissistic traits ourselves, simultaneously inflating our own authority and that of the 'experts' on whose professional judgement we are piggy-backing.

## *How identity politics encourages narcissism*

In my previous book, *The Tribe*, I used the term 'system of diversity' to describe how progressive identity politics has become embedded in our state and society, from the top levels of government to the way we think and conceive of ourselves.[11] In a sense this system is itself a form of society, consisting of a couple of standard relationships:

1. The outsourcing of authority by an overseeing class of diversity administrators to representatives of favoured identity groups, like feminists and race activists; and
2. Between those representatives and the mass of group members they represent, whose role is to appear as victims in need of special assistance.

The nature of these relations fosters behaviour which often appears narcissistic in different ways. At the managerial overclass level it fosters a sense of a right to rule based on assumed benevolence and higher knowledge. In the middle layer of group representatives, the outsourcing of power from above generates a sprouting sense of entitlement, dependent on the assertion of grievance and victimhood of the group. This often comes to revolve around the self, with any criticism received appearing both as an affront against the representative's authority and as a justification for their power in the first place. These people often behave like mini-dictators, without a shred of humility. At the bottom layer, a sort of 'standing reserve' of people is created who have no purpose but to serve as victims and justify the power of those above them in the power structure. These people are largely invisible in and of themselves. The messaging coming from above treats them like infants who depend on the systems of bureaucracy that reach down to them. This fosters a lack of initiative and even defeatism; a self-image defining itself through victimhood and exclusion from the rest of society.

The outsourcing of power from the overclass to group representatives also creates a large degree of fluidity and upward mobility for those who are willing to embrace the system in its 'intersectionality'. This is the space in which the Duchess of Sussex operates, mobilizing her own favoured attributes of female sex and non-white skin colour while standing as an ally to other favoured groups.

Writing up her interview for *The Cut*, journalist Allison P. Davis wrote of her, 'She understands what her ascent meant to Black Britons, for whom she's a sign of progress, and to women, for whom she's a working mom and a signal boost to the issues that affect them (paid parental leave, equal pay). Even though she avoids reading her own press, Meghan knows people see her this way.' In a controversial passage following this, Meghan told Davis that a South African cast member in *The Lion King*, who 'was just like light', told her that people rejoiced in the streets of South Africa when she married into the Royal Family, in the same way they did when Nelson Mandela was freed from jail.[12]

These claims piled one upon another – that black Britons see her as a sign of progress, that women do too, and that South Africans danced in the streets to celebrate her ascent – all work to assign the approval of others onto herself. They bless her as someone associated with *light*; and in doing so they also appropriate large groups of people to assent without their consent.

Mental health is a constant presence in Meghan's discourse. She claimed her own mental health had been damaged by the lack of support for her from the rest of the Royal Family, to the extent she had considered suicide. This is a common way for the activist to respond to resistance and opposition to their desires and interests. The British feminist writer Laurie Penny even diagnosed herself with Complex Post-Traumatic Stress Disorder (CPTSD) after some bad reviews for her book *Sexual Revolution*, which she described as consisting of coordinated personal attacks and betrayals: a 'misogynist, transphobic media monstering'.[13]

The trans writer Jack Monroe, who has described herself as 'a poverty + trauma survivor', regularly invokes mental and physical health problems when faced with opposition. Responding to accusations she had been lying about her past poverty, she said, 'I'm autistic, which my detractors well know, and part of that means I cannot stand untruths and injustice.'[14] Elsewhere, Monroe has claimed her autism as a 'kind of superpower' like Greta Thunberg has.[15] The intense victimhood she has claimed at the hands of society, combined with these special mental powers to decide right from wrong and truth from falsity, fit neatly into an old religious model. For Jesus as Messiah came to us as a victim. He also had special powers and professed to offer salvation to anyone who believed in him. Meghan's special ability to heal the world – and the 'light' she places on those who please and praise her – is just one of many examples that can be found around the world of progressive identity politics, tapping into a Jesus-like narrative and placing themselves in a Jesus-like role.

Christopher Lasch was calling mental health 'the modern equivalent of salvation' all the way back in 1979.[16] And, in the Christian religious style emulated by progressives, this salvation always remains over the horizon, in the future. It is something to orient activity towards, something for which 'more needs to be done': more of *us* and our works and less of *them* and theirs. It is a prop to justify action and intervention, including the suppression of opponents who might thwart its achievement.

State and private bureaucracies now regularly claim both right and ability to administer this salvation of mental health via therapeutic interventions, many lumped under the Diversity, Equity and Inclusion (DEI or sometimes EDI) banner.\* Beneath the personal interests of those at the elite level, DEI doctrines work as a sort of sacred text to help *save* others from the depredations of a fallen world, providing a weapon to cut down the edifices of colonialism, slavery and the domination of white cisgender men. These doctrines and the slogans that accompany them guide our modern secular missionaries – or revolutionaries – as they go about their work.

For white-skinned civil servants in the Department for Levelling Up, Housing and Communities in the early 2020s, the drive towards salvation meant having to watch a training video telling them to believe that their society and culture was racist, that 'white privilege' was a fact and instructing them to become an 'ally' of ethnic minorities.† Such a

---

\* Note how 'equality', a former staple of progressive identity politics, has been removed from the DEI nomenclature coming out of the United States. 'Equity', which has been inserted in its place, is meant to enforce rightness, justifying unequal treatment and also unequal outcomes.

† See pp. 147–8.

presentation, in which all white people appear as in need of re-education and all non-white people are trauma victims who need 'time to heal and recover', opens the way for significant further therapeutic intervention. Whites can attempt to redeem themselves by joining the 'allyship' programme. Here they are effectively enlisted as therapeutic assistants, their role being to listen without question, to not criticize or contradict – to indulge the ego basically. In this way, politics, social policy and workplace training all merge into an enveloping, simplistic therapy culture, with experts in society overseeing the whole thing and making their money.

In schools, colleges and universities, similar ideas have proliferated. In 2021, a report from the National Education Union (NEU), Britain's largest for the sector, claimed there was an 'urgent' need to further 'decolonise' school life. It said that there was a 'silence around British imperialism and racism' in the education system, with wider British culture 'saturated with a longing for return to Empire without any understanding into what Empire is/was'. 'From curriculum to routines to classroom layout', it claimed, 'our education system has been shaped by colonisation and neoliberalism.'[17]

The revolutionary implications of these words match the crudeness of the history and sociology behind the ideas. It assumes that, during the days of Empire, the fundamental nature of British society was of colonialism, which means that everything existing within it was a consequence of colonialism and should be purged now. The purging is 'urgent' in order to protect non-white students from a continuation of colonial oppression and white students from seeking to reconstitute Empire. As Joanna Williams concluded, 'Apparently, expecting pupils to face the teacher, to sit still and to listen perpetuates a colonial legacy.'[18] It is a classic example of how gross generalization can lead into similarly gross stupidity: encouraging the imprinting of itself everywhere it looks.

Many of the efforts to overturn school practices gather around the apparent oppression of specifically black students. The group No More Exclusions was set up in 2018 to campaign against school exclusions, blaming schools themselves rather than student behaviour for exclusions. It also claimed exclusions are inherently racist. A *Guardian* profile of co-founder Zahra Bei said, 'The racial disparities are stark, with exclusion rates for black Caribbean students up to six times higher than those of their white peers in some local authorities, according to a recent Guardian analysis.'[19]

Teacher and blogger Andrew Old criticized this statement for being based on 'cherrypicked data, almost certainly intended to mislead'. Of the data collated by *The Guardian*, he said: 'Ethnic minority groups were broken down into the smallest possible categories and those ethnic groups that had lower exclusion rates than white British pupils were ignored (despite being the overwhelming majority of ethnic minority pupils).' *The Guardian* presented the data 'as if it was about black pupils in general rather than black Caribbean pupils in a handful of LAs'. The real story, Old said, was that 'London has a unique problem with racial disparities in *suspensions* [my italics], and that this has happened in a city that stands out for having kept suspensions low.'[20]

Bei, a graduate in 'social justice and education' from the Institute of Education in London, said in her *Guardian* interview, 'Schools are a protective factor in children and young people's lives. You remove the protective factor and you are exposing them to all manner of risks.' Though seemingly at odds with the idea of school as an oppressive environment for black children, this framing has a similar utopian character in how it imagines an alternative. It regards the school as a place with a *therapeutic* purpose, to protect the most disruptive and dangerous pupils from the world outside, rather than as a place of learning for students who are able to abide by rules of decent behaviour (and who may struggle to learn in a context of constant disruption from others). Bei suggests that schools should be doing a lot more to deal with troubled children, who she describes as 'neurodiverse', with many having 'undiagnosed special educational needs and disabilities'.[21] This view sees the school as a place that would need experts in psychology (an inexact discipline at the best of times) to minister to these students, while keeping them in school and in the classroom. This is surely a recipe for costly confusion, but one that the new Labour government's Education Secretary Bridget Philippson seems wholly committed to.

## *The saviour complex*

We can see narcissistic traits in how activists invest huge power in the *self*: the good self, the right self, the victim self – and the evil self who must be defeated. In educational settings, the idea of the victim self confers on black students and staff a sort of blessed identity, of innocence and purity rather like Rousseau's conception of the 'noble savage' (and in that sense a racist stereotype). The assumption is that this nobility and purity (or 'blank slate' quality) can only be corrupted by the actions of white people or white-dominated culture – whether it be by exclusions from school or the colonialism implicit in the school curriculum and practices.

The good self of the activist-teacher is a sort of saviour self whose status is grounded in beliefs and theories, giving them the role of social therapist. This role is less about teaching knowledge and skills and more about saving the victims of oppression from their oppression. It is concerned with protecting the child from the big bad world of the Nigel Farages and Suella Bravermans, placing them in a cocoon through which only the right messages can break through.

Both these identities, of victim and saviour, work to boost the ego. They displace all negativity outside themselves, leaving only good inside. Victim and saviour identities also depend on each other. They often cohere within the same person, perhaps explaining why a great many progressive activists like to emphasize several victim identity traits (for example, female, Black and trans) while holding senior positions and qualifications in society, notably professorships and doctorates which give them intellectual authority. This positions them well to appear both as victim and saviour, as Jesus does in the Christian story.

Given their over-inflated theories and ambitions, it is perhaps unsurprising that many progressive activists report mental health troubles. Their consistent overreach in the way they address reality dooms them to failure and disappointment. The world consistently fails to play along. Pushback and conflict arise which can sometimes be disturbing. However, while reacting against it, the activist finds that such conflict also works to renew their sense of self, their burning sense of injustice and victimhood. Opposition offers possibilities for claiming victimhood, adding fuel to the narcissistic sense of self – justifying more of the same; and so the cycle continues.

Notwithstanding the boosts in ego that come from this process, from the group solidarity and the theory apparently confirming itself, feeding off an eternal recurrence of conflict and antagonism does not seem like an inherently healthy way to live. Indeed, activists can often appear strikingly childlike in their outbursts – reminding us of the child's narcissistic dreams for domination of its immediate world, now transposed onto society and institutions like the school by adults in a supposedly adult world.

The saviour complex of this modern-day progressive activist, often not long out of university and head full of totalizing theory, reflects a wider mind-made sense of self, one that finds meaning largely in theory and 'values'. For this form of selfhood, group membership does not revolve so much around things like family, community and nation as what you believe in. It concentrates on whether you are right or wrong, whether you have the right ideas and the right view of reality or the wrong one. This replicates a division in monotheistic religion between believer and unbeliever, righteous and reprobate. You are either on the right side of history or on the wrong side – and you will be judged by history later on.

The mind-made sense of self is always reaching out to the future because the present never meets its exalted standards. It is impatient and uneasy with the present moment and rejects the past as unbearably tainted and oppressive. It is always striving to get somewhere else. And when that new place, the secular equivalent of the new Jerusalem, fails to materialize, it lashes out against the unbelievers just like a little boy told he cannot have another biscuit.

# 12

# *Conclusions: How should we respond?*

There is a traditional Spanish saying, 'Que no haya novedad': 'May no new thing arise'.[1] It expresses an assumption that new things are by their nature dangerous and untrustworthy, showing an instinctual conservatism.

Such is the embrace of progressive ideology in much of the West nowadays that we may as well invert the expression to 'May *only* new things arise'. Our overseeing classes are always going on about the virtues of novelty, innovation and change (except when it comes to their overseeing power of course). Rather, it is the past, the old, the tried-and-trusted, that is dangerous and deserving of suspicion for them. And this is as true for top Conservatives as it is for the traditional progressives of the left.

We can see almost a reverence for change and transformation at these upper levels of society, in the spheres of politics, public service, business, media and education and all the rest. However I do not think much thought and reflection goes into this reverence. Rather, the progressive belief system seems to be imprinted on our leaders almost by their positions in society. Ideologies of progress propel them forward, like a currency of power. Anyone who explicitly rejects the currency appears like they are rejecting high society and immediately becomes an outsider.

I think this shows us the nature of progressivism as *a political force* rather than just a kind of theory about inevitable social improvement. The idea of progress is significant not so much for what it *says* as for what it *does*. It imprints optimism on power, along with a patina of intellectual and moral heft. At the same time power gives progress the attractions that power has always possessed: of access to wealth and status. There is a gathering of force here, one which is prevailing pretty much all over the world in different guises, from the totalitarian form of capitalism seen in Communist China to a more general economic progressivism across Asia and the rise of 'wokism' in the West.

## CONCLUSIONS: HOW SHOULD WE RESPOND?

The glamorous former Enron executive Rebecca Mark once told her employees, 'You never ever wake up in the morning without saying, "I will win today".' One of these employees once said of her, 'She came into the office every day never acting like anything other than the fearless leader who would lead you out of the darkness.' Bethany McLean and Peter Elkind say of her, 'That quality of unyielding optimism was her greatest strength. And it was also her greatest weakness.'[2]

This style, of belief in the future and your role in making it happen, confers a powerful conviction and confidence which can be a mixed blessing. It is a bit like a drug, injecting courage and belief into our veins. It is effective largely because we are all familiar with it even without necessarily being aware of its presence and our belief in it. Progress is woven into our language and our being, our ways of seeing the world and our public life and institutions. But it has largely detached from its status as theory, serving not so much in the game of truth as of power and authority, which it effectively manufactures as if in a factory.

In his *History of the Idea of Progress*, the American sociologist Robert Nisbet said, 'Nothing gives greater importance or credibility to a moral or political value than belief that it is more than something cherished or to be cherished; that it is an essential element of historical movement from past through present to future. Such a value can then be transposed from the merely desirable to the historically necessary.'[3]

This notion of 'credibility' is political. It has a purpose, to provide reassurance and authority. Nisbet refers later in his book to the 'strategic superiority' of progress in relation to political and social *action*.[4] In this way it appears as a tool, a weapon, a prop rather than a theory to take seriously in and of itself. Progress here is an idea that provides necessary *support* to something else: to authority rather than truth (since the future is by definition unknown).

The support provided by this prop of progress instils optimism and self-belief. It gives progressives a driving purpose which others might seem to lack. Think about the no-borders liberalism embraced by much of our overclass. Without the belief that it is *necessary* and historically-ordained, rational as well as moral and part of a movement that will inevitably prevail, it loses most of its motivating force. Without the blessing of this higher progressive authority, it stands rather sadly as the impractical 'luxury belief' that it is: committed to dismantling the basis on which a democratic society is constituted, the contours of the state and the meaning of territorial jurisdiction, the distinction between citizen and non-citizen and democratic rights within the state.

Progressive ideology patently inspires us to have faith in ourselves, to try things and attempt to make the world a better place. This is not to be sniffed at. However it also generates considerable hubris and self-delusion, of which the fate of Enron is a classic example. Through the framework of progress, beliefs and interests appear to merge into each other, making selfish acts into virtuous, unselfish ones. Progress promises the best of all possible worlds. As a framework to see the world – and our own place in it – it is attractive and seductive.

## *The risks of progressivism*

The risks are significant. The idea that we have progressed so far fools us into believing that things which mattered before no longer matter. Since we are in a new era now, the dialectic of progress tells us, there is no need to worry about things people used to worry about before. The concerns of previous eras are no longer relevant. Conflict has been transcended in this new era. It is now illegitimate unless it serves to push us further forward, away from the past, away from the bad people to be found in it. There is no need to make provisions to protect our people from the consequences of change, because these are not threats but possibilities to be embraced. Indeed, the words 'our', 'us' and 'we' are inherently suspect. They hold us back from a more advanced identity where we are part of a common humanity. Those who are pushing into the new world recognize that there is no 'us' anymore, because this would create a 'them' as a hostile 'Other', an unacceptable discrimination.

The only people to worry about are those people who are stuck in these ways of the past. They obsess about things like culture and national borders. But these things are relics of the old world and obstruct the full realization of our common humanity. Because the old, dangerous, tainted history is over, we do not need to worry about them, nor about such things as food, water and energy security. The lessons learned from the old world in which such things mattered do not apply anymore. Rather than banking the lessons learned (an active, alert stance), we banked the fact that lessons *have been* learned (a passive, sociological stance). We assumed it would be alright and forgot the difficult decisions required to make it alright. We became passive, stuck in our self-serving theories, attached to the world as we imagined it and unresponsive to the world as it is. All in the name of a better society, one of optimism and progress.

This optimism of progress depends on destruction. At the extremes, as we can see with liberal-left identity politics, progressive ideologies threaten to destroy much that we love and value. Indeed, that it is their purpose. To make systemic and structural change happen means destroying social systems and structures which support life now. Like arms manufacturers, the progress trap manufactures power and destruction. The assumption of progressives that they are right and good and therefore entitled to wealth and power gives them a driving energy to seek and destroy those they perceive as their opponents.

Progressive activists and technocrats have an unusual sense of certainty, faith and conviction about them, at least in public. They have convinced themselves that they are right about things and also right to dictate what should happen in the world. The most accomplished among them have an array of language tools available to support their authority and deter opponents from challenging it – from specialist economic terminology to accusations of various kinds of bigotry grounded in theoretical sociology.

The relatively few ideologues who genuinely believe in the inexorable march of history and how it is bending in their direction often exude a seemingly unshakeable confidence. By attaching ourselves to these true believers we can grab our piece of that pie, taking a bit of the self-certainty and thereby magnifying our own presence, confidence and self-belief. And so progressive ideology ends up successfully capturing many who do not believe in it, do not understand it and have little interest in it as theory.

Like anything, with prolonged exposure the customs and style of progressives are relatively easy to pick up. To be introduced into our public culture is to be introduced to a culture of progressivism. As detailed in Part One, I think we can divide it into a number of techniques, including: (1) self- and group-promotion; (2) assuming specialized knowledge over the whole of society (largely by association with other self-described experts); (3) making predictions that opponents will inevitably fail and your group will inevitably succeed; and (4) seeking to make opponents disappear from the world, including by denouncing them as self-evidently wrong and against all possible truth and goodness.

For anyone passing through a contemporary university, these things are likely to become second nature. But frankly, this style is everywhere. You can effectively become a progressive without knowing it and without choosing to be, just by turning on the radio or logging into your social media.

As Zygmunt Bauman has written, modernity 'constantly but vainly tries to "embrace the unembraceable", to replace diversity with uniformity and ambivalence with coherent and transparent order – and while trying to do this turns out unstoppably more divisions, diversity and ambivalence than it has managed to get rid of'.[5]

It may seem curious how progressives often fail to acknowledge or sometimes even notice that they are doing this. But this is because they are right, because they are prevailing and what is prevailing is right. Divisiveness for them consists of departing from *their* perspective, which is established and historically-ordained. It is a language trick, similar to the treatment of 'hate'. Attempts to combat hate are permeated by hate as a behaviour, but this does not count as hate because progressives are not hateful people in a sociological, historical sense. Needless to say, such double-think is easily exploited by the cynical and the extreme. And the same goes for their use of 'unity' and 'division'. It legitimizes their own form of divisiveness as a form of unity while damning opposing perspectives as divisive.

One form of division continuously reproduced by progressives is that between the young and the old. This arises almost naturally from the core progressive commitment to the future being better than the past. Older people are denigrated and disrespected for their association with the past, while young people are new and untouched by the past so look good in comparison. In this way progressive theory upends our conventional ideas of maturity: seeing it not in terms of an individual maturing as they get older but as *history* maturing. This perversely makes younger people more mature than their elders because they are arriving in the world at a later stage of historical development. Time retains its status as a vehicle of increasing maturity, but this no longer applies to individuals passing through life but rather to society: your maturity depends on the stage of social evolution at which you enter the world.

In this sense, far from your experience appearing as a valuable resource from which younger generations might learn, getting older actually means becoming less *relevant*. Young people are 'the future, not the past', as we can see from campaigns to give the vote to sixteen- and seventeen-year-olds and repeated complaints in Britain about how older voters have a nefarious influence on election results and referenda. From this perspective, far from having anything to learn from their ancestors, young people are responsible for overturning the inheritance that has been passed down to them. Their mission is to *change* society, even to *change the world*. And this often means rejecting their parents, backgrounds and cultural inheritance. As a progressive liberal society, these attitudes pervade British culture.

Speaking of young women who feel hurt from casual sexual encounters, Louise Perry writes:

> They've been denied the guidance of mothers, not because their actual mothers are unwilling to offer it but because of a matricidal impulse in liberal feminism that cuts young women off from the 'problematic' older generation. This means not only that they are cut off from the voices of experience, but – more importantly – they are also cut off from the person who loves them most in the world.[6]

The existential void created by rejecting parental authority offers space for other sources: including various forms of progressive ideology but also criminal and other damaging influences. This appears to be most pronounced among poorer, less educated families in which parents are more prone to demoralization.

There is a further level of concern to this. For the denigration of older people in what we call 'the West', especially the Anglophone part of it, is merging with other forms of identity politics to create concentrations of disfavour, towards white-skinned men in particular. Progressive identity politics naturally leans towards groups that appear to be new on the scene of power, like immigrants, non-white people in general, women, gay and transgender people. The straight white male here appears as an apparition that needs to be defeated as a nefarious force in the world, an oppressive leftover from the past. He was dominant in the bad old world and his influence is necessarily being consigned to the dustbin of history by the rising new groups. Demographically and culturally, these new favoured groups have a much greater concentration among younger people. The younger, newer groups, merged into a block, appear to have a destiny to prevail, bringing in a more just and fair society. To the rising progressive powers of our society, they appear as blank slates to be written on. As a recipe for social division and hostility, it would be difficult to conjure up anything better, yet this arises from a form of optimism.

Where successful politically, progressive politics has invariably been closely tied to some form (or forms) of identity politics: promoting some groups (thereby creating natural 'allies'), while seeking to clamp down on others as backward and reflexively hostile to social progress. This was the case in the Soviet Union with the proletariat being thrown against the bourgeoisie and kulaks. It was the case in Communist China with poorer peasants thrown against richer ones and students thrown against their teachers and parents.

Identity brings something essential to the progressive party: a connection to the meaningful, existential world where promises are made, interests created and the lines of battle drawn. It gives the dry theory of progress a politics or a 'praxis': a way of dividing what is supported from what is opposed. Through that, it attains a sense of purpose and meaning that anyone can understand. It obtains a tribalism. It also attains a tangible measure of what success means: group members gaining positions of power and money while those of the out-group are shut out and deprived of resources. When success is achieved, this confers momentum and further belief on the movement. For conventional Marxists over the years, the triumph of the proletariat or 'vanguard' has offered this measure. Nowadays, the post-Marxian left has largely dropped associations with the working class, rather seeking to exploit other groups, from Muslims and immigrants as a group to transgender people, pitching them as a coalition against an image of the dominant, older, white-skinned man, whose complaints it then labels 'divisive', discriminatory and an example of the 'culture wars'.

From the favouring of some groups to the denial of their own agency (as if their actions are not political), all of these activities count as 'praxis': theory converted into political practice. You do not need to understand or agree with progressive theory in order to engage in the practice, which makes it amenable to the bureaucratic environment – helping to make this a key locus for progressive identity politics in the contemporary Western world. Within bureaucracies, the 'diversity, equity and inclusion' (DEI) agenda is aided further by an idea of 'representation': an explicitly political idea which treats institutions themselves as political battlegrounds. As an alternative to democratic representation, progressive representation helps to embed progressive identity politics into the state and civil society. It coheres around the assumption that we attain our place in the world through other people in powerful institutions who share the same characteristics as us, including skin colour, sex (or gender), immigrant or non-immigrant status, sexuality and gender transition. For those groups treated as victim groups, an absence of such possibilities for representation in any instance (for example via the production staff of a TV programme) counts as a deficit of social justice that needs to be corrected by replacing people possessing the wrong characteristics with others who have the right ones.

That process is one of progress – and it means pushing experienced people out of the door, leading to the institution in question having less of what we might call 'institutional memory', leading to mistakes and misjudgements that would not have happened before. The poor state of the mass media, arts and academic sectors seems to be partly a consequence of this loss of experience and the promotion of younger people and more favoured identity groups to replace the older, experienced employees with unfavoured characteristics. In other words: progress causes regress, the *advancement of 'humanity'* generates what some call our present 'crisis of competence', plus rising feelings of stasis, decline and danger.

The widespread left-progressive capture of the 'intelligence' functions of Western society is particularly concerning. Universities, the media and arts bodies all have an important role in showing us to ourselves, in helping us to reflect on the world and our place in it. The fact of these sectors being effectively hijacked by political activists with little or no interest in truth means these intelligence functions are no longer working. We can see it in phenomena such as the large numbers of university academics variously celebrating and denying the atrocities of Hamas in southern Israel on 7 October 2023. However it is always present, showing itself indirectly, such as in the way that radical identity politics now appears constantly in mainstream public discourse in the guise of expertise, pushing itself forward with the authority of apparent knowledge and understanding rather than political commitment.

The decline in standards seems to be everywhere, not least in the institutions of state. It is evident in the Arts Council England (ACE), the state funding body for the arts in England, deciding to stop using the word 'artist', replacing it with 'creative practitioner'. As well as negating its own name, the move breaks down the barrier between art and non-art and between the role of artist and non-artist, subsuming all into a wider definition of 'culture' or 'creative' activity. Art and political activism, technology and the state, social theory and social work, public relations and advertising: all merge into variations of the same thing. The variety of life becomes reduced to a bland uniformity in which the same messaging is pumped at us wherever we go, from art gallery to train platform; from workplace training session to school parents' evening; from TV drama to our on-message friends on social media. For ACE, however, this loosening of definitions means that it can support a greater range of activity that is more amenable to its bureaucratic conditions and demands, establishing it as a sort of mini-alternative government all of its own.

As well as showing disregard for art, ACE has shown that it is not very keen on the country it is meant to be serving. Indeed, it tells us that one of its core missions is to break down the boundaries that separate England and the people who live there from other places. It wants the 'creative practitioners' it sponsors to be 'outward-looking and globally-connected', thereby aligning them to current Establishment-speak and marginalizing any artistic or cultural endeavour that is local, individual and distinctive. It seems that no one involved has stopped to think about these hackneyed phrases; of what it means to be an 'outward-looking' artist versus an 'inward-looking' one; of how those who go deep into the human situation – and indeed the British or English situation – might *have to be* rather inward-looking.

This sort of bureaucratic cant assumes that cultural and artistic activity is following a line of historical development, that whatever is currently fashionable in a globalized arts world should be seen as the 'cutting-edge' of social and cultural improvement, and that 'practitioners' themselves need to know and understand this in order for further improvements to occur. Sociology has become primary to the life of the artist, now

## CONCLUSIONS: HOW SHOULD WE RESPOND?

'creative practitioner'. They are to fit into an already-known world as an agent of change, largely stripped of individuality, just following whatever the bureaucratic consensus decides is historical change.

In this strange and sometimes febrile context, we might think of turning to the much less invasive, open, liberal form of progressivism advocated by Robert Nisbet among others. This perspective has much to recommend it, not least if you share Nisbet's superstition that we need faith in the future in order to face the future. It supports free expression and free association. It believes in the pursuit of knowledge as knowledge rather than to support a dogmatic orthodoxy. It lets the world breathe rather than gripping it by the neck.

However, I think that in practice this perspective is partly responsible for troubles caused by the more controlling form of progressivism. It has shown weaknesses in history, arguably aiding the rise of the Nazis in the 1930s through the complacent assumption that Hitler would eventually see sense and be reasonable. Nowadays liberal progressives take a similar attitude to radical Islamists who want to overturn the basis of liberal democracy and turn Western countries like Britain into quasi-Islamic states; also to other identity activists who want to turn the world around in order to benefit themselves.

In practice liberal progressives are serially naive and complacent, failing to think things through and too often falling back on the assumption that things will be alright in the end. As they happily outsource authority to the more invasive kind of progressive identity activists, all the things that they apparently value are put at risk, including freedom, tolerance and what we think of as basic human rights. They do little or nothing to protect liberal democratic society from hostile forces because those forces seem the wave of the future: and therefore appear to be blessed with a natural righteousness. The laziness and inattention of this perspective is a characteristic marker of the liberal wing of the Conservative Party.\* Superficially, it seems to be quite nice and reasonable, but it does not recognize threats out of a blithe faith that everything will work out in the end.

---

\* These liberal Tories call themselves the One Nation wing of the party, yet they believe in assisting the dissolution of the nation by outsourcing powers to forces which are hostile to it.

## *The politics*

### A form of imperialism?

Since the General Election of July 2024, the United Kingdom has found itself once more under an explicitly progressive government: the Labour Party, with former human rights lawyer and public prosecutor Sir Keir Starmer as Prime Minister. Labour's slogan for the last party conference before the election was 'Give Britain its Future Back'. For the campaign this switched to 'Change'. Then for the party's first conference in power it moved onto 'Change Begins'. In his speech to the latter, new Foreign Secretary David Lammy said: 'My job is to tell a new story about the United Kingdom abroad, a story of openness, of the future, of hope.'[7] He started his speech in the American rhetorical style, emphasizing humble beginnings and challenges faced in early life, including racism. His colleagues followed a similar formula: sentimental and formulaic. Rachel Reeves kept on telling us what a big deal it was that she was the first female Chancellor of the Exchequer. Education Secretary Bridget Phillipson claimed she had 'defied the odds' by attaining her position.

The message was one of self-congratulation: that they had made history just by being there. And they did it in public, as if the power of suggestion would draw us in to share in their happiness at being elected and appointed to their roles. Above all, they were telling us, their being in power was *right*. It represented a sociological and historical change for the better. To them, it seemed, they were blessed by history, their presence a tangible demonstration of social progress. Hence their irritation at criticism, including for accepting multiple 'freebies' from donors who were given privileged access to the corridors of power. Their bewildered responses seemed to be saying: 'What us? But we're the good people, the right people! We cannot be corrupt by definition. It's all for social justice!'

This sense of entitlement around Labour and other Western progressive parties can be deeply unattractive. However, at least it is visible and open to ridicule; also, ultimately open to judgement at the ballot box, as the American Democrats found to their cost in 2024. The same does not go for the 'permanent government' of the British Civil Service and associated quango-state, where progressive ideas and progressive power have entrenched themselves in recent decades.

The Civil Service's ability to obstruct, delay and destroy the policy of elected governments was immortalized through the figure of Sir Humphrey Appleby in the *Yes, Minister* series. But nowadays the force and scope of that obstruction and entitlement appears magnified. The embedding of progressive identity politics into its structure and organization, largely a result of the final and most domestically-significant act of the New Labour governments of 1997–2010, the 2010 Equality Act, has revolutionized the way our state sees itself.

In the name of equality and combating discrimination, the Act's Public Sector Equality Duty (PSED) mandated discrimination in the state sector in order to promote participation by certain identity groups, often translated into a responsibility to boost *representation*, which is a political concept. However, by treating the state as a locus for representation based on skin colour, gender and other categories, the PSED set up a tension with democratic representation via election. This *newer* form of representation confronted an older form and found it badly lacking, its sometimes tenuous democratic legitimacy knocked out of the park by the more assertive claims of social justice. And this was supported by a state structure whose power is permanent, while democratic power is only temporary.

Alongside these duties and the culture which has built up around it, ruling mandarins have come to see their impartiality as a form of partiality: their role as being to safeguard 'the country' and the 'values' of their organization; to protect against any scary 'populist' or 'right-wing' influence from the populace and the representatives they elect. Senior civil servants have become almost explicitly political figures, attaining a superior status for being 'above politics'.

As a result, while the Labour government's big majority could easily disappear in the next election, the party's twenty-first-century value system appears secure in the corridors of power, for now. The value system comes largely from the United States, reflecting the close attachment of senior Labour people over many decades to the US Democratic Party; also to the glamour and exalted sense of mission to be found over the Atlantic.

But, at its source, this value system appears to have collapsed with Kamala Harris's defeat to Donald Trump in the American Presidential Election. Suddenly and visibly, the bubble burst for the Western liberal-left ecosystem. Rory Stewart's blithe confidence that Kamala Harris would easily defeat Donald Trump (see pp. 105–6) exemplified progressive hubris. It was like a culminating point: the point at which reality finally put its foot down and refused to comply with its erstwhile masters. After Trump 2, progressives could no longer assume they could will their political desires into reality. Brexit and Trump 1 had suggested that they could hold out and use their institutional power to neuter the 'populist' threat. But this second iteration confirmed that they had not cauterized populism after all. If anything, they had made things worse by their actions, their presumptions and their arrogance.

In the way they speak, the way they make strategy and in their social analysis and policy prescriptions, the reflex of Labour people is to fall back on American styles and approaches, particularly those gathering around race and other identity markers. This is where the strange attempts to paint Britain as 'a nation of immigrants' comes from.* It treats Britain as a *new* country like America, so marginalizing any deep ancestral and cultural roots present in the country, treating such roots as if they do not exist, are irredeemably tainted or have no *relevance*. For the wider progressive left ecosystem now embedded in the state, the docking of the *Empire Windrush* with the first West Indian immigrants on board after the Second World War plays a crucial role, helping to adapt the redemptive American story for the British context. In what we now know as 'the UK', the *Windrush* signals *rebirth*; a point from which British society might be celebrated and admired. Here, history, in a magnified sense of *improvement*, seems to have begun in the British context.†

For anti-colonial historians, a similar renewal took place around the same time in their profession with the entry of increasing numbers of women and 'people of color', highlighting voices of the past that had been ignored by the white male practitioners who had dominated the discipline.

In her book *Time's Monster*, Professor Priya Satia of Stanford University promotes this story while claiming to reject the idea of historical progress

---

* *A Nation of Immigrants* is a book authored by John F. Kennedy in 1958, before the first wave of mass immigration to Britain.
† In 'The Whig Interpretation of History', as interpreted by Herbert Butterfield, the Protestant Reformation plays a similar role: consigning the ignorance of the 'Middle Ages' to the past and inaugurating a new history of increasing freedom and prosperity.

on account of its crucial ideological role in the British Empire. Rather than going along with the self-serving mystical talk of how 'history will judge', Satia thinks that she and her colleagues can judge perfectly well now. As far as she is concerned, the Court of History has delivered its Verdict: the British Empire, the British people and the state are *guilty* on all counts. And, because of this, historians can move on from the work of history to that of politics: making sure the right version of history *wins*. The first and last pages of *Time's Monster* reflect this preoccupation, being concerned not with the history of Empire but the role of the historian in influencing contemporary politics. As Satia puts it on her first page, 'While we might continue to strain after a world of policymakers well informed by history, the historian's more potent role in public debate is perhaps in speaking to the public, so that people may exert pressure on their elected representatives.'[8] She then adds that her hope is: 'to guide us to a more constructive vision of historians' possible public roles today, as we navigate the detritus of empire in the form of climate crisis, global inequalities, racism, diasporas, demands for reparations, and so on'.[9]

Satia's book is most concerned with the present, and the public role of the writer in it, rather than the past. Its final chapter consists of an extended whinge about how everything that is not really left-wing in Britain today is like the Nazis and needs to be condemned a lot more. And its most obvious practical policy suggestion is that of 'reparations': the transfer of wealth from the beneficiaries of the British Empire to its victims. On how this would take place, Satia is vague, suggesting the answer might be 'a combination of strategies that hold individuals, collectives and state institutions accountable'.[10]*

However, the main point here is that punishment, revenge, must be inflicted, with the crimes of the past (and present) to be punished in the righteous future. It is informed by a 'new culture', Satia explains, in which history-writing has become 'an instrument of redemption for the victims of modern history'.[11] This is quite different to what we might think of the historian's proper role, of giving a truthful account of the past, while hopefully providing some consolation on the way. Indeed,

---

* The mind boggles about how this would work in the multiracial, multinational Britain of today.

the role that she describes has a distinctly religious character: of providing *redemption* to certain types of people, *saving* them in a sense like the Christian God would. It is a story of progress, linking together an improvement in history-writing, embodied in the ascent of people like her, to the saving of souls; of victims who need recompense.*

This all helps to justify a new kind of imperial project, to pronounce on the affairs of a place far away, to demand that it be subjugated, its wealth extracted and people made to do 'penance'.[12] The imperial centre of this project, it appears, has been in the United States. And it has done its imperialism not just through direct political pressure but through academic history, social science and publishing, just as the British Empire did. Its perspectives are generally distant from – and often hostile to – the concerns of the people in the territories concerned. But it justifies this by treating those people and their concerns as backward and wrong.

In her book, Satia rightly talks about how many British colonialists suspended their consciences in doing the work of Empire, helped by the idea that they were instruments of progress. But she seems to be doing something similar: pronouncing from afar, seemingly based on stereotyped reports from journalists *on the ground* whose allegiance is to the Empire and its codes. American politicians who pronounce and dictate to foreign parts including Britain fulfil a similar role: dictating from above to their inferiors elsewhere. Their attitude is mirrored by the politicians, administrators and journalists of the territory concerned. Before Trump beat Kamala Harris, these could be found genuflecting to progressive America, desperately trying to please as if to their imperial masters. The language was all of right versus wrong, of the necessary triumph of 'democracy' versus a form of barbarism; but underlying it all were hard power, money and self-interest. The language of progress, as always, clears the way for the practice of power. But progressivism only makes sense if it is winning, helping to drive things *forward*. Once that relationship of belief and power breaks down, its justification falls apart and it stands naked: as after Trump 2.

---

* Race and gender provide a crucial source of authority here. As she has said elsewhere, white-skinned men must necessarily have a different perspective to hers and they need to be silent on certain issues on account of their 'positionality' (see Dr Bruce Gilley, 'Stanford's Priya Satia's open racism', *YouTube*, 7 April 2022).

Progress seems to be inherently related to forms of imperialism. However it is not a straight causal relation. Rather, progress acts like a catalyst, helping to facilitate forms of imperialism and colonization. As we have seen, it is much more than a theory. It is also a source of power in the world, one we should be wary of: and learn to resist when it turns on us.

We should reject progressivism for this link to power. We should reject it for the way it creates fake forms of intellectual and moral authority. We should reject it for the way some use this fake authority to try and dominate society. We should reject it for its role in subverting traditions of knowledge; also for its role in directing hostility to those who are thinking for themselves. We should recognize that it is inherently illiberal. And this goes too for softer, less invasive liberal versions of progressivism. These versions have nowhere near the dangers of the closed kind, but they instinctively ally to power and therefore fail to protect their apparent values when those values are under threat. They tend to mitigate the colonial or imperial tendencies of progressivism rather than oppose them.

## The Rebel Alliance

But how should we put this rejection into practice? Currently virtually all styles of our politics are progressive in some form or another: from lazy liberal Conservatism to extreme left-wing wokery. Opposition to 'progressive' politics meanwhile is fragmented. Many critics see the ultra-progressive turn in Western culture as an aberration against progress rather than as yet another example of it. Donald Trump, Elon Musk and the right-leaning wing of the 'techbro' crowd embody this perspective. New Conservative leader Kemi Badenoch has a not dissimilar viewpoint. Trump and Badenoch represent, in their different ways, more muscular, confrontational iterations of the liberal perspective, discarding the complacency that has marred liberalism for decades. They are looking at a politics of restoration: to defend and enforce liberal codes like meritocracy, in Trump's case if necessary by illiberal means. Pierre Poilievre is pursuing a similar course in Canada.

Then there are what we might call the 'regressivists', who think things are inevitably, inexorably getting worse and there is nothing to be done about it: the opposite of the core progressive belief. They are relentlessly defeatist and have effectively given up on practical politics, but they still make quite a lot of noise.

Many who are concerned with how things are going veer between those two points of view. One minute they assure themselves that sanity will be restored in time, maybe through the unlikely leadership of Donald Trump; the next they are fatalist and defeatist, seeing no hope. In truth, probably most of us switch between optimism and pessimism, faith and acceptance of defeat, like this. In any case, that old trusting liberal perspective is in clear retreat, at least for now. It stands old, tired and discredited. Politics is back to replace the fakery of post-politics. Who knows what it will bring? For now, in Britain, the old guard is still very much in control. But it is on notice.

Progressive techniques which strive to place opponents outside acceptable society have grown tired with overuse. Today's 'centrists' and far left have long needed the 'far right' to justify their policies, for reacting against the consequences of those policies. Much of the time this opposition has appeared to be at the mercy of progressives who have had many more channels to initiate activity and get their messaging out, who have been better organized and funded and are always working to punish opponents and send out warnings for others to not follow. The Western technocratic elite raised up 'populism' as a danger to civilization and good order, converting a potential threat against technocracy into something much bigger against which all should fight.

The social and financial implications of resisting progressive colonization have been serious for many: from losing your friends to losing your job and income. Getting denounced as an enemy of society and becoming a *persona non grata* is not an attractive proposition for most people, let alone those with families to house and feed. The rebellion against progressivism has therefore tended to come from social outsiders.

As Michael Lind writes:

> The weakness of populism is that it is literally reactionary. Populists react against what the dominant overclass establishment does, rather than having a positive and constructive agenda of their own.
>
> Today's populism is a counterculture, not a counterestablishment. A counterculture defines itself in opposition to the establishment. A counter-

## CONCLUSIONS: HOW SHOULD WE RESPOND?

establishment wants to be the establishment. Members of a counterculture relish their outsider status. A counterculture is the heckler in the audience. A counterestablishment is the understudy, waiting in the wings for a chance to play the title role.'[13]

Donald Trump may not be everyone's cup of tea, but his 2024 election win seems to have overturned this reality, primarily in the United States but also to an extent elsewhere. Unlike his first time in office, this time Trump seems to have a clue about what he is doing and some more convincing allies. Given the shared Anglophone media space, this has given a boost to British rebels too. Nigel Farage has a line to Trump and is able to leverage that relationship to his advantage in Parliament. His Reform Party was already more credible for having got himself and four colleagues into the House of Commons in the 2024 election.

Up until Trump 2, populism in Britain looked more like a group of countercultures, coming together at times as a sort of Rebel Alliance, rebelling against the dominant overclass culture before retiring back into its different fragments. That seems to have changed. *Unherd* political editor Tom McTague summed it up afterwards, saying: 'it is hard to open any social media app today – *pace* Bluesky – and not be struck by the sense that something has shifted in the zeitgeist. The right is winning and it's becoming cool. A new epoch has begun.'[14]

But in the British context, anti-progressives are still up against it. In institutional settings, they remain on the outside, looking in. Some are distinctly unattractive, deserving the accusations of bigotry thrown as a blanket over all opponents of progressive identity politics. The relentless politicization of race in the Western public sphere has led many resisters to fixate on their own race, rebelling against the dominant framing of 'Whiteness' as oppression and seeking to insert a positive *white identity* in its stead. These attempts are often merely defensive and truthful, but they surely have no future in any serious politics of resistance. Racial and ethnic essentialism is precisely what a politics of resistance should be resisting. Trump 2 strangely provides an example for this in showing a racial realignment, with many more Latinos and black people rebelling against their implicit ownership by the Democratic Party and coming over to Trump.

There is hope for the Rebel Alliance: and there is no doubt that Trump's second win has given it a boost. Progressives are now appearing in the role of *losers*. This adds another element to their constant struggle to legitimize themselves, to popularize the bizarre ruses they constantly come up with. They tend to overreach when in positions of power. Their policies on things like gender, race and immigration are broadly unpopular. And there has been some progress in the reaction in recent years. New institutions have emerged, while existing ones have realized that there is a rich seam of ridiculousness and danger to react against from progressives in power.

The most effective *political* reaction against progressivism, at least in Britain, has been the revolt against gender self-ID, a policy that has allowed biological males self-defining as women into female-only spaces. This revolt is significant and instructive for how it reached across the boundary between anti-progressive and progressive, uniting conservatives and 'gender-critical' feminists. Staunchly left-wing feminists, blocked from expressing their views about gender self-ID and trans activism in their normal outlets, found a home in rebellious and predominantly right-leaning new publications like *Unherd* (founded in 2017) and *The Critic* (2019). Moreover, they were successful in influencing both the Conservative government and eventually the opposition Labour Party to moderate policies and statements in favour of self-ID.

This issue was a reasonably straightforward one on which progressives in government, the state and closely-connected campaign groups like Stonewall clearly overreached. But it offers a basic template for how a successful anti-progressive politics might work. Quite simply, anti-progressives need to breach the walls which keep them out of mainstream and official discourse. To be effective in countering progressivism, it is not enough to remain on the outside, complaining to people who already agree with you, comfortable in the embrace of the existing group. The group needs to grow. And that means making alliances with progressives – both of the open and closed variety.

This is the political battle: and it is a subset of a wider intellectual battle. As with all political battles, the purpose is to minimize weakness (for example: outsider status and absence of a common platform) while maximizing strengths (greater honesty and recognition of reality). More of us who care need to contribute in whatever way we can. This may be through setting up new institutions ourselves, joining existing ones like political parties, or merely using our social media platforms to highlight the good and the bad.

Progressives have a strong funding base, not least from US Big Tech tycoons and legacy trusts in Britain which activists have appropriated. These need to be countered: putting our money, where we have it to spare, where our mouths are; not merely whinging but acting. Meaningful political movements take time to grow. It takes time for them to gather around that which works; and it takes time for durable leaders to emerge. This process is political more than philosophical. It is not just about having the right ideas but doing the right things to win: that *praxis* which has made progressives so effective.

## Techniques of resistance

In her book *Feminism Against Progress*, Mary Harrington shows us how progressivism can go to war with human nature, manically trying to break down boundaries and distinctions between people wherever it finds them. As she explains it, the libertarian version of this creed is striving to *liquefy* reality, not least in the desire to erase biological differences between males and females: gender self-ID on steroids. It employs a range of techniques, both political and technological. But, as she points out, 'Whether at the small or large scale, human nature refuses to be entirely liquefied. And this resistance prompts increasingly frenzied efforts by the proponents of liquefaction-as-progress to stamp out the last traces of resistance.'[15]

We might see in this passage how resistance to progressivism is largely a resistance of nature, of reality: of truth over falsity; of being over the excesses of the mind. Any such resistance is therefore not *extreme* as progressives often characterize it, but *normal*. Progressives get around this by pretending to stand *ahead* or *in front of* the rest of us. As they have it, they are already in the future, waiting for the rest of us to catch up. But this is an invention of the human mind and of language rather than a reflection of pre-existing reality.

The progressive imperialists of past centuries ultimately failed because subject populations would not accept being dictated to by remote and distant forces that were not of them, by them or for them. The Indian independence movement was particularly effective at exploiting the obvious contradictions of British imperialism, with many of its leading lights having visited and studied in Britain. Mahatma Gandhi was one. The doctrines he developed, of 'non-cooperation' and 'satyagraha' (non-violent resistance) might offer some promise as a means to challenge progressive hegemony in our own day. The same goes for the way the peoples of the Soviet Union and Eastern Bloc deployed humour to bridge the gap between reality and the daily propaganda pumped at them. Such humour already proliferates on social media in Britain; and we can expect it to spread more as Labour flails around in power; and while the comedy of the Establishment remains stuck in a 1990s rut.

Humour as rebellion is quite close to the idea of 'immanent criticism': of criticism that invokes the 'values' of those it is challenging against them, showing how the claims of power are different to the reality and often opposite (as with the use of terms like 'inclusion', 'kindness' and 'diversity' today). There are whiffs of a better society in such resistance: of active citizens willing to think for themselves; of the assertion of individual morality against the machine; and comedy that is generous and humorous rather than tired and cynical.

There are other techniques that we can use. One is quite basic: to accept, against all that progressives try to tell us, that *they are in power*. Progressives are not the victims of society; they *are* society. They oversee and police its most prominent parts. They are making things happen. They are present when the big decisions get made, while their opponents are largely absent. They are not bravely fighting against insuperable odds and external threats. They are the dominant force. They are the Establishment, the elite. The society they oversee is the society they have created. Its problems and reactions are theirs; they need to take responsibility for it.

Another technique is 'deconstruction'. This word is thrown around with scorn by some pro-Enlightenment reactionaries,* but it can be a useful tool in interrogating power. By literally *deconstructing* the claims of those in power, you pull apart that which comforts them, their self-justifications and self-deceptions. And this is not so far away from another

---

* It is one of the strange consequences of the current progressive turn that advocates of the Enlightenment appear in the reactionary camp, looking to the past and *resisting* change made in the name of progress.

technique from a very different tradition: the largely Anglophone 'analytic' school of philosophy with its old, pedantic demand: 'define your terms!' This practice can be insufferable. Like deconstruction, it lacks any positive vision of its own and can disappear up its own fundament. But it is mighty effective at pricking self-importance wherever it exists. Journalists and others could do worse than press progressives on what they mean by concepts like 'the future', 'history will judge', 'humanity', 'communities', 'diversity', 'inclusion'. Such terms generally pass by unquestioned, as if their meaning is clear and obvious. But they are anything but. Teasing their alternative, progressive, meanings apart will shed a lot more light on what our overseeing class is up to. Anyone invoking intellectual superiority from such concepts should be made to account for it.

Accurate description has a quality of its own. As Joseph Conrad said, 'My task which I am trying to achieve is, by the power of the written word to make you hear, to make you feel – it is, above all to make you see. That – and no more, and it is everything.'[16] This is what I have tried to do in this book. But understanding, being ready to understand, even just paying attention and taking things seriously, is more difficult than we assume. We easily fall back into the ways things are done, the things that *are focused on* around us and the language in which they are addressed. These ways often avoid probing the delicate parts, because they are the delicate parts of the progressive society; and progressive society needs to protect itself.

We might see the trap of progress as a form of corruption: of meaning and language; of institutions and their purpose. And it helps to facilitate the more familiar kind of corruption: that of law and of money.\* There still appears to be legal and political leeway in Western democracies to resist such corruption. But it is fragile, with constant efforts to curb free speech and even free association among unfavoured groups and wrong-thinkers, often supported by the authorities, as with the unholy mess that the world of 'hate crime' has developed into.† Left-progressives and

---

\* Self-interested forces exploit legal and rhetorical favouritism as night follows day. The multinational migration industry, subsidized by British taxpayers to the tune of £5.4 billion in accommodation and other 'support' costs alone in 2023–4, is just one example.

† One example of attacks on free association is the campaigns against formerly male-only spaces like the Garrick Club in London; applying a principle that rejects gender segregation in spaces where predominantly white men gather.

their allies have been broadly successful in deploying notions of 'hate' and '-phobia' to criminalize opponents, in rhetoric and increasingly in law too. These efforts must be resisted, as organizations including the Free Speech Union, the Academy of Ideas and Don't Divide Us have been doing in Britain. However more significant challenges lie in wait, not least the intense pressure on Labour to push through an 'Islamophobia' law with its large Commons majority. This could effectively criminalize opposition to Islamist bigotry and oppression: making the British state in some aspects an Islamic state with a *de facto* blasphemy law in place.

As a relatively new and rising force in the West, Islam can appear quite readily as a form of progress, or at least as part of the march of history.\* The progressive animus against religion is by no means absolute.

## Reconstitution

Given the array of interests attached to the state and its wider ecosystem, what Matthew Crawford describes in the American context as 'the public and private bureaucracies that make up a kind of sprawling para-state',[17] any government wishing to seriously challenge our current progressive consensus would get into immediate and substantial political trouble. Making such a challenge would therefore require extensive preparation, both in terms of the politics and through detailed, critically-examined policy proposals.

Here is not the place for such detail, but I think it is possible to outline a general theme plus a few policies.

The theme would be a need to *reconstitute* state and society. Many of our principal institutions, like the Civil Service, universities, NHS and BBC, have fallen so far down the progress trap that they may be irrecoverable. Through the pressure of progressive identity politics, their old core purposes often seem lost and marginal. As a necessary first step to reconstitution, we must restate that the duty of public services is to serve the public in their particular areas of concern, not to provide

---

\* Muslims sometimes claim that Islam is superior to Judaism and Christianity because it came along later than they did, helping it to remove the errors of these religions. In this and other ways it can appear surprisingly amenable to a progressive worldview.

political representation or engage in political promotion of some types of people over others. The Public Sector Equality Duty (PSED) part of the Equality Act should be repealed, at the very least. DEI commissar roles that have proliferated in public services and other major institutions must be abolished and institutions refocused towards their core functions: from catching and punishing criminals to providing healthcare and entertainment and telling us what is going on in the world. Institutions that are meant to provide representation should provide representation, while those that are for something else should be for something else.

Likewise international agreements and institutions like the European Court of Human Rights and associated 'legal' codes that constantly thwart the democratic will and put citizens in danger must be cut down to size: either forced to restrain their proliferating political ambitions or stripped of their role in law. Democracy is a chimera if governments cannot do basic things like deport dangerous foreign criminals.

On immigration, we could do with a 'pause' to allow society to settle down and get to know itself again.* A pause in positive net migration would help the existential links that make up society to re-form without the continuing pressure that further large-scale incomings bring. Such a reconstitution of society could take generations to achieve. We may worry that it will not happen at all given the scale of change and the emergence of significant parallel communities, not least Muslims with a separatist, supremacist ethic. But we must try.

Then there is the specific problem of the almost absolute capture of British, Anglophone and to a great extent 'Western' society's 'intelligence functions', like the media, the arts and universities, by intolerant forms of progressivism. How can you possibly make genuine *progress* in society when those who oversee these intelligence functions spend so much time falsifying reality so that anyone who is not ultra-progressive like them, or allied to them, qualifies as a far-right 'fascist' or 'Nazi' (movements that were, in their own way, ultra-progressive)? These people, whether cynically or not, mistake their own positional interests for right and truth, thereby creating a permanent warring tendency on matters of even basic

---

\* 'The mass immigration pause' is a policy of the UK's Social Democratic Party (SDP). However this still proposes net migration of up to 50,000 a year, meaning possible actual immigration of more than half a million a year.

reality. This has added rocket fuel to our society's crisis of competence, diverting masses of money and effort into damaging, futile attacks on what is often just human nature.

These institutions inform the public sphere, providing a platform to clarify what is going on, what is at stake and what should be done about it. But they are largely broken in their old core purposes: with more examples emerging every day and detailed in this book and elsewhere. In Britain, the PSED is clearly only one aspect of this problem. Much closer control and supervision from government seems necessary to ensure that different viewpoints are given space and protected, to allow for a properly vigorous intellectual space that should ultimately benefit us all. The former Conservative government's Higher Education (Freedom of Speech) Act 2023, immediately halted by the incoming Labour administration, was a tentative attempt to alter the balance, to prevent the 'cancellation' of alternative opinions in universities. Much more needs to be done along these lines: and a lot more dedicated thought needs to go into it.

Progressivism is not the single cause of all our troubles. Attempting to *eliminate* it would be laughably impractical. As a guiding idea of the modern world, progress is in the existential air that we breathe. We all fall back into it from time to time: not least in the idea of the happy ending, that eventually all will be well, right will be restored and the wrong-doers will get their comeuppance.*

Nevertheless, it is intriguing to imagine a modern world in which this idea – that has formed and shaped it – has been muted. We might fear the consequences of such a development, such a *progress*. Would we lose all confidence in ourselves? Would we lose hope? Would we be rendered incapable and lacking purpose? And I think the obvious answer to this is: have not a great many of us already reached this point, of being incapable, lacking purpose and confidence, precisely under the reign of progress? Did this not happen widely in the Soviet Union and Mao's China and Pol Pot's Cambodia: each of them assertively progressive regimes? Would shedding this pseudo-intellectual snake oil not make for a better world, one with less bullshit and more focus on the things that matter?

Would discarding the assumption of progress perhaps open the way for actual progress?

---

* Another one is the illusion of *boundless choice*: that you can be whoever you want to be.

# *Notes*

## *Preface*
1 Tweet: @GadSaad, 21 October 2023, 7.34pm.

## *Chapter 1: Introduction: From colonialism to decolonization*
1 Quoted in Thomas Pakenham, *The Scramble for Africa* (1991; Abacus, 1992), p. 21.
2 Adam Hochschild, *King Leopold's Ghost: A Story of Greed, Terror and Heroism in Colonial Africa* (1998; Pan Books 2006), pp. 44–5.
3 From Vanderwoude, *Conférence*, quoted in Pakenham, p. 22.
4 *Daily Telegraph*, 22 October 1884, quoted in Pakenham, p. 239.
5 Hochschild, p. 233.
6 Pakenham, p. 290.
7 Richard Dowden, *Africa: Altered States, Ordinary Miracles* (Portobello Books, 2008, 2009), p. 8.
8 Ibid., p. 279.
9 Pakenham, p. xxiv.
10 Robert Tombs, *The English and Their History* (2014; Penguin Books, 2015), p. 465.
11 Ibid., p. 538.
12 Quoted in Wade Davis, *Into the Silence: The Great War, Mallory and the Conquest of Everest* (Vintage, reprint edition, 2012), p. 47.
13 Tombs, pp. 268–9.
14 Quoted in Eric Hobsbawm, *The Age of Revolution. Europe 1789–1848* (Weidenfeld & Nicolson, 1962, 1995), p. 151 (italics in original).
15 Hobsbawm, p. 151.
16 George Catlin, *North American Indians* (1841; Penguin Books, 1989), p. 182.
17 Audrey Watters 'The history of the future', *Hack Education*, 24 April 2020.
18 Tombs, p. 361.
19 Quoted in Hannah Arendt, *On Revolution* (1963; Faber and Faber, 2016), p. 15.
20 Philip Caputo, *A Rumor of War* (1977; The Bodley Head, 2017), pp. 353–4.
21 Neil Sheehan in *The Vietnam War* (PBS, 2017), Episode 2, 'Riding the Tiger' (1961–3).
22 Quoted in various places.
23 Arendt, p. 71.
24 Quoted in Martin Sixsmith, *Russia: A 1,000 Year Chronicle of the Wild East* (BBC Books, 2011), p. 420.
25 Martin Sixsmith (with Daniel Sixsmith), *The War of Nerves: Inside the Cold War Mind* (Profile, 2021), p. ix.
26 J.B. Bury, *The Idea of Progress, An Inquiry into its Origin and Growth* (1920; e-artnow, 2020), p. 133.

27 See Robert Nisbet, *History of the Idea of Progress* (Basic Books, 1980).
28 Catherine Merridale, *Ivan's War: The Red Army 1939–45* (Faber and Faber, 2005), p. 262.
29 Nisbet, p. 171.
30 John Lewis Gaddis, *The Cold War: The Deals. The Spies. The Lies. The Truth* (2005; Penguin, 2007), p. ix.
31 'Mayoral statement: US election', Mayor of London, 6 November 2024.
32 Claire Lehmann, 'Revenge of the silent male voter', *Quillette*, 6 November 2024.
33 Ibid.
34 Niall Ferguson: 'The resurrection of Donald J. Trump', *The Free Press*, 6 November 2024.
35 E.H. Carr, *What is History?* (1961; Penguin, 1990), p. 142.
36 Ibid., p. 149.
37 Tanner Greer, 'The theory of history that guides Xi Jinping', *Palladium*, 8 July 2020.
38 Jonathan Rutherford, 'The left has an England problem', *New Statesman*, 29 August 2023.
39 Nicholas Boyle, 'The problem with the English: England doesn't want to be just another member of a team', *The New European*, 17 January 2017.
40 Ibid.
41 Nicholas Boyle, 'Brexit is a collective English mental breakdown', *Irish Times*, 16 January 2018.
42 'Fintan O'Toole: Brexit resurrects the English cult of heroic failure', *Irish Times*, 24 January 2017.
43 Tweet: @peterjukes, 13 December 2018, 4.24pm.
44 Ricken Patel, Avaaz campaign email, 22 June 2016.
45 Owen Smith MP, House of Commons, 27 February 2019.
46 Joris Luyendijk, 'How I learnt to loathe England', *Prospect*, 6 October 2017.
47 Tweet: @redhistorian, 11 September 2018, 12.36pm.
48 Quoted in Peter Baker, '"We the people": The battle to define populism', *The Guardian*, 10 January 2019.
49 Caroline Criado-Perez, speaking in clip promoted in tweet from @theJeremyVine, 8 September 2018.
50 Rosie Duffield, 'Brexit is a feminist issue: No deal is not an option for women', *New Statesman*, 30 January 2019.
51 Grace Campbell, 'Why I think Brexit is a man', *The New European*, 16 July 2018.
52 'Brexit vote "sparks rise in Islamophobia" against Muslim footballers at grassroots level', *Sky News*, 16 December 2017.
53 See for example, James Heartfield, *The Equal Opportunities Revolution* (Repeater Books, 2017), p. 159.
54 Ibid., p. 154.
55 Sheffield University, *Decolonising the curriculum: A guide for APS*, July 2020, p. 4.
56 Priya Satia, *Time's Monster: History, Conscience and Britain's Empire* (2020; Penguin, 2022), p. 275.
57 Ibid., pp. 279–80.
58 Ibid., p. 2.
59 Sheffield University, p. 6.

60 Ibid., p. 9.
61 Ibid., p. 11.
62 Ibid.
63 Ibram X. Kendi, *How to be an Antiracist* (2019), quoted in 'Ibram X. Kendi faces a reckoning of his own', *New York Times Magazine*, 4 June 2024.
64 Quoted in Ian Kershaw, *Hitler* (1998; abridged version, Allen Lane, 2008), p. 148.
65 Ibid., p. 148.
66 Timothy Snyder, 'The worldview of Hitler', *WORLD*, 30 January 2016.
67 Tweet: @HumzaYousaf, 6 November 2023, 6.05pm.
68 Tweet: @ProfSunnySingh, 24 September, 11.29am.
69 James Muldoon, 'Academics: It's time to get behind decolonising the curriculum', *The Guardian*, 20 March 2019.

## Chapter 2: Taking the place of God

1 Jeffrey M. Jones, 'Americans say history will be more kind than unkind to Obama', *Gallup.com*, 12 January 2017.
2 Address of President-Elect John F. Kennedy delivered to a Joint Convention of the General Court of the Commonwealth of Massachusetts, 9 January, 1961, John. F. Kennedy Presidential Library and Museum.
3 Robert F. Kennedy, Speech at the University of California at Berkeley, 22 October 1966, Robert F. Kennedy Human Rights.
4 Tweet: @Bonn1eGreer, 1 April 2023, 9.39pm.
5 Tweet: @Bonn1eGreer, 19 September 2017, 9.26pm.
6 'Mayor urges London MPs to do whatever it takes to stop no-deal Brexit', Mayor of London press release, 2 September 2019.
7 'Lee Anderson says public supports him over Sadiq Khan comments', *The Guardian*, 27 February 2024.
8 E.H. Carr, *What is History?*, p. 110.
9 Ibid., p. 135.
10 Robert Nisbet, *History of the Idea of Progress*, p. 173.
11 Karen Armstrong, *A History of God* (1993; Vintage, 1999), p. 357.
12 Nisbet, p. 173.
13 *Holding up a mirror to cricket: A report by the Independent Commission for Equity in Cricket*, June 2023.
14 'Equity in Cricket report: "Absolutely horrific" stories show "culture is rotten"', *BBC Sport*, 27 June 2023.
15 *Holding up a mirror to cricket*, p. 5.
16 Ibid., p. 6.
17 Ibid., p. 120.
18 https://www.britannica.com/biography/George-Floyd
19 Tom Holland, *Dominion: The Making of the Western Mind* (Little, Brown, 2019), p. xxi.
20 Matthew 20:16.
21 Tweet: @DawnButlerBrent, 18 June 2020, 2.42pm.
22 Holland, p. 85.
23 Ibid., p. 92.

24 Ibid., p. xxix.
25 'New churches are dropping the word "church", report finds', *Church Times*, 13 August 2024.
26 Nisbet, pp. 194–6.
27 James Simpson, *Permanent Revolution: The Reformation and the Illiberal Roots of Liberalism* (Harvard University Press, 2019), p. 25.
28 Quoted in Simpson, pp. 44–5.
29 Ibid., p. 92.
30 Holland, p. 32.
31 Armstrong, p. 25.
32 Ibid., p. 11.

## *Chapter 3: The uses of social science*

1 Tweet: @DrUmarAlQadri, 16 November 2023, 1.57pm.
2 Robert Nisbet, *History of the Idea of Progress*, p. 175.
3 J.B. Bury, *The Idea of Progress*, p. 169.
4 Ibid., p. 168.
5 Jack Hayward in D. Miller et al. (eds.), *The Blackwell Encyclopaedia of Political Thought* (Blackwell, 1991), p. 93.
6 'Stop Hate UK's Rose Simkins gives her thoughts after TUC report', *Sky News* (on Stop Hate UK Facebook page), 17 March 2017.
7 '"Brexit tensions partly to blame," charity claims, as racist offences double on TfL rail network in space of four years', *Evening Standard*, 5 May 2019.
8 Ibid.
9 Thomas Brudholm and Birgitte Schepelern Johansen (eds.), *Hate, Politics, Law: Critical Perspectives on Combating Hate* (Oxford University Press, 2018), p. 1.
10 Ibid., p. 5.
11 James O'Brien, *How Not To Be Wrong: The Art of Changing Your Mind* (W.H. Allen, 2020), p. 219.
12 Ibid., p. 111.
13 Ibid.
14 Ibid., p. 205.
15 Ibid., p. 208.
16 Emily Maitlis, 'We have to stop normalising the absurd', MacTaggart Lecture reproduced in *Prospect Magazine*, 25 August 2022.
17 Michael Oakeshott, 'Rationalism in politics', in *Rationalism in Politics and Other Essays* (1962; Liberty Fund, 1991), p. 16.
18 Ibid., p. 8.
19 O'Brien, p. 11.
20 George Orwell, 'The prevention of literature', The Orwell Foundation (originally from *Polemic*, January 1946).
21 Ibid.
22 Oakeshott, p. 5.
23 Ibid., p. 31.
24 Quoted in Max Hastings, *Nemesis, The Battle for Japan, 1944–45* (HarperCollins, 2007), p. 440.

## Chapter 4: Progressivism as promotion

1. Philip Caputo, *A Rumor of War*, p. xvi.
2. Ibid., p. 5.
3. Ibid., pp. 69–70.
4. Robert Dallek, *John F. Kennedy: An Unfinished Life, 1917–1963* (2003; Penguin, 2004), p. ix.
5. Ibid., pp. 275–6.
6. 'Lib Dems are the party of progress', letter to *The Guardian*, first published 28 April 2010.
7. 'Tony Blair: Without total change Labour will die', *New Statesman*, 11 May 2021.
8. Tweet: @guardian, 6 May 2021, 12.00pm.
9. Tweet: @theRSAorg, 13 March 2021, 3.34pm.
10. See 'Welcome to the University of WOKE! Leicester has ditched Chaucer, is "decolonising" its syllabus and marks "International Womxn's Week"... no wonder it's turning into a first-class failure, says Guy Adams', *Daily Mail*, 22 January 2021.
11. Justin Elderman, 'The BLM takeover of Whitehall', *The Critic*, 18 August 2020.
12. Marium R. Qureshi and Jade Williams, 'Allyship right now: #BlackLivesMatter', Twitter Help Center, 4 June 2020.
13. 'Britain's colonial legacy in Ireland under spotlight after Black Lives Matter protests', *BBC News*, 9 July 2020.
14. Ben Cobley, *The Tribe: The Liberal-Left and the System of Diversity* (Societas, 2018).
15. 'Funding for racial equity', *Candid* special issue, updated 12 October 2022.
16. Quoted in Thomas Edsall, 'The law of unintended political consequences strikes again', *New York Times*, 5 January 2022.
17. 'Funding for racial equity', *Candid*.
18. See for example, 'After raising $90 million in 2020, Black Lives Matter has $42 million in assets', *New York Times*, 17 May 2022.
19. Tweet: @ukblm, 21 September 2020, 4.27pm.
20. James O'Brien, *How Not To Be Wrong*, p. 96.
21. Ibid., p. 97.
22. Christopher Lasch, *The Culture of Narcissism: American Life in an Age of Diminishing Expectations* (1979; W.W. Norton, 2018), pp. 90–1.
23. Ibid., Introduction by E.J. Dionne, p. xxv.
24. Kelly Hogarth, *World Football Summit*, September 2022.
25. 'Tony Hall's resignation letter', *Media Guido*, 20 January 2020.
26. See 'BBC 100 Women 2019: Who is on the list this year?', *BBC World News* website, 16 October 2019.
27. 'Who owns the news? Market share analysis of UK print, online and broadcast news markets', *Press Gazette*, 25 November 2021.
28. 'Ballet star Precious Adams on balancing roles with being a role model', *BBC News*, 17 October 2019.
29. 'Britain's choice: Common ground and division in 2020s Britain', *More in Common*, October 2020, p. 10.
30. Peter Franklin, 'Who are the real tribes of Britain?', *Unherd*, 27 October 2020.
31. J.G. Ballard, *Miracles of Life: Shanghai to Shepperton. An Autobiography* (Fourth Estate, 2008), p. 259.

## Chapter 5: Eliminating opponents

1 Quoted in Martin Sixsmith, *Russia*, p. 306.
2 Ibid., p. 314.
3 Ibid., p. 414 and 414n.
4 Jung Chang and Jon Halliday, *Mao. The Unknown Story* (2005; Vintage Books, 2007), p. 398.
5 Ibid., p. 594.
6 Quoted in Bernard Fall, *Street Without Joy, The French Debacle in Indochina* (1961; Pen & Sword Military, 2005), p. 304.
7 Catherine Merridale, *Ivan's War*, p. 323.
8 Robert Tombs, *The English and Their History*, pp. 2, 3.
9 Tweet: @mrjamesob, 5 July 2020, 10.58am.
10 Martha Gill, 'Free speech isn't under threat. It just suits bigots and boors to suggest so', *The Observer*, 23 June 2019.
11 Twitter thread: @bariweiss, 9 December 2022, 12:15–1.40am UK time.
12 Joanna Williams, *How Woke Won* (Spiked, 2022), p. 171.
13 Tweet: @ucuedinburgh, 7 December 2022, 9.44pm.
14 See for example, 'Sussex University students campaign to have "transphobic" professor Kathleen Stock sacked', *The Times*, 7 October 2021.
15 Hadley Freeman, 'Mermaids' useful idiots', *Unherd*, 29 November 2022.
16 'Hundreds of staff at The Guardian have signed a letter to the Editor criticising its "transphobic content"', *Buzzfeed News*, 6 March 2020.
17 Williams, pp. 178–9.
18 Suzanne Moore, 'An exclusive interview with JK Rowling about her new project', *Letters from Suzanne (Substack)*, 12 December 2022.
19 Kathleen Stock, 'How I survived my annus horribilis', *Unherd*, 4 November 2022.
20 See for example, 'Christian doctor who refuses to call transgender woman "she" loses employment tribunal', *The Independent*, 3 October 2019.
21 'Mother, 38, is arrested in front of her children and locked in a cell for seven hours after calling a transgender woman a man on Twitter', *Mail on Sunday*, 10 February 2019.
22 J.B. Bury, *The Idea of Progress*, p. 162.
23 Zygmunt Bauman, *Postmodern Ethics* (1993; Blackwell, 1998), p. 226.

## Chapter 6: The politics of expertise

1 'ESRC announces extension of funding for the UK in a changing Europe and nine new Senior Fellows', ESRC press release, 19 June 2019.
2 Jonathan Portes and John Springford, 'Early impacts of the post-Brexit immigration system on the UK labour market', UK in a Changing Europe/Centre for European Reform, 17 January 2023.
3 Jonathan Portes and John Springford, 'The impact of the post-Brexit migration system on the UK labour market', UKICE working paper 01/2023.
4 Anand Menon and Jill Rutter, 'UK in a changing Europe: Injecting social science into a polarised political debate', *LSE blogs*, 18 August 2022.
5 'A beginner's guide to the European Union', UK in a Changing Europe, 2 November 2022.

6 Christopher Lasch, *The Revolt of the Elites and the Betrayal of Democracy* (1995; W.W. Norton, 1996), p. 174.
7 Ibid., p. 11.
8 Tweet: @anandMenon1, 30 March 2022, 10.01pm.
9 Tweet: @iain_w_anderson, 13 February 2023, 7.03am.
10 'Daniel Radcliffe responds to J.K. Rowling's tweets on gender identity', *The Trevor Project*, 8 June 2020.
11 Reported in 'What Hilary Cass needs to tell schools: Social transition is incompatible with safeguarding', *Sex Matters*, 29 July 2022.
12 Runnymede Trust website home page.
13 'Barrister at head of panel to tackle police racism wanted to defund police, bragged of her "hatred" for the Tories and called for officers to be more "woke"', *Daily Mail*, 25 May 2022.
14 'Leaked email says Sky hiring only BAME or women correspondents', *Media Guido*, 25 February 2021.
15 See tweet: @SholaMos1, 21 June 2021, 3.47pm.
16 'Sky adviser on psychological safety says those who criticise take-the-knee are "sub-human"', *Media Guido*, 15 July 2021.
17 Joanna Williams, *How Woke Won*, pp. 178–9.
18 Hadley Freeman, 'Mermaids' useful idiots', *Unherd*, 29 November 2022.
19 'Guidelines for psychological practice with transgender and gender nonconforming people', *American Psychologist* (published by the American Psychological Association), December 2015, p. 832.
20 Ethan Watters, *Crazy Like Us: The Globalization of the Western Mind* (2010; Robinson, 2011), p. 2.
21 Ibid., p. 65.
22 Ibid., pp. 76–7.
23 Ibid., p. 100.
24 '"We are living in a racism pandemic," says APA president', American Psychological Association, 29 May 2020.
25 Lasch, p. 207.
26 Ibid.
27 Quoted in *The New Penguin Dictionary of Quotations* (ed. J.M. and M.J. Cohen, Penguin, 2002), p. 64.
28 Twitter thread: @RoryStewartUK, 3 November 2024, 10.37pm and 4 November, 7.13am.
29 The Rest is Politics Livestream: 'America decides'. See tweet: @RestIsPolitics, 6 November 2024, 8.59am.
30 Tweet: @RoryStewartUK, 8 November 2024, 7.08am.
31 See Robert Dallek, *John F. Kennedy*, p. 90.

## *Chapter 7: From art to activism*

1 Taken from tweet: @tonyprinciotti, 15 September 2022, 5.20pm.
2 Quoted in Norman Lebrecht, *The Companion to 20th Century Music* (Simon & Schuster, 1992), p. x.
3 Ibid., p. 45.

4 Ibid., p. 308.
5 Harold C. Schonberg, *The Lives of the Great Composers* (3rd ed., 1997; Abacus, 2006 reprint), p. 669.
6 Ibid., p. 669.
7 Ibid., p. 675.
8 Letter VWL1680, from Ralph Vaughan Williams to Ferdinand Rauter, 16 August 1942, Vaughan Williams Foundation.
9 Quoted in Schonberg, p. 301.
10 Ibid., pp. 301, 317.
11 Hannah Arendt, *New Yorker*, 12 September 1970. Taken from the *New Penguin Dictionary of Quotations* (ed. R. Andrews, 2006).
12 Schonberg, p. 609.
13 'Turner Prize 2019 awarded to collective of this year's nominees Abu Hamdan/Cammock/Murillo/Shani', *Turner Contemporary*, 3 December 2019.
14 'Turner prize awarded four ways after artists' plea to judges', *The Guardian*, 3 December 2019.
15 'Joint Turner Prize winners criticise Tories for "hostile environment"', *ITV News*, 4 December 2019.
16 See tweet: @Tate, 3 December 2019, 9.43pm.
17 'In shock move, all four nominated artists win Turner Prize 2019', *The Art Newspaper*, 3 December 2019.
18 Holly Race Roughan, 'Our Henry V is very dark', *The Stage*, 3 November 2022.
19 'Five questions with . . . Euella Jackson, Rising Arts Agency', *Arts Council England*, 8 October 2020.
20 *Let's Create: Strategy 2020–2030*, Arts Council England, 2021, p. 9.
21 Ibid., p. 12.
22 Ibid.
23 Claire Mera-Nelson (Director, Music, Arts Council England), 'Diversity in classical music', *Arts Council England blog*, 6 February 2020.
24 Ibid.
25 *Let's Create*, p. 15.
26 Ibid., p. 49.
27 Ibid., p. 8.
28 Ibid., p. 53.
29 J.G. Ballard, *Miracles of Life*, pp. 233–4.

## Chapter 8: Progressive capitalism

1 Bethany McLean and Peter Elkind, *The Smartest Guys in the Room: The Amazing Rise and Scandalous Fall of Enron* (2003; Penguin, 2004), p. 3.
2 Ibid., p. 71.
3 Quoted in McLean and Elkind, p. xxi.
4 Quoted in McLean and Elkind, p. 173.
5 Ibid., p. 216.
6 Jacob Bronowski and Bruce Mazlish, *The Western Intellectual Tradition: From Leonardo to Hegel* (1960; Pelican, 1963), p. 397.
7 Ibid., p. 399.

8. Robert Nisbet, *History of the Idea of Progress*, p. 177.
9. John Locke, *Two Treatises on Government* (1689; ed. P. Laslett, Cambridge University Press, 1988), p. 292.
10. Ibid., pp. 297–8.
11. Taken from Kristian Niemietz, 'Housebuilding targets: Britain becomes a NIMBYocracy', *IEA*, 6 December 2022.
12. Figures from the Official for National Statistics (ONS) and Eurostat.
13. Quoted in tweet: @Steven_Swinford, 5 March 2023, 9.24am.
14. BBC *Daily Politics*, 2 April 2023.
15. 'Alan Manning: "Achieving growth by just having more people is not what we should aim for"', *Financial Times*, 8 March 2023.
16. Bronowski and Mazlish, p. 394.
17. Karl Polanyi, *The Great Transformation: The Political and Economic Origins of Our Time* (1944; Beacon Press, 2001), Introduction by Fred Block, p. xxvii.
18. 'HSBC "Home to so much more" by Wunderman Thompson', *Campaign Live*, 22 January 2020.
19. Alessandro Manfredi, 'Why Dove is stepping up its "actionist" approach', *Campaign Live*, 11 May 2021.
20. Ibid.
21. 'Math suffers from white supremacy, according to a Bill Gates-funded course', *Newsweek*, 23 February 2021.
22. Stephen Daisley, 'Is this Wickes's Gerald Ratner moment?', *Spectator*, 16 June 2023.
23. Tweet: @sainsburys, 1 October 2020, 3.22pm.
24. Tweets: @HalifaxBank, 28 June 2022, 9am and 3.10pm.
25. Charlotte Gooch, 'Why diversity in the workplace is a must', *neuroworx*, 9 September 2021.
26. James Esses, 'The horrors of the "Pink News Trans Summit"', *TRANSparency*, 15 June 2023.
27. John Gray, *Straw Dogs: Thoughts on Humans and Other Animals* (Granta, 2002), p. 163.
28. Ethan Watters, *Crazy Like Us*, p. 217.
29. Ibid., p. 252.
30. Ibid., p. 253.
31. Christopher Lasch, *The Culture of Narcissism*, p. 140.

## Chapter 9: The technocratic state

1. Jacob Bronowski and Bruce Mazlish, *The Western Intellectual Tradition*, p. 249.
2. Ibid., p. 245.
3. *Compact Oxford English Dictionary of Current English, Third Edition*, revised (ed. C. Soanes and S. Hawker, Oxford University Press, 2008), p. 1063.
4. *The Wire*, Season 4 DVD Box Set, Episode 11 (HBO, 2007).
5. All from, 'Civil servant who blew the whistle on political activism wins £100,000 settlement', *The Telegraph*, 27 May 2023.
6. 'Civil Servants trained to accept Britain is racist', *The Times*, 29 July 2022.
7. Letter from Matthew Rycroft to Rt Hon Priti Patel (accessible), *Gov.uk*, published 16 April 2022.
8. Sir David Normington featured in tweet from @BBCNewsnight, 14 April 2022, 5.29pm.

9 'Archbishop of Canterbury's speech in Lords debate on UK asylum policy', *The Archbishop of Canterbury*, 9 December 2022.
10 Tweets: @Daaronovitch, 14 April 2022, 12.42pm and @maitlis, 5.01pm same day.
11 Twitter thread: @benandjerrysUK, 8 June 2022, 4.36pm–9 June, 1.29pm.
12 Peter Hennessey, *Whitehall* (1989; Fontana, 1990), p. xiii; originally from 'Thatcher's 3000 days', *BBC 1 Panorama*, 4 January 1988.
13 Ibid., pp. xvi, xvii.
14 Perry Anderson, 'Ever closer union', *London Review of Books*, Vol. 43, No. 1, 7 January 2021.
15 Ibid.
16 Bruno Waterfield, 'EU-Qatar corruption scandal's no surprise – Brussels encourages sleaze', *The Times*, 16 December 2022.
17 Wolfgang Streeck, 'Ins and outs', *New Left Review*, 19 January 2021.
18 Anderson, *LRB*.
19 Quoted in Anderson, *LRB*.

## Chapter 10: Nationalisms, good and bad

1 Ralph Vaughan Williams, 'Who wants the English composer?', in D. Manning (ed.), *Vaughan Williams on Music* (Oxford University Press, 2007), online abstract.
2 David Manning, 'Introduction', in above, online edition (Oxford Academic, 2011).
3 Ibid., refers to p. 41 of print edition.
4 Jan Brachmann, 'Der Soldat als Hirte, "A Pastoral Symphony" von Ralph Vaughan Williams', *Deutschlandfunk Kultur*, 6 January 2019.
5 Letter No. VWL1537 from Ralph Vaughan Williams to Lord Kennet, 20 May 1941, Vaughan Williams Foundation.
6 Hugh Morris, 'I know, but: "Fantasia on a Theme by Thomas Tallis": Seeing past the pastoral in Ralph Vaughan Williams', *Van Magazine*, 18 March 2021.
7 Elizabeth Botcherby, 'Lark descending: Time for superior classical works to take the Hall of Fame spotlight', *Medium.com* (date not available, since deleted).
8 Tweet: @rafaelbehr, 14 May 2020, 9.57pm; replying to deleted tweet from @mePadraigReidy.
9 Philip Clark, 'This isle is full of noises: The trouble with "English music"', *The Guardian*, 11 December 2019.
10 Tweet: @Andrew_Adonis, 19 April 2018, 5.46am.
11 J.G. Ballard, *Miracles of Life*, p. 121.
12 Ibid., p. 123.
13 Ibid., p. 126.
14 Ibid., pp. 126–7.
15 Ibid., p. 125.
16 Maya Jasanoff, 'Mourn the Queen, not her empire', *New York Times*, 8 September 2022.
17 Jan Fleischhauer, 'Watching a country make a fool of itself', *Spiegel International*, 19 October 2018.
18 Jasanoff, *New York Times*.
19 Tweet: @carlbildt, 2 April 2015.
20 Taken from a tweet posted by @cbbc, 31 January 2020, 9.05am.
21 Tweet: @DanielaNadj, 15 February 2022, 5.27pm.

22 Tweet: @DanielaNadj, 21 March 2022, 11.35pm.
23 Zoe Williams, 'English nationalism has a champion in No 10. But it's a very fragile concept', *The Guardian*, 15 December 2020; 'Emma Thompson says UK is "A cake-filled misery-laden grey old island" as she warns against Brexit', *HuffPost UK*, 16 February 2016; Tweet: @ProfBrianCox, 8 August 2020, 9.20pm; two tweets from: @RichardDawkins, 27 March 2017, 1.39am and 30 November 2017, 10.18am.
24 V.S. Naipaul, *Guerrillas* (1975; Penguin, 1977), pp. 47–8.
25 From 'Micheál Martin has "no time" for a UK-style "toxic" discussion on trans issues', *thejournal.ie*, 24 June 2022.
26 'Paul Hosford: Ireland doesn't need or want toxic culture war "debate" on trans people', *Irish Examiner*, 28 June 2022.
27 John McGuirk, 'The two sides of Irish tribalism', *GRIPT*, 13 October 2022.
28 Taken from John Wilson Foster, 'What's Hecuba to him?', *Dublin Review of Books*, March 2019. Referring to Fintan O'Toole, *Heroic Failure: Brexit and the Politics of Pain* (Apollo, 2018).
29 Wilson Foster, *Dublin Review of Books*.
30 Ibid.
31 Tweet: @BrigidLaffan, 1 July 2022, 11.27am.
32 Tweets from @KeohaneDan, 28 February 2021, since deleted, as was his apology on 1 March 2021.
33 Conor Fitzgerald, 'Goodboyism: An Irish political neurosis', *Medium*, 20 May 2020.
34 Tweet: @ruth_wishart, 18 April 2022, 8.58pm.
35 Tweet: @ruth_wishart, 12 October 2022, 3.37pm.

## Chapter 11: Playing Jesus: The activist as narcissist

1 Allison P. Davis, 'Meghan of Montecito', *The Cut*, 29 August 2022.
2 Ibid.
3 Ibid.
4 'Narcissus, definition & myth', https://www.britannica.com/science/narcissism
5 Christopher Lasch, *The Culture of Narcissism*, p. 251.
6 Lasch, *The Revolt of the Elites*, p. 207.
7 Ibid., pp. 208–9.
8 Ibid., p. 273.
9 Lasch, *The Culture of Narcissism*, p. 260.
10 Ibid.
11 Ben Cobley, *The Tribe*.
12 Davis, *The Cut*.
13 Twitter thread: @PennyRed, 6 March 2022, 6.19pm–11.48pm.
14 Tweet: @BootstrapCook, 3 August 2022, 1.02pm.
15 Jack Monroe, 'Go, Greta. Autism is my superpower too', *The Guardian*, 27 April 2019.
16 Lasch, *The Culture of Narcissism*, p. 22.
17 'Decolonise your desks, demands teaching union in "sinister" new escalation of culture wars', *The Telegraph*, 3 July 2021.
18 Joanna Williams, 'The divisive plan to "decolonise" our schools', *Spiked*, 5 July 2021.
19 '"I got fed up with my students ending up in prison or dead": The teacher fighting to end school exclusions', *The Guardian*, 19 May 2022.

20 'Are exclusion rates for black Caribbean students up to six times higher?', *Scenes from the Battleground* (WordPress), 31 May 2022.
21 *The Guardian*, 19 May 2022.

## Chapter 12: Conclusions: How should we respond?

1 Encountered in Patrick O'Brian: *The Far Side of the World* (1984; HarperCollins, 2003), p. 202.
2 Bethany McLean and Peter Elkind, *The Smartest Guys in the Room*, p. 257.
3 Robert Nisbet, *History of the Idea of Progress*, p. 4.
4 Ibid., p. 171.
5 Zygmunt Bauman, *Postmodern Ethics*, p. 5.
6 Louise Perry, *The Case Against the Sexual Revolution: A New Guide to Sex in the 21st Century* (Polity, 2022), pp. 189–90.
7 David Lammy speech at Labour Party Conference 2024, 22 September 2024.
8 Priya Satia, *Time's Monster*, p. 1.
9 Ibid., pp. 2–3.
10 Ibid., p. 276.
11 Ibid., p. 2.
12 Ibid., p. 275.
13 Michael Lind, *The New Class War: Saving Democracy from the Metropolitan Elite* (2020; Atlantic Books, 2021), p. 83.
14 Tom McTague, 'Jeremy Clarkson: Populist tribune', *Unherd*, 20 November 2024.
15 Mary Harrington, *Feminism Against Progress* (Forum, 2023), p. 79.
16 Joseph Conrad, *The Nigger of the 'Narcissus'* (1897); quoted in Philip Caputo, *A Rumor of War*, p. 351.
17 Matthew Crawford, 'The sexual holy war is coming for you', *Unherd*, 24 July 2023.

# *Index*

Aaronovitch, David 149
Academy of Ideas, the 204
activists, activism *viii*, 38, 39, 43, 56, 65, 72, 73, 82, 83, 87–8, 99, 100, 103, 115, 135, 138, 149, 150, 171–81, 185, 189, 190, 191, 200, 201
   as 'independent' 'experts' 23, 96, 98, 103, 151
   as therapists 173–4
   mental health troubles 180–1
   merged with academic work 37, 51, 53
   merged with art 114–19, 121
   'saviour complex' 179–81
Adams, John 6, 40
Adonis, Lord Andrew 159
*Adult Human Female* 83
Africa, Africans 2–3, 13
'allyship' 66, 73, 98n, 99, 147–8, 176, 177–8
Al-Qadri, Shaykh Dr Umar 47
Amazon 136
America *see* United States of America
American Psychological Association (APA) 101, 102
Americans, Native 130
   Mandan tribe 5
'analytic' school of philosophy 203
Anderson, Iain 97
Anderson, Lee, MP 34
Anderson, Perry 152, 154
anti-Semitism *vi*, 24, 52, 88n, 113
Applbaum, Kalman 141–2
Apple 136
Appleby, Sir Humphrey 193
Archewell 171
Arendt, Hannah 7, 113
Armstrong, Karen 44, 45
Arsenal Football Club 65
art, artistic activity (including music) *viii*, 64, 72, 111–24, 156, 189, 190, 205
Arthur Andersen 126
Arts Council England (ACE) 118–23, 190–1
   as a sort of alternative government 122

   outward-looking versus inward 190
   replacing 'artist' with 'creative practitioner' 119, 190–1
   role of sociology for 120
'assaultive speech' 100
Augustine, Saint 41
Australia 101–2, 122
Avaaz 17
avant-garde 157
Ayoade, Richard 134

Badenoch, Kemi, MP 148, 197
Bakhtin, Mikhail 62, 76
Ballard, J.G. 76, 123, 159, 160
Balshaw, Maria 117
Barber, Lionel 96
Bartolini, Stefano 152
Bauman, Zygmunt 89, 186
BBC 36, 54, 55, 57, 58, 66, 98, 158, 162, 167
   as a promotional organization 73–5
   BBC Allies 98
   reconstitution of 204
   staff networks 75
Behr, Rafael 158
Bei, Zahra 178–9
Belgium 1–2
Ben and Jerry's Ice Cream 149–50
Bhattacharya, Dr Jay 82
Bickerton, Professor Chris 154
Biden, Joe/Hunter 136
Big Tech 67, 71, 135, 136, 201
Bildt, Carl 162
Bill & Melinda Gates Foundation 67
Black History Month 72, 137
Black Lives Matter (BLM) 37, 38, 65–70, 65n, 72, 76, 99, 135, 137n, 147, 168
Black Lives Matter Global Network Foundation (BLMGNF) 67
BLM UK list of demands 68
Blair, Tony 2–3, 18, 64, 72
Boers, The 4

# INDEX

Bohr, Niels 104
Botcherby, Elizabeth 158
Boulez, Pierre 111
Bowers, Shalomyah 67
Boyle, Professor Nicholas 16
Brachmann, Jan 157
Braverman, Suella, MP 148, 150n
Brexit and referendum *vi*, 54–5, 56, 57, 74,
    92–4, 96, 107, 122, 132, 134, 145, 152,
    165, 167, 169, 194
  as crisis of identity 16, 135
  as English pathology/sickness 16–18, 21, 158,
    162, 166
  'behind the times', etc. 21–2, 33, 159n, 161,
    167
  'in the room', 'at the top table' 154
  Northern Ireland Protocol 167
  'perfect storm of identity politics' 15–19,
    48–51, 56n, 162
  'war of position' over 16
Brighton Pride 137
Bristol 118–19
  Bristol City Council 118
Britain, British, the *see also* United Kingdom, the
    British stat*e*
  after WWII 159–60
  armed forces 160
  diluting meaning of 117, 131, 134–5, 162
  disease 164
  elites/'Establishment' 154, 156, 161, 163,
    164, 166, 169, 198
  'Global Britain' 161
  guilt 53, 161, 195
  'heroic failure' 16
  historical versions of progress 2–5, 15, 22
  music 156–9
  people 21, 50, 162–3
  rebirth/redemption via migration 194
British Academy 16
British Empire, imperialism 2, 4–5, 15, 16,
    21–2, 66, 156, 161, 162, 164, 178, 195,
    196, 202 *see also* colonialism, European,
    historical; imperialism, European
  as a continuing reality 21, 178
  'the key to glory and wealth ... and the means
    of service to mankind', etc. 4
Britten Sinfonia 120
Bronowski, Jacob 128, 133, 144
Brudholm, Thomas 51, 52
Bruguera, Tania 114–15
*BT Sport* 65

Bukharin, Nikolay 77
Bury, J.B. 8, 48, 88
Bush, Governor (later President) George W.
    125
Butler, Dawn, MP 38
*Butterfly* 100
Butts, Cindy 36, 37, 38

Cadwalladr, Carole 96
Calamy, Edmund 44
Calvinism 44
Cambodia 122, 206
Campbell, Grace 18
Canada 122, 197
'cancel culture' 54, 80
Candid 67
Cape Colony 4
capitalism 8, 19, 25, 43, 125–43
  as a colonial force 142
  inherently progressive 127–8
  manufacturing the consumer 140–3
  regulation 153
  territorial colonization 128–34
  totalitarian form 182
  'woke' 134–9
Caputo, Philip 6, 62
Carlyle, Thomas 3
Carr, E.H. 12–13, 34–5
Cass, Dr Hilary 98
Catlin, George 5
causation 6, 17, 19, 54, 56–60, 70, 72, 74, 100,
    122, 144 *see also* social science; sociology
Centre for European Reform (CER) 92, 167
'centrists' 198
Chang, Jung 78
charities *see* non-governmental organizations
Charles III, King 149
China/Chinese, Communist/Maoist *vi*, 8, 14,
    19, 34, 43, 44, 61, 78, 88, 119, 182,
    188, 206
  Cultural Revolution 23
Chineke! Orchestra 120
Christianity, Christian stories 2, 4, 9, 38, 39,
    43–4, 70, 87, 89, 127, 134, 149–50,
    180, 204n
  aligned to progressivism 2, 34–5, 39–40, 44,
    104, 149–50, 177, 196
  different to progressivism 40–3
  Last Judgement 32, 34
Church of England 40, 149
Churchill, Winston 22

# INDEX

CIEO 82
citizenship, citizens 115, 116, 139, 152, 161, 202, 205
   'Citizens of Change' 64
   submission, diluting meaning of 9, 143, 145, 150, 154, 184
Civil Service (Britain) 56, 67, 96, 147–52
   as 'agents of change' etc. 19–20, 151
   'permanent government' 151, 192
   reconstitution of 204
Clark, Philip 158
Classic FM 158, 170
classical music 111–13, 120–1, 156–9, 157n1, 157n2, 169–70
   'diversity in' 120–1
Clinton, Senator Hillary 33
Cold War, The 8, 10
College of Policing *see* police
colonialism, European, historical 1–5, 13, 129, 142, 196 *see also* imperialism; progressivism – contemporary imperialism, colonialism
   contemporary associations with 63, 66, 78n, 177, 178, 180
   progressive 4, 35
Comcast 99
commissars 20, 151, 205
Communism 6, 7, 8, 14, 41, 43, 44, 60, 79, 146, 151, 166, 188
   Chinese Communism *see* China/Chinese; Communist/Maoist
   Communist Party of the Soviet Union *see* Soviet Union
   Vietnamese Communism *see* Vietnam
Comte, Auguste 35, 48, 55, 88
Condorcet, Nicolas de 7
Congo, The 1–2
Conrad, Joseph 203
Conservative Party, Conservatives 34, 56, 97, 117, 149, 182, 197
   European Research Group 56
   in government 38, 64, 75, 76, 94, 98, 99, 117, 147, 200, 206
   immigration 117, 131–2, 133, 134, 148, 150
   liberal or 'One Nation' wing 191, 191n
conservatives 55, 64, 81, 82, 86, 200
   pessimism about human nature 41
Counterpoints 115
Coutts 137
Covid-19 pandemic 65, 82, 93, 96, 118, 147

Cox, Professor Brian 163
Crawford, Matthew 204
Criado-Perez, Caroline 18
cricket 36–7, 38
'crisis of competence' 189, 206
*Critic, The* 200
critical race theory (CRT) 24, 25, 150
Cullors, Patrisse 67
'culture wars' 80, 97, 165, 188
Cummings, Dominic 148
Curzon, Lord 4

Dallek, Robert 62
Darwin, Sir Charles 23
Davis, Allison P. 176
Davis, David, MP 148
Dawkins, Richard 63
decolonization 20–7, 34, 47, 64, 161
   as a form of colonization/imperialism *viii*, 26–7
   genocidal impulse 26
'deconstruction' 202
democracy 56, 60, 64, 70, 77–8, 94, 105, 145, 153, 163, 191, 193, 203
   against populism 106, 145, 152, 196
   as a chimera 205
   democratic society 33, 79, 150, 183–4
   representation 189, 193
Democratic Party, The 62, 193, 199
Department for Education 65
Department for Environment, Food and Rural Affairs (DEFRA) 65
Department for Levelling Up, Housing and Communities (DLUHC) 147
Department for Work and Pensions (DWP) 147
depression 101, 102, 141
dialectic 35, 184
DiAngelo, Robyn 24, 147
Diversity, Equity and Inclusion (DEI/EDI) 20, 37, 41, 151, 177, 177n, 189, 205
'division', divisiveness 50, 139n, 163, 165, 186, 188
   between young and old 186
Don't Divide Us 204
Dorsey, Jack 82, 136
Dove 135
Dowden, Richard 3
Dublin Pride 164
Duchess of Sussex, the *see* Markle, Meghan
Duffield, Rosie, MP 18

# INDEX

eBay UK 132
Economic and Social Research Council (ESRC) 91–2, 95n
Edinburgh International Television Festival 56
education, general 68, 135, 178, 180, 182 *see also* schools; universities, general
Elizabeth II, Queen 161, 162
Elkind, Peter 125, 183
Ellis, Havelock 172
*Empire Windrush* 194
Engels, Friedrich 61
England, the English 38, 50, 65, 118, 131, 163, 167, 168, 169, 190
    'Anglophobia' 165
    as a centre of progress, civilization 3–4, 5
    as backward, reactionary 16–17, 158, 159–60, 161, 162, 166, 170
    association with whiteness 17, 118
    diseased, dirty 16, 17, 118, 159–64, 166
    'exceptionalism' 158, 163
    folk song 157
    men's cricket team 36
    men's football team 37, 39, 68
    'Middle England' 158
    music 156–7, 157n
    nationalism 118, 118n, 159n, 166
    Reformation in 43, 44
    rejection of history, traditions 15, 79, 121, 156, 163, 190
England and Wales Cricket Board (ECB) 36–7
English National Ballet 74
English National Opera (ENO) 120
Enlightenment, The 3, 22, 35, 202n
    'pro-Enlightenment reactionaries' 202
Eno, Brian 63
Enron 125–7, 183, 184
environment, the 127
    expansion into 131
Equality Act (2010) 26n, 193, 205
Equitable Math 136
European Central Bank 153
European Convention on Human Rights (ECHR) 148
European Court of Human Rights 149, 205
European Union (EU) 15, 18, 91–4, 92n, 96, 163, 165, 166, 167, 168, 169
    *acquis communitaire* 152, 153
    as a technocratic empire 152–5
    as a totem of progress/the future 15, 153
    EU Customs Union 153
    European Central Bank (ECB) 153

European Commission 94, 96
European Council
European Court of Justice (ECJ) 153
European Parliament 152
European Single Market 153
    free movement 51, 93, 94, 132
    member states 152, 154, 161
expertise 16, 51, 91–108, 189–90
    expert in society 54, 104, 173
    identity politics as 97–103, 189
    nature of 103–5
    protects against contradiction 57, 103
EY (formerly Ernst & Young) 137

Fabian Society, The 4
'false consciousness' 79
family, the ix, 72, 78, 86, 102, 140, 181, 187, 188
far right, the vi, 11, 43n, 52, 55, 198, 205
Farage, Nigel 51, 52, 53, 137, 180, 199
Farquharson, Alex 118
Farrand Carrapico, Helena 96
feminism, feminists 18, 84, 86, 135, 172–3, 175, 201
    gender-critical (aka. 'terfs') 84, 85, 86, 87, 200
    'girlboss' 171
    'liberal feminism' 187
Ferguson, Professor Niall 11
*Financial Times, The* 96
Finkelstein, Tamara 65
Fitzgerald, Conor 168, 169
Floyd, George 36–9, 65, 67, 102, 119, 147
    'post-Floyd moment' 39
football 19, 37, 39, 65, 69, 99, 156, 165
Football Association (FA) 19
Ford Foundation 67
*Fortune* (magazine) 125
Foster, Francis 137
France, the French 3, 3n, 7, 57, 78, 79
    civilizing mission 2, 3
    French Revolution 7, 14, 35, 44, 79, 128
Franklin, Benjamin 40
Franklin, Peter 75
free speech 48, 60, 81, 85, 203, 206
    as 'an imperialist capitalist white supremacist cis heteropatriarchal technique' 25
Free Speech Union (FSU) 137, 204
free trade 4
freedom/liberty 4, 5, 6, 8, 9, 10, 12, 24, 44, 48, 96, 128, 153, 191, 194n
Freeman, Hadley 85

222

# INDEX

Gaddis, John Lewis 10
Gallup 31
Gandhi, Mohandas Karamchand (Mahatma) 202
Garrick Club 203n
*GB News* 51
Genesis, Book of 149
genocide 26
Germany, Germans 4, 19, 113, 157, 159
    pre-WWI jingoism 157n
    supremacy of German music 112
Gill, Martha 81
Gilley, Bruce 196n
Gladstone, William Ewart 4
GlaxoSmithKline (GSK) 141
Global Butterflies 98
Globe, The 118
Glock, William 158
'Glorious Revolution', the 43
Gödel, Kurt 46
Goëldhieux, Claude 78–9
Google 135, 136, 137
    NGram Viewer 31
government, role in manufacturing workers 139
Government Equalities Office (UK) 96
Gray, John 140
Green, Susie 85, 100
Greer, Bonnie 33
*Guardian, The* 17, 64, 73, 85
    skewed ethnic analysis of school exclusions 178–9

Halifax Bank 137
Halliday, Jon 78
Hamas *vi, vii*, 24, 25, 47
Hamilton, Emily 138
Haringey, London Borough of 20
Harrington, Mary 201
Harris, Kamala 105–6, 193, 194, 196
Harry, Prince, Duke of Sussex 171
'hate' and 'hate crime' 100, 186, 203
    as thought-crime 87n
    opaque definition 52, 53, 87
    reporting/statistics 49, 50, 162
    sociology of 48–53
    tool in activist armoury 87, 204
Headlong Theatre 118
Heartfield, James 20
Heaton-Harris, Chris (former MP) 131
Hegel, G.W.F 35, 48
Heine, Heinrich 157n
Henley, Darren 121

Hennessey, Peter 151
*Henry V* 118
Hertz, Noreena 63
Higher Education (Freedom of Speech) Act 2023 206
historian, history, role of 12, 13, 22, 33, 34, 89, 195
    'instrument of redemption' 195
Hitchens, Peter 41
Hitler, Adolf 19, 24, 113, 191
Hobsbawm, Eric 5
Hodges, Dan 99
Holland, Tom 38, 39, 44
Home Office, The 39n, 148
Hope Not Hate 51
'horizontal' relationships among elites 153
Hosford, Paul 164
Howard Hughes Medical Institute 67
HSBC 134–5
human resources (HR) 138, 139, 146
human rights 150, 153, 191, 192
Human Rights Act (1998) 148
humanitarian movement 1, 2
Hunt, Jeremy, MP 148

identity politics, general 15, 90 *see also* progressivism – identity politics
'immanent criticism' 202
immigration and asylum 39, 45, 50, 68, 93–4, 131–2, 133, 148, 158, 162, 168, 170, 194n, 200
    abolition of border controls 68
    alliance between liberals and the left over 134
    immigrants as a class *vi*, 187, 188
    'nation of immigrants' 194, 194n
    'pause' 205, 205n
    record numbers 93, 131, 132
impartiality 1, 58, 73, 92, 94, 96
    as a form of partiality 57, 94–5, 96, 99, 146, 151–2, 193
imperialism, European *viii*, 4–5, 18, 20, 40
    *see also* colonialism; progressivism – contemporary imperialism, colonialism
    contemporary 94, 122, 151, 154
    ultimate failure of 201–2
    use in contemporary discourse 15, 16–17, 21, 25, 153, 160, 161, 166, 167, 170, 178
Independent Commission for Equity in Cricket (ICEC) 36–7, 38
Independent Commission on UK–EU Relations 96

# INDEX

'Independent SAGE' 96
Indian independence movement 201
individualism 5, 60, 79, 130
Industrial Revolution 128, 133
intellectual/intelligentsia 7, 44, 59, 63, 104, 108, 111, 113, 114, 150, 157–8, 163, 180, 182, 197, 200, 203, 205
   'snake oil' 206
   subject to external authority 9, 22, 23, 60, 61
intelligence functions of society
   capture of 189, 205
   no longer working 189
intersectionality 123, 176
Ireland/Irish 79, 98, 163
   Anglophobia 165
   as a progressive nation 164–9
   association with the EU 15, 167–9
   'goodboyism' 168
   integration in Britain 165–6, 167
      with British ruling class 164, 166, 168
   link to Black Lives Matter 66
   nationalism 168, 170
   'Official Ireland'/the establishment 168, 169
   Women's Football Team 165
Irish Muslim Council 47
Irish Republican Army (IRA) 161, 165
Islam
   as a form of progress 204, 204n
   Islamism *vi*, 34, 43n, 47, 52, 191, 204
Islamophobia *vi*, 19
   law, pressure on Labour to introduce 204
Israel *vi, vii*, 24–5, 34, 47, 52, 189
Israelites 42
*ITV* 100

Jackson, Euella 118
Japan, Japanese 61, 141–2
Jasanoff, Professor Maya 161, 162
Javid, Sajid, MP 131
Jefferson, Thomas
Jesus Christ 149, 150, 177, 180
Jews, Jewishness 19, 24, 34, 35, 52, 113, 149
   as an oppressor group 25, 47
   for the Nazis 166
Jinping, President Xi 14
Johnson, Abimbola 99
Johnson, Boris (former MP) 17n, 51, 52, 53, 93, 97, 148, 161, 167
Johnson, Sasha 99n

Kaepernick, Colin 65
Kendi, Professor Ibram X. 24, 147
Kennedy, President John F. 31–2, 62–3, 194n
Kennedy, Senator Robert F. 32
Keohane, Daniel 167
Kershaw, Professor Ian 24
Khan, Sadiq 11, 33, 34, 54
Khatun, Nurjahan 39n
Khrushchev, Nikita 7, 78
Kick It Out 19
Kimberley diamond mines 4
Kirk, Charlie 92
Kirmayer, Dr Laurence 141
Kisin, Konstantin 137
Kumar, Nish 162

Labour Party 11, 17, 38, 51, 56, 68, 73, 97, 99, 200
   attachment to American styles 193, 194
   in government 2024 179, 192, 193, 202, 206
   Islamophobia law, pressure to enact 204
   New Labour governments 1997–2010 26n, 72, 94, 193
   sense of entitlement 192
Laffan, Brigid 167
Lambell, Murray 132
Lambeth, London Borough of 20
Lammy, David, MP 66, 192
land
   appropriation of 129–30
   as a commodity
   as a resource 128, 130
   of Britain
language, corruption of 203
Lasch, Christopher 142, 172–4
   *The Culture of Narcissism* 71, 72, 172, 174, 177
   *The Revolt of the Elites* 95, 102–3
Lay, Kenneth 125, 127
le Carré, John 63
Lebrecht, Norman 111, 112
left-wing, foundations of 43, 44
Lehmann, Claire 11
Lenin, Vladimir 7
Leninism (Marxism-Leninism) 7, 111
Leopold II, King of Belgium 1–2
Lesseps, Ferdinand de 1
LGB Alliance 137
Liberal Democrats (Lib Dems), the 63–4

224

# INDEX

liberalism, liberals *vi*, 8, 9, 45, 60, 82, 93, 101, 130, 133, 144 *see also* progressivism –
    open liberal form of
    'liberal democracy' 106, 191
    'liberal institutions' 85
    more muscular, confrontational versions 187
    'no borders liberalism' 183
liberty *see* freedom
Libs of TikTok 82
Lind, Professor Michael 198–9
Livingstone, David 2, 3
Locke, John 131
    justification for appropriating land, 128–30
    theory of government 144
London Metropolitan University 25
Longden, Fraser 137
Lord Kerr 96
Lord Mountbatten 161
Lord Wolfson 93
Lovegrove, Stephen 65
Luyendijk, Joris 17

Macaulay, Thomas Babington 4
Macron, President Emmanuel 2, 57, 96
Maitlis, Emily 55–7, 58, 59, 149
Mama Cash 98
Manfredi, Alessandro 135
Manning, Professor Alan 132
Manning, David 156
Mao Zedong 23, 26, 61, 78
    and elimination of horticulture 78
Mark, Rebecca 183
Markle, Meghan, Duchess of Sussex 171–2, 173, 176–7
Martin TD, Micheál 164, 169
Marxism, Marxists 7, 10, 12, 14, 79, 99, 106, 188
Matthew, Book of 38
maturity, upending ideas of 186
May, Theresa (former MP) 161
Mazlish, Bruce 128, 133, 144
McGuirk, John 165
McLean, Bethany 125, 183
McTague Tom 199
media (mainstream) 10, 26, 53, 55, 67, 69, 70, 73, 76, 84, 85, 87, 95, 163, 165, 182, 189, 205
    defending against populism 56, 58
    expert slots 96, 97, 141
    shared Anglophone media space 199
Menon, Professor Anand 91, 94, 95, 95n

mental health 82, 100, 101–2, 141, 176, 177, 180
    industry 101
    'the modern equivalent of salvation' 177
Mermaids 85, 98, 100
Merridale, Professor Catherine 9
Microsoft 136
Mill, John Stuart
    'harm principle' 22, 82, 101
mind-made sense of self 181
Ministry of Defence (UK) 65, 98
modernism 111, 157, 158
modernity 45, 89–90, 160, 186
    revolutionary 44
Monbiot, George 63
Monroe, Jack 176–7
Moore, Suzanne 85
Mordaunt, Penny (former MP) 148
Morris, Hugh 158
Mos-Shogbamimu, Shola 99
Mounk, Yascha 18
Muldoon, James 26
musicology 114, 157
Musil, Robert 77
Musk, Elon *vi*, 11, 75n, 81, 82, 136, 197
Muslims 38, 89, 188, 204n
    separatist, supremacist ethic 205

Nadj, Daniela 163
Naipaul, V.S. 164
narcissism 171–81
    as a culture 172–5
    definition of 171, 172
    identity politics and 175–9
National Education Union (NEU) 178
National Health Service (NHS) 98, 204
National Infrastructure Commission 96
National Police Chiefs' Council (NPCC) 99
Nazis, The 19, 22, 56, 149, 166, 191, 195, 205
Neil, Andrew 105
Neuroworx 138
*New York Times, The* 85, 161, 162
Newton, Isaac 144
'nimbys' 133n
Nisbet, Robert 9–10, 13, 35–6, 40, 48, 128, 183, 191
No More Exclusions 178
non-governmental organizations (NGOs)/ charities 3, 42, 49–51, 85, 98, 100, 103, 147, 150
Norman Conquest 118n

225

Normington, David 149
Northern Ireland 94
  unionists 167
Nott, John (former MP) 151

Oakeshott, Michael 58–9, 60
Obama, President Barack 31, 32, 33, 54, 168
O'Brien, James 53–5, 56, 58, 59, 68, 80–1
Ó Cathasaigh, Marc 165
Office for Budget Responsibility (OBR) 96, 107
Old, Andrew 179
O'Neill, Deirdre 83
original sin 41–2
  progressive identity politics adaptation of 42n
Orwell, George vii, 53, 60, 87n
Osborne, George (former MP) 96
O'Toole, Fintan 16–17, 166–7, 169
Otto, Rudolf 45
overclass/overseeing class 158, 160, 164, 169, 175, 176, 183, 198, 199, 203

Paine, Thomas 40
Pakenham, Thomas 2, 3
Paraorchestra 120
'para-state' 204
Patel, Priti, MP 99, 148, 149, 150n
Patel, Ricken 17
PayPal 137
Penny, Laurie 176
Perry, Louise 187
pharmaceutical industry 102, 141–2
Philippson, Bridget, MP 179
Pink News Trans Summit 137–8
Poilievre, Pierre, PC MP 197
Pol Pot 206
Polanyi, Karl 134
police 49, 53, 68, 87, 88, 88n
  British Transport Police (BTP) 49, 50
  brutality, general 66
  College of Policing 99
  defunding/abolition of 37, 68, 99
  in the United States 37, 39, 65, 146
  Independent Scrutiny and Oversight Board (ISOB) 99
  Metropolitan Police 147
  training 51
policing, as behaviour 20, 86, 114, 202
population, maximizing 130, 131, 132
populism 18, 53, 193, 198–9
  as a disease 18, 194
  weakness of 198–9

Portes, Professor Jonathan 92–4
post-politics/post-political 146, 198
post-traumatic stress disorder (PTSD) 101, 176
praxis 106, 188, 201
Predict and Provide 107
Premier League 65
progressivism
  and democracy 145, 146, 150, 183–4, 189, 191, 193, 196, 203, 205
  as a catalyst 197
  as a form of corruption 123, 203
  as historically necessary 9, 10, 183
  as technical expertise 91, 103–4, 105
  attractive and seductive 14, 70, 141, 182, 184
  closed, controlling form 8, 9, 9n, 12, 14, 48, 197
  Progress as Power 9, 10
  consequences/risks of vii, 58, 83, 131–2, 133, 184–191, 198, 202n
  contemporary imperialism, colonialism 4, 20–7, 116, 121, 122, 143, 163, 192–7
  denial of agency 47, 56–7, 174, 188
  denial of reality vii, 61, 71, 79–80, 108, 201, 202, 205
  destructive force 27, 89, 141, 141n, 185
  dialectic of 35, 184
  economic 45, 104, 125, 126, 128, 131, 133, 139, 182
  hubris and self-delusion 184, 194
  identity politics 15–16, 19–20, 25, 56n, 73–4, 98, 98n, 99, 100, 123, 135, 138, 143, 148, 151, 177, 177n, 187, 188, 189, 193
    amenable to bureaucracy 188–9, 190
    as apolitical 97
    destructive power 185, 204
    discriminating with justification 19
    opponents, sceptics of 148, 199
    outsourcing of authority 136n, 175–6
    representation see representation, via identity
  libertarian 201
  liquefaction-as-progress 201
  manufacturing authority 32, 57, 58, 90, 183, 185
  open, liberal form 8–10, 11, 43, 191, 192, 197, 200
    defers to power 10
    in retreat 198
    lazy, naive, complacent 191, 197
    Progress as Freedom 9, 10
    triumphalism 10

# INDEX

predictions, role of 105–8
rejection of 197
resistance to 86, 87, 176, 199, 201–4
scientific 48, 128, 142
techniques of 25–7, 57, 58–61, 75–6, 78–9, 80, 88, 91, 145, 185–6, 198
  overuse 198
  woven into our lives 79, 186, 206
Prokofiev, Sergey 77
property 19
  individualism in 5
  market, UK 141–2
  rights 129, 144
  role in marginalization 142
Protestantism 4, 9, 10, 43, 194n
  Protestant ethic 131
  the 'social gospel' 173
Providence 6, 35, 40, 127, 128
psychology 23, 48, 54, 55, 99–101, 102–3, 166, 171, 172, 179
  merging with advocacy 101
  progress as a psychological law 88
  'psychological first aid' 102
  psychological safety 99
Public Sector Equality Duty (PSED) 123, 193, 205, 206
Publicis 137
Puritans, Puritanism 9, 40, 43, 44
  proto-revolutionary movement 44
  work ethic 129
Putin, Vladimir vi, 14, 34, 79, 80

Quangos, the quango-state 92, 96, 192

Raab, Dominic (former MP) 148
Race Roughan, Holly 118
racism vi, 11, 17, 20, 21, 48–9, 52, 63, 65, 69n, 72, 78n, 99, 147, 163, 166, 178, 180, 192, 195, 196n
  accusations of 23, 51, 68, 80, 99, 134, 150, 162
  as a weapon 69
  defining 100
  'pandemic' 102, 147
  systemic/'racist society' 21, 37, 39, 53, 66, 68, 148, 177
Radcliffe, Daniel 97–8
Raichik, Chaya 82
rationalism 55, 58–8, 60–1, 97
'Rebel Alliance' 197–201
  bigotry within 199

  counterculture or counterestablishment? 198–9
  racialism within 199
  revolt against gender self-ID 200
reconstitution of institutions 204–5
Rees-Mogg, Jacob (former MP) 148
Reeves, Rachel, MP 192
Reform Party, The 34, 199
Reformation, The (Protestant)
  as start of progress 194n
  double movement of 43
'regressivists' 197–8
Reidy, Padraig 158
'relevance' 104, 120, 184, 187, 194
'Remainers' 34, 153
reparations 68, 195
representation, via identity 23, 74–5, 138, 139n, 175–6, 189, 193, 205
  in advertising 135
  of historical improvement 13
  'representation and portrayal' 74
  tension with democratic representation 193
  'under-representation' 26n
reverse mentoring 23, 138
Rhodes, Cecil 4
Rising Arts Agency 118–19
Robert Wood Johnson Foundation 67
Robespierre, Maximilien 7, 35
Rousseau, Jean-Jacques 7
  idea of the 'noble savage' 160
Rowling, J.K. 86, 97
Royal College of Music (RCM) 156
Royal Family, The 163, 171, 176
Royal Society of Arts (RSA), The 64
RTÉ 164
'rule of law' 42, 88
Runnymede Trust, The 99
Rutherford, Jonathan 16
Rutter, Jill 94
Rwanda, 148–9
Rycroft, Matthew 149

Sainsburys 137
Saint-Simon, Henri de 35
salvation 10, 177
  mental health as 177
  progressive version of 42
Salvation Army 156
Satia, Professor Priya 21–2, 194–6, 196n
'satyagraha' 202
Saunders, Robert 18

# INDEX

Schepelern Johansen, Birgitte 51, 52
schizophrenia, creeping 78
Schmitz, Oskar Adolf Hermann 157n1
Schoenberg, Arnold 111–12, 113
Schofield, Peter 147
Schonberg, Harold 112, 113
schools 20, 25, 68, 82, 85, 87, 94, 147, 178–9, 180, 181, 190
    as centres for therapeutic intervention 102, 174, 179
Scotland, Scottish 24–5, 79, 91, 163, 170
    'on the right side of history and humanity' 25
    Scottish Enlightenment 3
    Scottish independence referendum 91
    Scottish nationalism 15, 161, 170
Scottow, Kate 87
Second World War 6, 79, 107, 111, 160, 194
Seeley, John 5
serialism (music) 111, 113–14
Shakespeare, William 118
Sheehan, Neil 6
Shostakovich, Dmitri 77
Shullman, Sandra L. 102
Silicon Valley Community Foundation 67
Simkins, Rose 49–50
Simpson, Professor James 44
Singh, Professor Sunny 25
Sinn Féin 169
Sixsmith, Martin 8, 77, 78
Skilling, Jeffrey 125, 126, 127
Sky 99
    *Sky News* 19, 48–9
    *Sky Sports* 65
Slater, Jonathan 65
slavery, slave trade 1, 2, 4, 21, 22, 63, 162, 177
    Arab-Swahili 2
    Britain bans 2
Smith, Adam 127–8, 133, 139
Smith, Owen, MP 17
Snow, Edgar 61
Social Democratic Party (SDP) 205n
social media/new media 56, 73, 75, 76, 85, 87, 89, 136, 174, 186, 190, 199, 201, 202
social science 36, 37–61, 70, 72, 108, 122, 196
    social scientist-historian 12, 12n2, 89
socialism, socialists 7, 8, 34, 149
    founding of 35
sociology 12, 12n1, 47, 52, 54, 64, 100, 120–1, 166, 178, 185, 186, 190, 192
    as a cog in the progressive wheel 13, 50, 72, 82, 122

    merging with politics 52, 60, 61, 118
    as a science, systematic 35, 48
    as technique 58–61
    policing function 89
    foundations of 48
    morality as variation of 89
    opinion as primary to 88
    passive style 184–5
South Africa 122, 176
Soviet Union 7–8, 9, 19, 20, 34, 43, 77, 79, 88, 119, 122, 151, 188, 206
    artistic and intellectual activity 113, 124
    humour as resistance 202
    Soviet psychiatry 78
*Spectator, The* 51
Spencer, Herbert 36
*Spiegel, Der* 161, 162
Springford, John 92–3
Sri Lanka 101–2
SSRI (selective serotonin reuptake inhibitor) antidepressants 141
Stalin, Joseph 7, 77
Stanley, Henry Morton 1
Starmer, Sir Keir, MP 37, 68, 192
Steinem, Gloria 173
Stewart, Rory (former MP) 105–6, 194
Stock, Kathleen 84, 86
Stonewall 98, 136, 137, 147, 200
    UK Workplace Equality Index 136–7
Stop Funding Hate 51
Stop Hate UK 49–50, 51
Stravinsky, Igor 111
Streeck, Professor Wolfgang 153
Suez Canal 1
Sunak, Rishi, MP 17n, 148
'system of diversity' 66, 99, 175

Tate Modern 114–16
    Tate Exchange 114
    Tate Neighbours 114–15
Tavistock Gender and Identity Development Service (GIDS) 98
'techbros' 197
technocracy, technocratic approach 105, 142, 144–55, 185, 198
    conflicts with democracy 105, 150
    definition 145–6
    integrating rationality and morality 150
    of opinion 88, 96
    tendency towards 48, 55, 58
technology *viii*, 12, 119, 127, 160, 190

# INDEX

knowledge as 59
role in Global Great Game 8
role in social change *vi*, 140, 141n, 201
*Telegraph, Daily* 1
temporality 34–6, 39
'terfs' *see* feminists – gender-critical
*The Cut* 176
therapy
  education as 179–80
  merged with social justice politics 101, 103, 172–4
    administration via DEI 177–8
    healing the world 173
  therapeutic authority 102–3
  therapeutic morality 174
*The Wire* 146
Thomas, Anna 147–8
Thompson, Emma 163
'thought-crime' 87n
Thunberg, Greta 73, 177
Tide Bank 137
Timothy, Nick (now MP) 148
Tocqueville, Alexis de 10
Tombs, Professor Robert 3–4, 5, 6, 79
Trades Union Congress (TUC) 48–9
'Trans in the City' 138
transgender 73, 98, 100, 136, 164–5, 170, 176, 180
  transactivism 82–7, 200
  'trans-affirmative' and 'trans-inclusive' practice 101, 137
Trevor Project, The 97
Triggernometry 137
Trump, President Donald *vi*, 11–12, 18, 33, 52, 54, 56, 75n, 105, 122, 168, 172, 193–4, 196, 197, 198, 199, 200
Turner Prize, The 116–18
Twitter/X *vi*, 66, 75, 75n, 76, 81, 136
  'Twitter Files' 82

UK in a Changing Europe (UKICE) 91–6, 95n
UK Research and Innovation (UKRI) 92
Ukraine 26, 79, 80
*Unherd* 199, 200
Unilever 135
United Kingdom, the British state 17–18, 56, 91–2, 146–52, 167, 192, 204
  detaching from territorially-bounded population 139, 142, 150, 192
  dissolution of 17, 191n

guilt of 17, 195
vulnerability of non-conformists 148
United States of America 7, 8, 9, 11, 31, 37, 62–3, 65, 67, 70, 129, 138, 160, 161, 172, 173, 177n, 193, 199
  American Revolution 6, 7, 128
  civil rights movement 52, 63
  Constitution 144
  consumerist culture 172
  forefront of progress 6, 142, 194
  Founding Fathers 40
  frontier spirit 5–6, 12, 63
  imperial centre 196
  invincibility 62
  land, conflicts over 129–30, 144
  national myth 5, 6, 32
  publicity and promotion 62, 76, 107, 107n, 192
  2024 Presidential Election *vi*, 105–6, 193
universities, general 10, 20, 22, 23, 26, 52, 76, 81, 82, 84, 85, 114, 178, 186, 189, 204, 205, 206
University and Colleges Union (UCU)
  Edinburgh branch 84
  Sussex branch 84
University of Edinburgh 83
University of Leicester 64
University of Sheffield 20–1, 22–4
University of Sussex 84

van Middelaar, Luuk 152
Vance, JD 11
Vaughan Williams, Ralph 112–13, 156, 157, 157n1, 158, 159
  nationalism 158, 159n, 169
  relation to modernism, avant-garde 157, 157n2
  support for European Federal Union 159n
  *The Lark Ascending* 169–70
Verrier, Anthony 151
*Vicar of Dibley, The* 66
Victoria, Queen 162
Viet-Minh 78
Vietnam Wars 6, 62, 78, 107
  My Lai massacre 6
Viner, Katherine 85
Voltaire 35, 128

Wagner, Richard 113
Wallace, George 6
Waterfield, Bruno 152–3

# INDEX

Watson, Emma 98
Watson, James 23
Watters, Audrey 5–6
Watters, Ethan 101–2, 141–2
Wayne, Mike 83
Weber, Max 10
Webern, Anton von 111, 112, 113
Weiler, Joseph 152
Weiss, Bari 82
Welby, Justin 134, 149
Welsh, the 156
Welsh National Opera (WNO) 120
Whig Interpretation of History, The 4, 15, 194n2
'whiteness' 15, 21, 24, 25, 65, 199
  'white privilege' 177
Wickes 137
Williams, Joanna 82, 86, 100, 178
Williams, Zoe 163
Wilson Foster, Professor John 166–7
Wishart, Ruth 170

W.K. Kellogg Foundation 67
'wokism' 41, 182
Women and Equalities Select Committee (UK House of Commons) 98
Woof, Robyn 83
working class 14, 142, 160, 188
workplace 19, 20, 23, 26, 98, 136, 138, 139, 174
  removing 'institutional memory' 189
  training 178, 190
Wunderman Thompson 134–5

*Yes, Minister* 56n, 193
Young, Toby *137*
young people 48, 179, 189
  as agents of change 140, 187
  as more mature than older people 186
  blank slates 186
  identity politics of 15, 188
  'the future, not the past' 187
Yousaf, Humza, MSP 24–5
*YouTube* 137